FLESH

&

The Triangle Fire and Its Legacy

BLOOD

SO

CHEAP

GIRLS
WANTED

Also by ALBERT MARRIN

FDR and the American Crisis

Thomas Paine: Crusader for Liberty

A Volcano Beneath the Snow: John Brown's War Against Slavery

Black Gold: The Story of Oil in Our Lives

This book was generously
provided by:

A JOINT PROJECT WITH

jetBlue

RANDOM HOUSE
CHILDREN'S BOOKS

FLESH & BLOOD SO CHEAP

The Triangle Fire and Its Legacy

Albert Marrin

A Yearling Book

For picture credits, please see page 177.

Front cover images: The photograph of women sewing used on the front cover is an example of a new-model factory; this one is in Syracuse, New York, as no usable images of the intact interior of the Triangle Waist Company exist. The inset drawing of the burned-out Triangle Shirtwaist building, titled "Girls Wanted," was created by artist Henry Glintenkamp as a commentary on the fire after the official investigation report was released.

Visit us on the Web! randomhouse.com/kids

Educators and librarians, for a variety of teaching tools, visit us at RHTeachersLibrarians.com

The Library of Congress has cataloged the hardcover edition of this work as follows:
Marrin, Albert.
Flesh and blood so cheap : the Triangle fire and its legacy / Albert Marrin. — 1st ed.
        p. cm.
Includes bibliographical references and index.
ISBN 978-0-375-86889-4 (trade) — ISBN 978-0-375-96889-1 (lib. bdg.) — ISBN 978-0-307-97660-4 (ebook)
[1. Triangle Shirtwaist Company—Fire, 1911. 2. Clothing factories—New York (State)—New York—Safety measures—History—20th century.
3. Industrial safety—New York (State)—New York—History—20th century. 4. New York (N.Y.)—History—1898–1951.] I. Title.
F128.5.M122 2011
974.7'1041—dc22
2010021533

ISBN 978-0-553-49935-3 (pbk.)

MANUFACTURED IN CHINA

10 9 8 7 6 5 4 3 2 1

First Yearling Edition 2015

to their memory

The land flourished because it was fed from so many sources—
because it was nourished by so many cultures and traditions and peoples.

—President Lyndon B. Johnson
at the Statue of Liberty,
October 3, 1965

CONTENTS

FROM THE ASHES

From the ashes of the Triangle Company fire began to rise one of the most dramatic and far-reaching [changes] in American history—one that would . . . eventually redefine forever the role the government played in the lives of ordinary people.
—Ric Burns and James Sanders,
New York (1999)

New York City, Saturday, March 25, 1911. One of those sparkling early-spring afternoons New Yorkers so enjoy after a cold, dreary winter. Under the cloudless blue sky, strong, bracing gusts of wind blew across Manhattan Island from the East River. The air smelled fresh and clean, and it felt good to be alive. It would also be a day of tragedy that would weigh on the hearts of witnesses and survivors for the rest of their days.

People flocked to Washington Square, a ten-acre park named for our first president. A century earlier, the site was a wasteland on the city's northern outskirts. Back then, it served as a cemetery for unclaimed bodies and the poorest when they died; even today, the bones of some twenty thousand people lie under its lawns and paths. After the cemetery closed in 1825, a group of elegant town houses called "the Row" rose on the north side of the square. This area lay in "the country," and the rich spared no expense to escape there from the bustling city. Although the Row still

"The Row" along Washington Square in 1936.

exists, by 1911 Washington Square had become a green oasis amid grimy factories and immigrant neighborhoods.

On this Saturday, families from the tenements strolled the tree-lined paths. Children ran around, played on the grass, or stood on the playground swings and "flew to the moon." Lovers walked hand in hand. Students from nearby New York University sat on the benches reading, thinking great thoughts, arguing, flirting.

Miss Frances Perkins, thirty-one, was visiting a friend at her home in the Row. A social worker by profession, Perkins led the Consumers' League, an organization devoted to improving working conditions in factories. The two women were about to have tea when they heard fire engines. Opening the front door, they saw smoke rising behind a New York University building across the street from the east side of the square. The top three floors of an adjoining ten-story building at the corner of Washington Place and Greene Street were ablaze. These floors housed the Triangle Waist Company, a manufacturer of shirtwaists, a kind of women's blouse that was at the height of fashion.

Hearts pounding, the friends ran across the square, joining the crowd racing toward the smoke. Moments later, they came upon a scene that seared itself into their souls. By twos and threes, workers, some with their hair and clothes on fire, were jumping from the windows. "We got there just as they started to jump," Perkins recalled in 1961, the fiftieth anniversary of the disaster. "I shall never forget the frozen horror which came over us as we stood with our hands on our throats watching that horrible sight, knowing that there was no help. . . . The firemen kept shouting for them not to jump. But they had no choice; the flames were right behind them, for by this time the fire was far gone."[1]

Within minutes, 146 workers died, broken on the sidewalk, suffocated by smoke, or burnt in the flames. Most were young women ages fourteen to twenty-three, nearly all recent immigrants, Italians and Russian Jews. Dubbed the "Triangle Fire," for ninety years it held the record as New York's deadliest workplace fire. Only the September 11, 2001, terrorist attacks on the World Trade Center took more lives.

Frances Perkins was shaken by what she saw that day. It was a life-changing

Frances Perkins, circa 1911.

experience. The sight of people jumping from windows affected her so deeply that she vowed such a horror could not, *must* not, be allowed to happen again. She would devote the rest of her life to

Fifth Avenue, an area of wealth and luxury in New York City, circa 1900.

making her vow a reality. Yet the Triangle Fire is more than a tragedy. It is part of a larger story, one woven into the very fabric of American life. Without understanding that larger story, we cannot fully understand the disaster and how it influences us today.

The Triangle Fire occurred during the greatest mass movement of people in history. People leave their homeland for various reasons, or "pushes," as historians call them. Pushes include natural disasters, crop failures, poverty, war, persecution, or simply the desire for change. Those who leave go to places they think will offer a better, happier, more interesting future. We call such reasons "pulls." Thus, in the years 1870 to 1900, about twelve million immigrants arrived in the United States, nearly all from Europe. During the next decade, 1901–10, another nine million— 75 percent of the total of the previous three decades—reached our shores. Most of these entered through New York City.

By the start of the twentieth century, America's growing industries had made the nation into a world power. Oil tycoon John D. Rockefeller. Automobile maker Henry Ford. Steel baron Andrew Carnegie. Inventor Thomas A. Edison. These and hundreds of others rose from humble backgrounds. Through hard

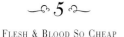
work, ambition, and knowledge, they became fabulously wealthy. But these were the lucky few.

The problem: life for most Americans was an endless grind, a harsh struggle for existence. Men and women, old and young, native-born and immigrant, worked long hours for little pay. Experts calculated that a family of four needed between $650 and $800 a year for its basic needs: food, clothing, housing, medical care. Yet in the year 1900, three out of four lived in poverty, defined as a family income of $553 a year or less.

To make matters worse, work was often dangerous, even deadly. In 1911, for example, over 50,000 people died on the job—that is, about 1,000 each week, or 140 a day, *every* day. This figure includes boys and girls who worked in every major industry from coal mining to textile manufacturing. (In 2008, by contrast, 5,071 American adults died of work-related injuries and diseases.)

If you were hurt or killed at work, that was too bad. The "safety net" we now take for granted did not exist. No health insurance or Medicare. No old-age pensions or Social Security. No

A cramped Lower East Side street.

unemployment benefits. No laws regulating hours and wages, safety and sanitation.

The Triangle Fire shocked Americans as no other job-related tragedy ever had. For many, it became a powerful emotional symbol of what seemed wrong about America. In doing so, it raised big questions in a way that gave force to a moral crusade. Was labor a product, something bought and sold like a stick of chewing gum or a newspaper? Or was labor something different—something human? What was our country coming to when workers, often young children, died so horribly? Must things go on this way? What changes were needed to realize the promise of America? How should these changes come about? Who should lead the drive for change?

School textbooks usually focus on "famous" names—kings, presidents, politicians, generals—as the shapers of history. Yet these are only part of the picture. The names of others, often equally important, seldom get the recognition they deserve. American history textbooks may, for example, mention Frances Perkins in a few sentences. For in the 1930s, she became secretary of labor, the first woman to hold a cabinet position, under President Franklin D. Roosevelt. We look in vain for other names—Jacob Riis, Clara Lemlich, Rose Schneiderman, Mary Dreier, Alfred E. Smith, Alva Belmont, and Anne Morgan, to mention a few. It is as if they had never existed or done anything worth remembering. Still, each in their own way, they helped create the America we know today.

I

HUDDLED MASSES

Give me your tired, your poor,
Your huddled masses yearning to breathe free,
The wretched refuse of your teeming shore,
Send these, the homeless, tempest-tost to me,
I lift my lamp beside the golden door!
—*Emma Lazarus,*
"The New Colossus" (1883), inscription on the pedestal of the Statue of Liberty

Immigration Old and New

In the spring of 1903, Sadie Frowne, age thirteen, and her mother sailed into New York Harbor aboard a steamship crowded with immigrants from Europe. Finally, their voyage had ended. As the passengers gathered on deck, Sadie recalled, they marveled at a giant green figure that seemed to rise out of the water. She never forgot "the big woman with the spikes on her head and the lamp that is lighted at night in her hand." Thus, the Statue of Liberty welcomed the newcomers to the United States and, they prayed, to a better life.[1]

Although America has always been a land of hope, immigrants have come from different places, at different times, for different reasons. This has led historians to divide immigration into two phases: old and new. The old immigration began in colonial times, more than a century before the United States existed as an independent nation. Over the generations, immigrants came from western and northern Europe: England, Scotland, Ireland, Holland, Germany, Norway, Sweden, Denmark. Except for Irish Catholics, most "old" immigrants were of the Protestant faith and could read and write their native language. Despite hardships, these people soon found their place in America.

The shift from the old to the new immigration began in the 1880s. While immigrants continued to arrive from the familiar places, a flood of humanity also came from southern and eastern Europe: Italy, Greece, Hungary, Romania, Poland, Russia. By 1910, people from these countries made up seven out of ten immigrants entering the United States, chiefly through New York City. Of these, the vast majority were Italians (mainly Catholic) and Jews from Russia. Because nearly all the victims of the Triangle Fire were from these two groups, we must look at them closely.

The Land Time Forgot

Educated Americans had always admired Italy as a land of beauty and culture. Each year, thousands of tourists visited its ancient cities—Rome, Florence, Milan, Venice—to see their splendid churches, museums, and art galleries. Music lovers filled the opera houses and concert halls. Yet few Americans realized that Italy was really two countries.

Northern Italy, the area tourists favored, was more advanced economically than the southern areas. The nation's industries, banks, and major businesses were based in the north. Since the government was in Rome, the capital, northerners made the laws, controlled the courts, and commanded the police. For them, the south was little more than an uncivilized colony, an extension of Africa.

Southern Italy forms the heel and toe of the Italian "boot." The boot, in turn, "kicks" Sicily, an Italian island in the Mediterranean Sea. Known as "the land time forgot," the south was a region of small farms and villages that lagged behind the industrial north in all things but *la miseria*—misery.

Misery ruled southern Italy. The majority of its people were among the poorest in Europe. Peasants, or farmers, did not own the land, but worked tiny parcels rented from wealthy landlords, chiefly nobles and northern businessmen. Landlords demanded high rents, so peasants could not afford to buy fertilizer or machinery. Instead, they tilled the soil with hand plows and hoes that were old when their grandparents were children. Peasant families were large and worked together, including children, who were given small chores nearly from the moment they could walk. Youngsters attended school

A map of Italy. Most immigrants came from the southern regions.

briefly if at all, for they had to help in the fields. Large families lived in tiny, cramped cottages, merely shacks with earthen floors, typically shared with a prized goat or rooster.

A street macaroni restaurant in Naples, in southern Italy.

Northerners had little respect for southerners, nicknamed "Black Italians" in a racist epithet meant to show their "inferiority"; they called Sicilians "Africans." The government in Rome cheated the south in countless ways. It built no modern roads or bridges there. Instead, it acted like a gigantic straw, sucking out whatever money it could. Heavy taxes collected in the south were spent in the north. Worse, justice was a cruel farce. If wronged by a landlord, a peasant was out of luck. Courts and police served the landlord. This, in turn, made peasants cynical, convinced others acted only for selfish reasons. Proverbs expressed their outrage: "The gallows is for the poor man, the law courts for the fool," "The law works against people," "The fat pig pays no taxes." If one person killed another, the victim's family took justice into its own hands, vowing to "wash blood with blood."[2]

Mother Nature herself seemed to turn against the land time forgot. Massive cutting down of forests for firewood and building materials harmed the environment. Without tree roots to hold the soil in place, rain washed away fertile soil, causing crop failure and hunger. Elsewhere, swamps formed. Mosquitoes breed in swamps. If a certain species of mosquito bites a person, it may inject a microscopic organism that causes malaria. This disease has killed more people than all history's wars, famines, and natural disasters combined. By the 1880s, malaria had become epidemic in southern Italy.

Disasters burst from within the earth, too. In 1905, earthquakes shook the region, collapsing buildings and burying their inhabitants under the rubble. The next year, Mount Vesuvius erupted. Located just east of Naples, this volcano had a fearsome history. An eruption in the year AD 79 buried the cities of Pompeii and Herculaneum, killing all their inhabitants. The 1906 eruption sent "explosions of red-hot stones" a half mile into the air. "The end of the world has come!" people cried in panic. "The inhabitants of the villages in the vicinity of Mount Vesuvius are in a condition of terror," said the *New York Times.* "Many homes have been abandoned for the open air, although there has been a thick fog all day and the atmosphere has been dense with volcanic ashes and the fumes of subterranean fires." Hundeds died, and over 150,000 fled, often struggling through knee-deep ash drifts.[3]

An earthquake that began miles under the bed of the Mediterranean Sea caused the worst disaster. In June 1908, it sent a tidal wave, or tsunami, roaring through the Strait of Messina, a narrow passage between Sicily and the Italian mainland. The wall of water reached back forty miles on the mainland and thirty miles in Sicily. It leveled the mainland city of Reggio di Calabria and Messina in Sicily. "Both places," said the *New York Times*, "are today vast morgues of the dead, and the air for many miles out to sea is polluted. Vultures are congregating to prey upon the dead." The tsunami also washed away hundreds of villages. In all, it killed some one hundred thousand people, leaving countless others homeless.[4]

Extreme poverty and natural disasters pushed Italians out of their country. Between 1880 and 1921, about 4.5 mil-

Mount Vesuvius. The volcano erupted in 1906, displacing more than 150,000 people.

lion, chiefly southerners, reached the United States. Only Jews from Russia came in numbers anywhere near those of the land time forgot.[5]

No Place for Jews

Like Italians, Russian Jews fled poverty. Unlike Italians, however, nature did not torment them with flood and fire. Their greatest threat was religious hatred.

Ever since the ancient Romans had driven Jews from their homeland in Palestine, most had lived in the countries of western Europe: England, Spain, France, Italy, the Netherlands, and the German lands. Good citizens, they obeyed the laws, paid their taxes, and prospered as merchants, traders, and artisans. Yet Christians often resented Jews because they held different religious beliefs. Resentment easily turned to hatred, and hatred to violence. In the early 1100s, Jews began to flee eastward in large numbers to Poland. Its kings welcomed them not only from kindness, but because they had skills needed to develop the country.

Russia was different. Poland's eastern neighbor banned Jews from its territory. Russians followed the Eastern Orthodox faith, a branch of Christianity. They despised Jews, calling them "Christ killers," Poles because they were Roman Catholics, and Muslims because they were not Christians at all. When Jewish merchants came to trade, the czars, or emperors, warned them to stay away or die. They meant it. In the year 1563, soldiers drowned Jewish "intruders" on orders from czar Ivan the Terrible.

In the late 1700s, Poland's stronger Russian, Austrian, and German neighbors forcibly partitioned, or divided, the country among themselves. Russia seized eastern Poland, the largest section, where the largest number of Jews also lived. Although the czars did not want any Jews in their lands, they got them anyhow. So, when we discuss

The Pale of Settlement, showing the Russian territories to which most Jews were restricted, where nearly five million Jews lived by 1900. The Pale contained hundreds of small towns called shtetls *and several cities; some of the major ones are indicated here.*

Russian Jews, we mean those who were originally Polish Jews. (Poland would not regain its independence until 1918, at the end of the First World War.)

The czars decided to segregate, or separate, the Jews from Russians by creating the Pale of Settlement. Originally, the word *pale* meant "fence" or "barrier." But instead of building a real fence, the czars separated the mainly Jewish areas from Russia proper by a line drawn on a map. The Pale of Settlement—Pale for short—held the territories along Russia's western border. It stretched from Russian-ruled Poland in the center to the traditional Russian lands along the Baltic Sea in the north and the Black Sea in the south. Several thousand Jewish merchants and skilled artisans had special permission to live in Russian cities. The rest dared not leave the Pale, or step "beyond the Pale." For if the police caught them, the czar took all their property and sent them to prison. By the year 1900, the Pale held 4.8 million Jews.

Russian Jews at a market, 1903.

The Pale was dotted with hundreds of *shtetls.* Most Jews lived in a *shtetl,* the Yiddish word for "small town." East European Jews often knew three languages. The first was Hebrew, the language of the

Bible and prayer but not of conversation; the second was the language of the country in which they lived and spoke to gentiles. The third, Yiddish, or "Jewish German," was the language of everyday life. When Jews first came to Poland from Germany, they spoke the German language. Over time, German mixed with Hebrew, Polish, and Russian words, forming Yiddish. However, Yiddish is written in Hebrew characters from right to left, like Hebrew. A vivid language, it can express everything from joy to grief with power and emotion.

All *shtetls* seemed cut from the same pattern. One looked much like another. A traveler described a *shtetl* as "a jumble of wooden houses clustered higgledy-piggledy about a market place" that served the gentiles living in the countryside. Peasants brought their cows and chickens, hides and wool, timber and grain to market. Jewish merchants traded these for goods manufactured in cities: clothing, boots, lamps, pottery, cutlery, nails, tools. Also, the *shtetl*'s own artisans kept small shops or worked out of their homes.[6]

Women played a key role in these activities. Wives not only ran the home, they and their daughters helped the menfolk earn a living. A traditional Yiddish marriage song mentions just a few of their duties:

> *Cobblers' wives must make*
> *the thread . . .*
> *Tailors' wives must sit up*
> *late . . .*
> *Butchers' wives must carry*
> *the meat . . .*
> *Weavers' wives must throw*
> *the spindle . . .*
> *Filers' wives must turn*
> *the [stone-sharpening]*
> *wheel . . .*
> *Painters' wives must mix*
> *the paint . . .*
> *Carpenters' wives must*
> *saw the boards . . .*[7]

Despite the Jews' important economic role, Russians never let them forget they were outsiders. Russia was the only country where anti-Semitism, hatred of Jews, was official government policy. Ordinary Russians, egged on by their rulers, spat out the word *Zhid* (Jew) like a foul curse.

No country persecuted Jews like Russia. Its laws limiting Jewish rights filled a book of nearly a thousand pages. By the 1880s, Jews could not be army officers or judges or serve on juries. Not one Jew taught in the Russian school system or was a university professor. Only one in ten high school or university students could be Jewish. The law banned Jews from owning land outside a *shtetl*—even for a graveyard. Nor could they deal in oil, coal, or gold or do business on Sundays. Jews who had received permission to live in Russian cities a century before had to return to the Pale, leaving their possessions behind.[8] None of these limitations existed in England or other western European countries. There, the "career open to talent," the right to follow any calling and rise as high as one's abilities could go, was the law of the land.

Many Jews, finding it impossible to earn a living in the *shtetls*, moved to slums in large cities within the Pale. They settled in cities most Americans had never heard of, places with strange-sounding names: Warsaw, Vilna, Lodz, Minsk, Grodno, Bialystok. But city jobs were scarce, too. Many Jews were so poor they said, half joking, they lived on air. Small wonder that Yiddish is rich in words for poverty and bad luck. One grammar book has nineteen columns of words for *misfortune*.[9]

Yet there were worse things than poverty. In the name of "keeping order," the czar's Cossacks, fierce horsemen, swept into *shtetls* to whip and loot, rape and burn. If anything went wrong, Russia's rulers made Jews scapegoats, those who bear blame for the sins of

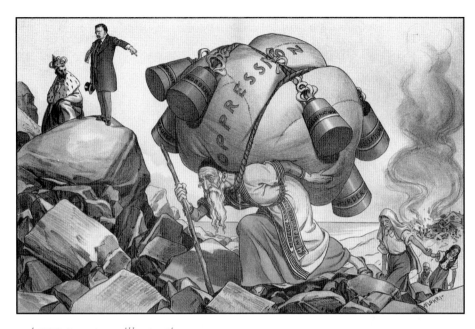

A 1904 cartoon illustrating the plight of the Jews in Russia, where they were constant victims of the czar's Cossacks in numerous pogroms. Note President Theodore Roosevelt admonishing the czar to stop the oppression.

others. In bad economic times, for example, officials directed popular anger away from the government and toward the Jews. People unleashed their anger in pogroms, from a Russian word meaning "riot" or "devastation." A pogrom, in effect, was a license to commit murder.

In April 1903, around the time Sadie Frowne saw the Statue of Liberty, the *New York Times* described a typical pogrom. "There was a well-laid plan for the general massacre of Jews on the day following the Orthodox Easter," its reporter noted. "The mob was led by priests, and the general cry, 'Kill the Jews,' was taken up all over the city [of Kishinev]. . . . The scenes of horror that attended this massacre are beyond description. Babes were literally torn to pieces by the frenzied and bloodthirsty mob. The local police made no attempt to check the reign of terror."[10]

Only after the massacre did the police step in—to arrest Jews who had tried to defend their families by force. From 1903 to 1906, during the reign of Czar Nicholas II, some 3,100 Jews lost their lives in pogroms. A single month, November 1905, saw no fewer than six hundred pogroms, an average of twenty a day. It is not surprising that many Jews decided that Russia was no place for them.

Crossing the Big Water

Jews had found refuge in America since colonial times. In 1654, several families from Holland settled in New Amsterdam, re-named New York a decade later to honor its English conqueror, the Duke of York. During the War for Independence, New York banker Haym Salomon used his fortune to support the patriot cause, and as many as two hundred Jewish men served in the Continental Army. In the years following independence, America's Jewish population rose slowly, to 4,000 in 1820 and 250,000 by 1880. Then came the deluge, as "American fever" swept the *shtetls*. Between 1881 and 1914, over 2.1 million Jews left the Pale and elsewhere in Eastern Europe.[11]

Everyone knew something about America from newspaper articles and letters of relatives who had already gone there. Although Jews also went to Canada, Australia, and South America, the United States was by far their favorite destination. Parents sang their children to sleep with a lullaby:

In America, they say
There is never any dearth.
It's a paradise for all
A real heaven on earth.[12]

An immigrant named Mary Antin recalled, "'America' was in everybody's mouth. Business men talked of it over their accounts; the market women made up their quarrels that they might discuss it from stall to stall; people who had relatives in the famous land went around reading their letters for the enlightenment of the less fortunate folks [and] children played at emigrating." Antin added that "scarcely anybody knew one true fact about this magic land."[13]

She was right. The real America was no paradise. Its streets were not paved with gold, as rosy reports often led would-be immigrants to believe. Many hardships awaited the newcomer. But America *was* a land of opportunity and, thank God, it had no czar. Its constitution

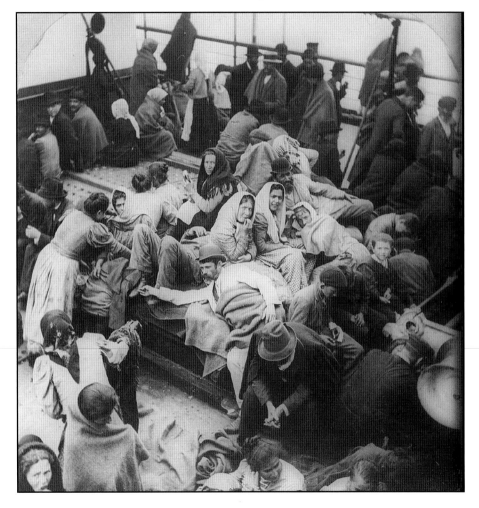

Emigrants on board a ship bound for the United States of America, circa 1905.

guaranteed religious freedom, the right to worship (or not) as one pleased.

Going to America was easier than it had ever been. In the days of wooden sailing ships, crossing the Atlantic Ocean was a dreadful ordeal. Travelers often made their wills before sailing, for you never knew if you would reach the far shore alive. Voyages took from six weeks to five months, depending on weather and luck. Storms blew immigrant vessels off course. Wind gusts tore sails to shreds and toppled masts. Mountainous waves capsized ships or pounded them to bits, drowning all aboard. Even on a "normal" voyage, ships swarmed with disease-carrying vermin: rats, mice, lice, fleas, roaches. A disease called "ship fever" often killed half the passengers and crew. Some ships reached port with scarcely a person able to stand on their own.

By 1903, iron steamships had greatly improved ocean travel. In that year, Russian Jews sailing from Hamburg in Germany or Italians from Naples could count on spending six to seventeen days aboard ship. The cheapest ticket cost thirty-four dollars. Even so, ocean travel was far from pleasant. Immigrants did not have separate cabins. Instead, they crowded into the steerage, or lowest deck, which housed the steering cables that controlled the ship's rudder. They slept on iron or wooden bunks, in three tiers, each with a straw mattress and no pillow. Between two hundred and four hundred people shared two toilets that stank to high heaven. There were no showers or bathtubs. Immigrants had to wait until they reached shore to wash. "Everything," one recalled, "was dirty, sticky, and disagreeable to the touch."[14]

Sailors called first-time passengers "landlubbers," because they had never been aboard an oceangoing vessel. Most had never seen a stretch of water broader than a river or lake. Once their ship left port, the land quickly vanished over the horizon. The open Atlantic, seemingly endless, was terrifying; on a "quiet" day the ship rocked constantly.

During storms, the winds howled like demons. Even the largest steamship heaved and tossed, bounced and rolled like a crazy cork. Crew members slammed the hatches shut to keep out the water. The air belowdecks grew stale, reeking of dampness and sweat. Food spoiled; drinking water grew scarce.

Even without storms, the ship's rocking made nearly every passenger seasick. On bad days, you could hardly walk without stepping into a puddle of vomit. An immigrant recalled that "hundreds of people had vomiting fits. . . . I wanted to escape from that inferno but no sooner had I thrust my head forward from the lower bunk than someone above me vomited straight upon my head. I wiped the vomit away, dragged myself onto the deck, leaned against the railing and vomited my share into the sea, and lay down half-dead upon the deck."[15] The ship's "heads," or toilets, often backed up. The filthy overflow

An immigrant family observes the Statue of Liberty from Ellis Island, 1900. It was a beacon of hope to millions reaching U.S. shores.

covered the area, filling the air with dreadful odors. Crossing the Atlantic in steerage was not for softies.

Eventually, seagulls appeared overhead. A shoreline became visible in the west. Hours passed. The ship steamed into a vast harbor teeming with vessels of every size. To its right, docks lined the shore far as the eye could see, like the teeth of a comb jutting into the water. Behind the docks rose rows of soaring towers—"skyscrapers." To the ship's left stood the big woman with the spikes on her head and the lamp in her hand.

INTO THE MAGIC CAULDRON

What, indeed, is a New Yorker? Is he Jew or Irish? Is he English or German?
Is he Russian or Polish? He may be something of all these, and yet he is wholly
none of them. Something has been added to him which he had not had before. He is
endowed with a briskness and an invention often alien to his blood. He is quicker
in his movement, less trammeled in his judgment. . . . The change he undergoes is
unmistakable. New York, indeed, resembles a magic cauldron. Those who are cast
into it are born again.
—*Charles Whibley, English journalist,* American Sketches *(1908)*

Ellis Island

The thrill of seeing Lady Liberty passed quickly, overcome by other sights and feelings. New York City was known as the "Golden Door," the immigrants' main port of entry into the United States. Their first stop, however, was not the city itself, but a low-lying island in the harbor.

Throughout the 1880s, immigrants arriving in New York entered at Castle Garden, a huge, run-down building at the tip of Manhattan Island. In 1892, the federal government opened a new reception center on Ellis Island. Named for Samuel Ellis, the original owner, it was once called Gallows Island by

*Ellis Island,
early twentieth century.*

New Yorkers, because pirates were hung from gallows that stood on its shore. Executions were a popular attraction. On hanging days, men, women, and children scrambled onto boats to watch the spectacle from the water's edge. When the federal government took over, eight out of ten immigrants, twelve million in all, passed through Ellis Island until the reception center closed in 1924. Today, it is a national historic site, part of the Statue of Liberty National Monument.

Ships carrying steerage passengers anchored at the main dock. The uniformed officers who met them as they came ashore seemed cold and unfriendly. No smiles. No hearty "Welcome!" These had no place in the reception center. For Ellis Island was a giant filter designed to admit workers for the nation's growing economy and reject any who might become a burden on taxpayers.

Immigrants had reason to call Ellis Island the Island of Fears. After checking their luggage, they entered an immense hall divided by rows of iron railings. Officers had them form dozens of lines and file past the waiting doctors. The process seemed like an assembly line, only it handled human beings, not manufactured goods. The first doctor listened to each person's heart with a stethoscope. Down the line, others checked for signs of tuberculosis, smallpox, and similar "loathsome diseases." Next, a doctor examined eyes for trachoma, a contagious disease. He did this with a buttonhook, a metal tool used to button gloves. Using the hook, he pulled each eyelid back to look for signs of the disease.

Finally, an inspector asked a series of questions. Have you any money or

Passengers on the steerage and upper decks of an immigrant ship, 1902.

Immigrants arriving at Ellis Island, waiting on the first of many lines in the arduous process to enter the country, 1904.

relatives in the United States? Do you have more than one wife or husband? Where will you live? Ever spend time in a jail or an insane asylum? These questions were not only meant to get facts. They tested intelligence and, the law said, ruled out "idiots, imbe- ciles or morons and other deficient persons."[1]

Rejection for any reason meant returning to Europe at the expense of the steamship company that brought the person. This often involved a painful choice, since a family mem-

A United States health inspector performing an eye examination on Ellis Island.

An Italian family looking for lost baggage, 1905.

ber's rejection forced the others to decide whether to leave, too. Most immigrants, however, passed through Ellis Island within a day. Ferries ran around the clock, taking them to Manhattan to begin their new lives.

The Empire City

What the immigrants found was different from anything they had ever seen or imagined. By the early 1900s, America had become a nation of fast-growing cities. With a population of 3.5 million, New York was the second-largest city on earth; only London, England, was larger. Cities had become centers of the Industrial Revolution, the changeover from the artisan's hand labor to machinery powered by steam or electricity. Manufacturers built their factories in cities because they had an abundant labor supply.

Growing cities brought growing problems. Traditional buildings of wood, stone, and brick could not be very tall without collapsing under their own weight. How, then, to put more people, more buildings, more factories—more everything—into a limited area? Reach for the sky! "When they find themselves a little crowded," William Archer, an English visitor, said about New Yorkers, "they simply tip a street on end and call it a skyscraper."[2]

In the 1880s, architects, experts who design and make building plans, began using new materials to create the skyscraper. This type of building had a skeleton of iron beams bolted together and connected to iron columns reinforced with concrete. A structure of this kind might soar hundreds of feet above the ground. Its iron skeleton easily supported brick walls pierced by windows made of mass-produced plate glass to flood the interior with natural light.

Chicago built the first skyscrapers, achieving the stunning height of ten

The teeming streets of the Lower East Side, 1907.

Manhattan construction workers, two hundred feet above the ground on the skeleton of a skyscraper, in 1907.

The Woolworth Building under construction, circa 1910. Notice the steel framework.

stories, about 110 feet. Yet Manhattan, ever short on space, quickly took the lead in skyscraper construction. By 1913, it had the tallest building on earth, the fifty-five-story Woolworth Building. When seen from a ship's deck, Manhattan's skyline amazed English novelist H. G. Wells. "The skyscrapers, that are the New Yorker's perpetual boast and pride . . . stand out, in a clustering group [to form] the strangest crown that a city ever wore."[3]

Skyscrapers were both tall and convenient, thanks to other inventions. Elevators sped passengers to the top floor within seconds. Telephones allowed people to speak to each other from anywhere in the city. In the early 1900s, telephone wires were not buried in the ground, but hung in metallic "cobwebs" from lines of wooden poles placed along the streets. An English visitor, W. G. Marshall, marveled at New York's "perfect maze of telephone and telegraph wires crossing and recrossing each other. . . . The sky, indeed, is blackened by them, and it is as if you were looking through the meshes of a net."[4]

Old-time cities were "walking cities"—that is, small enough to allow a healthy person to walk anywhere in about an hour. Ferries and wooden bridges allowed one to cross streams and narrow rivers. Those who could afford them rode horses or went about in horse-drawn buggies. Horse-drawn "omnibuses" carried ordinary folks for a penny or two; horse-drawn wagons hauled goods from place to place. Horses, however, left behind tons of manure each day, more than sanitation workers could clear away. Things got so bad that women in the wealthy Beekman Hill section of Manhattan complained about a manure pile twenty-five feet high. When it rained, streams of liquefied manure turned streets into gooey, evil-smelling swamps. In dry weather, the wind blew the filth, turned to fine dust, into people's faces, homes, and food. Dozens died each year from inhaling poisonous "street dust."[5]

As cities grew, they built modern transportation systems. Again, New York took the lead. In 1883, the Brooklyn Bridge opened. Then the world's longest bridge, it stretched more than a mile across the East River, connecting

The Brooklyn Bridge, looking from Brooklyn toward Manhattan, showing the 1901 skyline.

A 1909 illustration depicting the brand-new New York City subway, which opened in 1904.

the town (later borough) of Brooklyn and Manhattan. Gradually, electrified "street cars" replaced horses and horse-drawn vehicles. So did automobiles.

Starting in the 1870s, elevated railways made mass transit a reality, and a bargain at five cents a ride. Riding was an adventure. "The tracks are lifted to a height of thirty feet (in some places higher) upon iron pillars," wrote W. G. Marshall. "As you sit in a car on the 'L' and are being whirled along, you can put your head out of [the] window and salute a friend who is walking on the street pavement below. In some places, where the streets are narrow, the railway is built right over the sidewalks . . . close up against the walls of the houses." At night, the trains seemed to run "at full speed on nothing through the air." In 1904, New York opened its first underground rail line, or "subway."[6]

Rich folk did not ride the subway. When they went about town, it was in luxurious carriages and the most expensive automobiles, like royalty. The

A sumptuous banquet in New York City, circa 1900. Note the wreaths in the guests' hair.

wealthy felt entitled to everything they had, because God supposedly made them "better" than ordinary folk. Showing off their wealth proved their superiority, making others give them the respect they claimed to deserve.

New York's wealthiest lived on "Millionaires' Row," a row of mansions along Fifth Avenue, opposite Central Park. For example, Andrew Carnegie's home had eighty rooms on four floors. The steel baron, however, also gave

The Easter Parade along Fifth Avenue, 1906, where the wealthy could see and be seen.

thick carpets. For hours, they stuffed themselves with lobster, guzzled champagne, and, after dessert, smoked cigarettes rolled in hundred-dollar bills. Others gave "dog dinners" at which their pets wore gold collars and ate the best cuts of steak. Immigrants lived more simply.[7]

The World of the Greenhorn

Immigrants often passed through New York, bound for other places where they had relatives and friends. Most Italians and Russian Jews, however, chose to stay in the city, in neighborhoods with people like themselves. There, at least, "greenhorns" (unseasoned newcomers) could feel comfortable speaking their native language and practicing familiar customs. Italians headed for Little Italy, near the southern end of Manhattan Island, around Mulberry Street. Russian Jews settled in the adjoining district, the Lower East Side, bordering the East River.

generously to charity. Too many others spent fortunes on nonsense. Some gathered on horseback in elegant dining rooms with crystal chandeliers and

New York City had been founded at

the southern end of Manhattan. Over the years, it spread northward, toward Washington Square and beyond, as well-to-do families sought more space and privacy. Yet their old houses still had value. To meet the rising demand for immigrant housing, landlords cut these into tiny apartments. Sometimes, they rented cellars or built another house, little more than a shack, in the backyard. Thus, greenhorns crowded into districts never intended to house such large numbers. Every building, an English visitor wrote, "seemed to sweat humanity at every window and door."[8]

To make things worse, in the 1880s landlords built "dumbbell" tenements. Five or six stories high, these took their name from an indentation on each side; viewed from above, the indentations made them look like weight lifters' dumbbells. The idea was to create an air shaft, or passage for letting fresh air in, between tenements built up against each other. This meant that only one room on

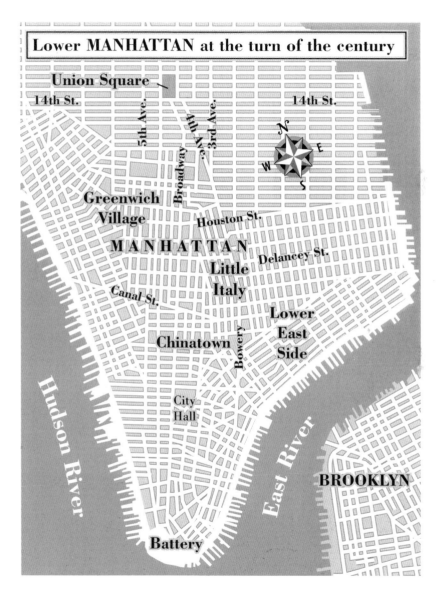

Lower MANHATTAN at the turn of the century

Adjoining dumbbell tenements. Note the air shaft between them.

the tenement's narrowest side had direct light from the street. A child once described her home as "a place so dark it seemed as if there weren't no sky." Air shafts also became huge garbage cans for household trash and rats.[9]

Designed to house as many people as possible, the dumbbell tenement had four apartments on a floor. Each had three or four rooms, the largest just ten by eleven feet. As many as seven people might live in such a room. A four-room apartment rented for twelve dollars a month; a three-room apartment cost eight dollars. Those costs may seem small by today's standards. In the early 1900s, however, they took a large bite out of workers' wages, often more than half. If you missed one or two rent payments, the landlord would evict you—that is, have his movers put all your belongings out on the sidewalk. There they lay until you found another place to live, or thieves stole them, or rain ruined them.

Tenement hallways had toilets (two per floor) and a water faucet. Apartments had no showers, so adults washed with a sponge dipped in a basin of water from the faucet. Mothers bathed small children in a basin or the kitchen sink. You never knew what to expect when you turned a faucet handle. "Once," said Rose Halpern, of Stanton Street, "I was washing my hands in

Dumbbell Tenement

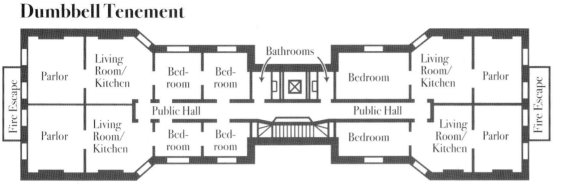

A floor plan of a dumbbell tenement.

the sink and a rat dropped right into my hands."[10]

Lack of toilets forced residents to relieve themselves wherever they could. "In the evening," said an official report, "every [parked] wagon becomes a private and public lavatory, and the odor and stench . . . is perfectly horrible." Many did not bother to leave their apartment. An old-timer recalled: "Every apartment had chamber pots. You used to crap in the pot instead of going downstairs. . . . They used to throw the stuff out the windows. You'd get nailed with it. That was very common."[11]

Only the lucky few had beds of their own. With space so limited, children slept two or three, even four to a bed. Often their parents took in boarders, men or women, relatives or strangers, to share the rent. Boarders slept wherever they could stretch out. Some slept in the kitchen on two chairs with boards laid across. Come morning, they had to remove the boards so others could walk into the kitchen or to the hallway toilets. Other boarders might sleep on a straw-filled sack on the floor, on the bare floor, or, in warm weather, on the fire escape. "In summertime," a social worker reported, "the children sleep on the steps and on covered chicken coops along the sidewalk; for inside the rooms are too often small and stifling."[12]

Tenements' narrow stairways and wooden stairs made them firetraps. In 1890, pioneer photographer Jacob Riis set out to document immigrant life. Using the newly invented flash powder, Riis went into tenements, basements, and alleys at night. The result was *How the Other Half Lives*, a classic picture-and-word study of immigrant life in New York. Riis described a typical tenement fire:

> *A fire panic at night in a tenement . . . is a horror that has few parallels in human experience. I cannot think without a shudder of one such scene in a First Avenue tenement. It was in the middle of the night. The fire had swept up with a sudden fury from a restaurant on the street floor, cutting off escape. Men and women threw themselves from the windows, or were*

carried down senseless by the firemen. . . . A half-grown girl with a baby in her arms walked among the dead and dying with a stunned, vacant look, singing in a low scared voice to the child. One of the doctors . . . patted the cheek of the baby soothingly. It was cold. The baby had been smothered with its father and mother; but the girl, her sister, did not know it. Her reason had fled.[13]

A child getting a bath in a tenement home.

Not everything was so bleak and miserable. Immigrants, fleeing cramped apartments, spent much of their time in the streets. Outdoors, the air fairly crackled with human energy. Every-body seemed in a hurry. "I never saw so many people on the streets, shouting, going in all directions," a visitor wrote.

An illustration of New Yorkers coping with a heat wave.

JACOB RIIS, Photojournalist

Jacob Riis created what we call today photojournalism. A Danish immigrant, he lived hand to mouth for a few years, then became a reporter for the New York *Evening Sun*. Riis had a tiny office on Mulberry Street. No mulberries grew on Mulberry Street anymore, for it lay in the heart of Little Italy. From his office, Riis set out to explore the city's dark side with his camera. Until the 1880s, it was impossible to take pictures at night or in poorly lit places, like tenement hallways and apartments. A German invention called flash powder, ignited by an electric battery, lit up a space for an instant, allowing the photographer to take his picture. Riis's "pictures of Gotham's crime and misery by night and day" became the basis of a lecture called "The Other Half: How It Lives and Dies in New York." The photographer-reporter expanded the lecture into a book, *How the Other Half Lives*, a powerful document reformers used to arouse public opinion to the need for reform of living conditions in tenements.

This photograph by Jacob Riis shows a rear view of tenements on Roosevelt Street, circa 1895. Lines were strung between buildings for hanging clothing since there were no mechanical dryers.

Apart from the street signs, written in English, greenhorns might imagine themselves back in the old country.[14]

Depending on the neighborhood, most shop signs were in Italian or Yiddish. People shopped and gossiped, argued and courted in their native language. "In the doorways, and on the steps of the staircases, on little wooden and straw stools almost in the middle of the street, women . . . nurse their young, sew . . . untangle and arrange one another's hair." On rooftops, weather permitting, they air-dried their hair after washing it.[15]

Immigrants complained of hardships, not boredom. There was always something to do after work. Readers might spend hours poring over newspapers printed in their native language. These not only reported events in the old country, but gave advice about getting along in the new one. The *Jewish Daily Forward*, for example, had a famous column, the "Bintel Brief," Yid-

Note the Yiddish sign in the background. In the foreground, tenants have been evicted.

dish for "Bundle of Letters." This answered readers' questions on every subject with common sense and humor. For example, a young man writes that he loves a woman, but a *shtetl* superstition keeps him from marrying her. "She has a dimple in her chin, and it is said that

The crowds at Coney Island, a day of entertainment for many New Yorkers.

people who have this lose their first husband or wife." The editor's reply: "The trouble is not that the girl has a dimple in her chin but that some people have a screw loose in their heads."[16]

Despite hardships, Little Italy and the Lower East Side enjoyed a rich cultural life. Each neighborhood had many small restaurants and social clubs where people could gather and socialize. In Little Italy, traveling theater com-panies staged performances about everyday life. Italians laughed at comedies like *Pasquale, You're a Pig,* and wept as poor Giovanni learned that his mother had died in Sicily. As in the old country, street puppeteers entertained children and adults with age-old tales of fair maidens rescued from evil bandits by gallant knights in shining armor. At the end of each show, viewers showed their appreciation by putting a few pennies on a plate passed around by a puppeteer. If Italians managed to save a little money or got lucky in the lottery, they might splurge on a real treat—a ticket for standing room at the famous Metropolitan Opera.

The Yiddish theater was the crown jewel of Lower East Side entertainment. By the first decade of the twentieth century, Second Avenue had become the Yiddish Broadway. The place blazed with lights. Wherever you turned, you saw colorful posters advertising current shows and coming attractions. There was some-

A poster for the play King Solomon, *performed in the Yiddish theater.*

thing to appeal to everyone's taste. Plays like *King Solomon, or the Love of the Song of Songs* and *Solomon's Judgement* had Bible themes. There were historical plays like *Bar Kokhba*, about the hero of a revolt against the Romans, and plays about work life, such as *Anna the Finisher*, whose heroine was a garment worker. Yiddish translations of classic plays by William Shakespeare—*Hamlet, The Merchant of Venice, King Lear*—drew large audiences. Theatergoers roared at the antics of *shtetl* characters like Tevye the Milkman and cried at the fate of kin during a pogrom. As an actor recited a letter to his mother in Russia, "the whole audience found it impossible to hold back the tears." Sometimes, the audience got into the act. When a singer gave out with *"Amerika ist ein frei land"*—"America is a free country"—the audience sang the phrase over and over. Yiddish actors were celebrities, like latter-day rock stars. When the famous Jacob Adler went out for a stroll, crowds followed him, "their faces shining with adoration and enchantment and awe."[17]

Movies were equally popular with native-born Americans and immigrants. New York, not Hollywood, was the first capital of the American film industry. Until the 1920s, more films were made in the "Empire City" than anywhere else in the world. Immigrant neighborhoods had many movie theaters, or nickelodeons, so called because of the five-cent admission charge. Owners put up posters with catchy come-ons:

> If you are tired of life,
>   go to the movies,
> If you are sick of troubles rife,
>   go to the picture show,
> You will forget your unpaid bills,
>   rheumatism and other ills,
> If you stow your pills and go to the
>   picture show.[18]

Although movies were silent, they helped greenhorns become Americanized. Their brief subtitles introduced them to the English language in a written form that followed the action on the screen. Before the age of air-conditioning, however, theaters and

Lend Me Your Words

Immigrants influenced their adopted country in many ways. Among these was their impact on American English, or the English language as spoken in the United States. This was to be expected. For close contact between communities that speak different languages often leads to the adoption of *loanwords*—that is, words taken over by speakers of one language from a different language.

Certain words contributed by Italian immigrants have become common in American English. Among these are *balcony, broccoli, buffoon, casino, espresso, confetti, duo, graffiti, inferno, extravaganza, pasta, macaroni, spaghetti, pizza, mustache, soprano, studio, solo, zucchini, umbrella* ("little shadow"), and, of course, *opera*, meaning "the work," as in a musical performance, and *cello*, a stringed musical instrument.

Some familiar Yiddish loanwords are *chutzpah* (shameless nerve), *kibitz* (offer unwanted advice), *kvetch* (whine, complain), *lox* (smoked salmon), *klutz* (clumsy person), *schlock* (cheap, shoddy), *schnook* (stupid person), *glitch* (a technical problem, a snag), *glitz* (flashiness), *schmooze* (chat), *spiel* (argument meant to persuade), *meshuga* (crazy), *schmeer* (smear).

Translations of Yiddish phrases passed into American slang. Among the most familiar are "Get lost," "You should live so long," "All right already," "It shouldn't happen to a dog," "Okay by me," "He knows from nothing," and "I need that like a hole in the head."

nickelodeons stood empty during the blazing summer months. On weekends, as many as a half-million people flocked to Coney Island, in Brooklyn, to cool off at the seashore. Often they arrived before sunrise and stayed until late at night. More than one married couple first met "on the seashore, by the beautiful sea."

The Bowery attracted those with less wholesome tastes. *Bowery* is a Dutch word for a country lane lined with farms and orchards. When George Washington led his victorious army into the city in 1783, Bowery farmers cheered and waved. A century later, the only thing that remained of the old Bowery was the name. Now it was New York's center of sin. Every street had its gangster hangouts, drug dealers, prostitutes, pool halls, flophouses, and gambling dens. Music blared from sleazy dance

A view of the Bowery. Note the "el"—elevated railroad—on each side of the street.

halls. Drunken men stumbled out of saloons; they lay on the sidewalk until they awoke on their own or the police took them to jail for the night. A song told of an out-of-towner who got more than he expected on the Bowery:

> *I was out to enjoy the*
> *   sights,*
> *There was the Bow'ry*
> *   ablaze with lights;*
> *I had one of the devil's own*
> *   nights! . . .*
> *The Bow'ry, the Bow'ry!*
> *They say such things,*
> *And they do such things*
> *On the Bow'ry! The*
> *   Bow'ry!*
> *I'll never go there*
> *   anymore!*[19]

Tenement children flocked to their neighborhood streets. Unable to afford store-bought games and toys, they used their imagination to invent their own.

Boys played stoopball with a rubber ball thrown against the edges, or "points," of the outer steps of a tenement and stickball, the street version of baseball, with a broomstick bat. They also liked prisoner's base, a form of tag, tug-of-war, and blindman's bluff. Girls went in for jacks, potsy (hopscotch), beanbag, and jump rope. Those who lived near stables had other "games." Blanche Levy, of Cherry Street, recalled: "I used to play on the dead horses. They'd just leave 'em layin' on the street, and then we'd play king of the hill on there. After a while, the smell didn't bother us."[20]

The streets taught life lessons. Immigrant children got "street smarts," wisdom about people and city ways and how to survive there. These youngsters, public school teachers said, had "old heads," common sense beyond their years.

Public schools were public—open to all. No fees. No entrance exams. No religious quotas. Having faced discrimina-

Boys playing stickball in an alley, circa 1910.

Children playing near a dead horse.

tion in Russia, Jews took advantage of the public schools more than any other immigrant group. Learning, they believed, was their passport to a better life. Jewish parents brought their children to the first day of school "as if it were an act of consecra-

tion," a blessing. Mothers who could not speak English would take their children to the local public library and hold up their fingers to indicate the number of cards they wanted. "Go, learn, read," they told the youngsters.[21]

Italians did much the same. A newspaper article urged: "Let us do as the Jews . . . invade the schools, teach ourselves, have our children taught, open to them the school paths by means of the hatchet of knowledge and genius."[22]

That "hatchet" cut deeply. Like those who had come before and would come after, the new immigrants found that America's genius lay in its ability to change millions of greenhorns into productive citizens. Yet this did not happen by waving a magic wand. It demanded willpower, sacrifice, work—and time.

⌇ FLESH AND BLOOD SO CHEAP ⌇

Oh, God! That bread should be so dear,
And flesh and blood so cheap!
—*Jacob Riis,* How the Other Half Lives *(1890)*

Work

Immigrants understood that unless they found work, and quickly, they could not survive, let alone prosper. Early-twentieth-century America had nothing like the social "safety net" we take for granted today. No unemployment benefits. No old-age pensions. No Social Security. No health insurance or Medicare. Apart from help from a few private charities, the rule was the same as in 1607 for settlers at Jamestown, Virginia: "He that doth not work shall not eat."

Since immigrant groups had different backgrounds, when they first arrived, they favored different occupations. Most men from the land time forgot had been country folk, peasants. This limited Italians to unskilled jobs in the cities. Chiefly manual laborers, they took, bigots snarled, "work no white man could stand." Yet such bitter resentment ignores a key fact: they did work that had to be done if America was to grow and prosper.

Those who knew the score appreciated the newcomers. "We need these strong and willing Italian laborers who are doing the hard work of the nation," said a journal for engineers. "They have strong arms and willing hearts, and they give the country their strength and their health in return for a living." Ital-

A group of Italian street-construction workers beneath the Sixth Avenue elevated railway, 1910.

ian dockworkers loaded and unloaded ships. Italian construction workers dug tunnels and sewers, put in water mains, and built skyscrapers.[1]

New York City owes its subways mainly to former peasants who earned a dollar a day for dangerous, back-breaking work. Although some sections needed special machines to bore through solid rock, wherever possible engineers favored the quicker "cut-and-cover" method. With picks, shovels, and jackhammers—power drills that use a hammering action—workers dug a deep trench in a street. Then they covered the trench with wooden planks to support traffic. After completing the steel-and-concrete tunnel and laying the tracks, they removed the planks and repaved the street above. Building subways was dangerous. Cave-ins buried men alive. Accidents with dynamite blew men apart. Moving trains were always a menace. "The slaughter of Italians . . . yesterday was simply awful," a

newspaper reported after a train hit a group of track workers. "The men were torn and mangled and their blood was scattered all over the tracks."[2]

Ambitious workers tried to save a few pennies from their weekly wages. Eventually, they invested in a fruit stand, a small bakery or grocery store, perhaps even imported favorite foods like olive oil and cheeses from Italy. Others, like shoemakers, followed trades learned in their villages, opening shoe repair shops; their boys might earn a little money by shining shoes and selling newspapers at subway entrances.

Russian Jews came from a different background than southern Italians. Many were already skilled artisans and small-time merchants when they left the *shtetl*. Fired by ambition to succeed in their new country, they might start as peddlers, carrying their wares in a sack or basket. Day in and day out, they climbed rickety tenement stairs and knocked on doors. In Yiddish or broken

English they pleaded, "Suspenders, collah buttons, matches, hankeches—please, lady, buy."[3]

One might also rent or buy a push-cart. This carryover from the *shtetl* was a two-wheeled cart pushed from street to street or, more likely, parked in a marketplace. In New York, that was the Chazir-mark, Yiddish for "Pig-market," located on Hester Street in the heart of the Lower East Side. Shoppers could find anything in the Pig-market but

Mulberry Street in Little Italy, 1900.

pork. (Pigs are not kosher—that is, ritually pure, according to Jewish law.) The term may have come from the street being crowded as a pigpen.

Pushcarts stretched far as the eye could see. Jacob Riis reported:

The Pig-market is in Hester Street . . . and up and down the side streets two or three blocks, as the state of trade demands. . . . There is scarcely anything that can be hawked from a wagon that is not to be found, and at ridiculously low prices. Bandannas and tin cups at two cents, peaches at a cent a quart, "damaged" eggs for a song, hats for a quarter. . . . Frowsy-looking chickens and half-plucked geese, hung by the neck and protesting with wildly strutting feet even in death against the outrage, are the great staple of the market. . . . Here is a woman churning horse-raddish on a machine. . . . Beside her is a butcher's stand with cuts and prices [uptowners] never dreamed of.

Old coats are hawked for fifty cents, "as good as new," and "pants" . . . at anything that can be got.[4]

Beside these items, Pig-market vendors offered dried codfish and salt herrings and pastrami—slabs of smoked beef seasoned with herbs and spices. Tall barrels stood brimful with pickled cucumbers, at two for a penny, in salty brine. Pick

Pushcart peddlers on Hester Street.

your pickle; roll up your sleeve and reach into the barrel as far as you can! Thirsty? Spend a few cents for a bottle of seltzer, or *belchwasser* (belch water), or an egg cream, a mixture of seltzer, milk, and chocolate syrup. Pushcarts featured mounds of sour Polish bread, made from coarse, whole rye and black as tar. Also heaps of bagels, hard rolls made of dough shaped into a ring, and bialys, rolls with a depressed center that are covered with onion flakes, just as in Bialystok, Poland. During times of unemployment, families often had little more than potatoes to fill their bellies. As the song put it:

> *Sunday, potatoes*
> *Monday, potatoes*
> *Tuesday and Wednesday, potatoes*
> *Thursday and Friday, potatoes*
> *Saturday, for a change, a potato*
> *   pudding,*
> *And Sunday again we have*
> *   potatoes.*

Eyeglasses sold briskly, at thirty-five cents a pair. Jewish men prized eyeglasses because, apart from helping them see better, they "said something" about the wearer; sidewalk photographers kept them on hand so that clients might pose as learned, book-reading gentlemen. Whatever the item, buyers tried to get sellers to lower their prices. Bargaining was part of the game of buying and selling. A good bargainer gained respect. A poor bargainer was a *schlemiel*, Yiddish for "pushover," a bumbling fool of a creature.

Peddling and selling from pushcarts were important occupations; however, Jewish immigrants' chief work lay in "rags," slang for the clothing industry.

Rags

Humans have three basic needs: food, shelter, clothing. Until modern times, most people made their clothes in their own homes. Each garment was unique, its various parts cut with shears, fitted to the individual wearer, and then sewn together by hand. Wealthy men had their clothes "tailor-made" by traveling or town-based tailors; seamstresses made women's dresses. In cities, the poor usually wore clothes discarded by their social "betters." Dealers visited affluent neighborhoods, ringing a bell and calling, "I buy old clothes for cash." Later, they sold these to shopkeepers or pushcart vendors, who then sold them to the poor.

Ready-made, or ready-to-wear, clothing had existed since the 1700s. By the end of sea voyages, often lasting a year or more, sailors had worn their canvas work clothes to shreds. Returning to port, they needed replacements before shipping out again. Some tailors' families worked together, making "slops," sailor slang for cheap, loose-fitting smocks and baggy trousers sold in "slop shops." Slops came in one size. If he was handy with needle and thread, the sailor took them in or let them out to suit himself. Families also specialized in making clothing for slaves. Southern plantation owners found it cheaper to buy ready-made clothing rather than have slaves spend time away from the fields being fitted.

The Civil War (1861–65) ended slavery in the United States, its most important contribution to American life. Yet it also made a contribution that is often overlooked: it changed the way people dressed.

When the Civil War began, the U.S. government paid to have soldiers' uniforms custom-made in workers' homes. But as armies expanded, so did the demand for mass-produced uniforms. Measurements taken of thousands of soldiers allowed tailors to make uniforms in various sizes. After the war, these measurements became standard for men's civilian clothing. Manufacturers adopted standard sizes for women's clothing, too. Thus, for the first time, consumers could buy "off-the-rack" clothes in standard sizes; chemical dyes developed in laboratories by scientists made it possible to produce clothes in a wider variety of colors than ever before. Off-the-rack, in turn, led to specialized stores that sold men's, women's, and children's clothing. For farmers and others who lived in the countryside, firms like Sears, Roebuck and Company sold all kinds of goods—tools, toys, false teeth, patent medicines, clothing—by mail-order catalog.

Two inventions turned ready-made clothing into a big business. First, in the 1850s, Isaac Merritt Singer and other in-

An advertisement for ready-to-wear clothing for men of different heights and sizes, circa 1890.

ventors began to sell their version of the sewing machine. Powered by a treadle, a pedal worked by foot, these sewing machines enabled an operator to sew up to four hundred stitches a minute; a skilled person could sew only thirty-five stitches a minute by hand. While the sewing machine made it easier to make clothes for oneself at home, it had the greatest impact on production for the mass market. The second invention came in the 1870s, when the cutter's knife replaced shears. This razor-sharp blade cut up to sixteen layers of cloth at a time, each piece exactly like the other. These inventions did more than lower clothing prices. They helped change the way people saw themselves.[5]

An English proverb went, "Clothes make the man," and the woman, too. Traditionally, clothing did more than cover the body. Well-made, elegant clothing was an advertisement, revealing at a glance the wearer's social rank and thus the respect due from the

An 1892 advertisement for Singer sewing machines.

Sweatshop
Steps in Making a Cotton Garment

Cotton crop planted and harvested
Raw cotton spun into thread
Thread dyed and woven into cloth
Manufacturer buys cloth from textile mill
Designer makes a model garment
Model used to make paper patterns for cutters
Cutting contractors make various parts of garment
Shleppers carry parts from shop to shop
Each shop does its own special task or tasks
  Basting
  Sewing
  Finishing
  Pressing
Shleppers carry garment to shops at each stage of production
Manufacturer inspects garment and has his label sewn into it
Garment shipped to retail stores
Customer buys garment

"above their station," while "gentle-folk" must dress according to their rank in society. All this changed with the rise of ready-made clothing.[6]

Ready-made was not only cheaper than tailor-made; it was an expression of democracy. For if people looked alike because they dressed alike, it followed that they were equal and should enjoy the same rights. Producers easily copied styles originally designed for the elite. Although they did not use the finest, most expensive fabrics—silk, satin, velvet, linen—wool and cotton were good enough for the mass market. Upper-class Europeans, however, thought it outrageous that ordinary American workers were so "overdressed" when not on the job. They complained of the difficulty, if not the impossibility, of distinguishing an office clerk from a banker, a housemaid from a gentlelady, by their clothes. Most Americans ignored these complaints. As a clothing manufacturer explained, ready-made

"lower orders." For example, in 1853 W. E. Baxter, a wealthy English merchant, noted that "it is no mark of gentility to wear a dress unsuitable to one's means and employment." In other words, people should know their "place." Workers should not dress had given Americans "that style and character in dress that is essential to the self-respect of a free democratic people." In short, it made them look and feel like "fine" people.[7]

New York was the nation's capital of ready-made. By the 1890s, more than 70 percent of American women's and 40 percent of men's "rags" came from Manhattan. Nearly all garment manufacturers were Jewish men who had learned their trade in the Pale of Settlement.

Rise of the Sweatshop

A clothing manufacturer's production line began on plantations in the southern states. It rested on the backs of abused workers, including young children. Miserably paid whites and blacks, descendants of freed slaves, grew and harvested cotton, the chief clothing fiber, also used for socks and underwear. Railroads brought the raw cotton mostly to mills in the New England states, chiefly Massachusetts, to be spun into thread and colored in steaming vats of chemical dyes. Textile workers, often nine- and ten-year-olds, tended

A young cotton picker in the fields of Oklahoma, 1916.

the looms that wove the thread into cloth. Textile machines lacked safety devices like guardrails and automatic shutoff switches. A machine might pull in a child, grown drowsy and careless with overwork, crushing limbs or

*Children working at a
Georgia cotton mill, 1909.*

worse. From the mill, the cloth went to the clothing manufacturer.

A manufacturer employed several types of contractors, people who agree to do a task for a fixed price, to make the finished product. He began by buying bolts of fabric, which he sent to a cutting contractor. These were garment-industry princes, because they made the difference between profit and loss. The chief cutter and his helpers began by stretching layers of fabric, one on top of another, on a long table. Next, they placed paper patterns on the top layer. Each pattern outlined part of a garment, as drawn by the garment's designer. Let's say they had to cut men's trousers, size 38. Cutters moved the pattern papers—right leg, left leg, waistband, lining, pockets—like pieces of a jigsaw puzzle. The idea was to fit each paper as close to its neighbor on the fabric as possible, thus reducing the amount of waste; it was impossible *not* to have some waste material. However, any scrap, multiplied by the number of layers, translated into lost profits. Thus,

Other Things Made in Sweatshops

Garment sweatshops produced only clothing. Other sweatshops produced a wide range of items, including the following:

artificial flowers	purses
wallets	umbrellas
collars	buttons
ties	feathered hats
cigars	Christmas decorations
handmade cigarettes	mops and brooms
cardboard boxes	envelopes
fur trimmings	costume jewelry
toys	elastic garters
feather dusters	dolls
shoes and slippers	gloves and mittens

manufacturers said, good cutters were worth their weight in gold. Nowadays, the "gold" comes less from men's keen eyes than from computer-made patterns that waste the absolutely smallest amount of fabric.

After cutting, the manufacturer might assemble the trousers in his own place, called a "shop." However, he usually found it easier, and cheaper, to give different tasks to different contractors in their own shops. For example, basters assembled each pair of trousers by hand-sewing its cut pieces with long, loose stitches to prepare them for further work. Next, sewing machine workers, called "operators," stitched the basted pieces permanently. Finishers added the "finishing touches," such as linings, decoration, and buttons. Pressers used heavy irons, heated on a stove and weighing up to twenty pounds, to remove wrinkles from completed garments. Finally, the trousers went to the manufacturer for inspection. If they passed, he put on his label and sold them to a retailer, who sold them to the consumer.

Garments did not get around by themselves. At each stage of production, *shleppers*, Yiddish for "draggers" or "car-riers," took them from shop to shop. Every day, on the Lower East Side, you saw men and women rushing along the streets, shlepping heavy bundles over their shoulders or balanced on their heads. Boys and girls carried lighter loads.

The manufacturer set garment prices. Naturally, by paying contractors less, he increased his profits. While this was good for him, it put contractors in a bind. To make a living, they had to "sweat" their employees. Although em-

A female shlepper on Lafayette Street, near Astor Place.

A boy shlepper,
New York City, 1912.

ployees might perspire on the job, sweating as a business method had nothing to do with perspiration. It had everything to do with squeezing as much work out of them as possible while paying them as little as possible. Sweating took place in a "sweatshop." In his own mind, the sweatshop owner justified his actions, for manufacturers took advantage of him. In time, if he was smart and ruthless enough, he might become a manufacturer himself.

Sweatshop owners, the contractors used by manufacturers, were immigrants themselves. They hired workers who spoke their language and desperately needed a job. Young Jewish women suited them perfectly. Everyone knew that an owner seeking a worker would stand at a certain place in the Hester Street Pigmarket. "Need a girl?" a woman would ask. "Girl" was the term for any female worker. In those days, teenagers and married women with children were called, and called themselves, "girls."

A Jewish family working on garters in a tenement sweatshop, 1912.

Going to work, a woman recalled, was "as inevitable as eating and breathing and finally dying. It was just part of the scheme of life." She had no choice in the matter. Russian Jews were often too poor to go to America as a family group. At first, like many southern Italians, a husband scraped together enough money to go alone. Months, even years, later, he had saved enough to send for his wife and children. Many Jewish families, however, decided to send a daughter first so the father could care for his family back in the homeland until they could leave. The first daughter to arrive acted as a kind of "human anchor." She found a job, saved, and bought a steamship ticket for another sister or brother. Eventually, they brought over the entire family.[8]

*Girls taking a lunchtime
break from work, 1915.*

Young workers in a tenement sweatshop, circa 1910.

After the family arrived, daughters still had to help with its expenses. In most families, their earnings were not their own. Daughters gave their unopened pay envelopes to their parents, getting an allowance in return. Despite their longing for an education, they often had to leave school to earn money. "When I had to quit school in the fifth grade," one recalled, "I felt terribly abused though I accepted it as part of life for a girl of a poor family."

Her earnings not only helped put food on the table and pay the rent, but sent brothers to high school, even to college. Jewish immigrants usually attended the tuition-free City College of New York, run at public expense. It was known as the "Jewish Harvard," after Harvard College, the oldest and most famous college in the land. Since college graduates earned more than sweatshop workers, they had a better chance of helping their families climb out of poverty.[9]

The path to the sweatshop often led from the Pig-market to a tenement apartment. A sweatshop owner usually worked in his own home, employing family members and hired help. If he did well, he might expand his operation by renting an apartment to use only as a shop. Anyhow, as many as fifteen people worked in a tiny home workshop. Nobody knew how many garment sweatshops there were in New York, because its government did not keep count. However, there must have been thousands on the Lower East Side.

Jacob Riis left a vivid word picture of sweatshop life. He began with a ride on the elevated railroad that ran along Second Avenue.

Every open window of the big tenements, that stand like a continuous brick wall on both sides of the way, gives you a glimpse of one of these shops as the train speeds by. Men and women bending over their machines, or ironing clothes at the window, half-naked. . . . The road is like a big gangway through an endless work-room where vast multitudes are forever laboring. Morning, noon, or night, it makes no difference; the scene is always the same. . . . Let us get off and continue

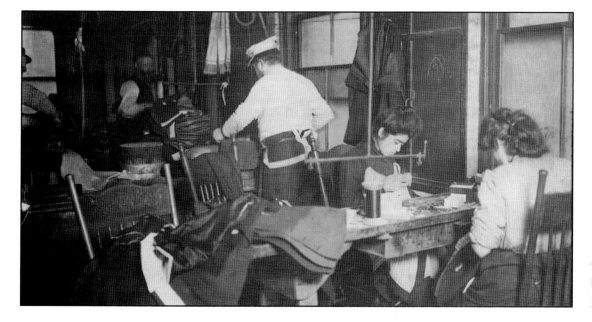

A group of sweatshop workers toil at worktables, 1908.

our tour on foot. . . . [We see] men stagger along the sidewalk groaning under heavy burdens of unsewn garments, or enormous black bags stuffed full of finished coats and trousers. . . .

Let us follow one to his home. . . . Up two flights of dark stairs . . . whirring sewing machines behind closed door betraying what goes on within, to the door that opens to admit the bundle and the man. . . . Five men and a woman, two young girls, not fifteen, and a boy . . . are at the machines sewing knickerbockers [short, loose-fitting trousers gathered in at the knee]. The floor is littered ankle-deep with half-sewn garments. In the alcove, on a couch of many dozens of "pants" ready for the finisher, a bare-legged baby with pinched face is asleep. A fence of piled-up clothing keeps him from rolling off on the floor. The faces, hands, and arms to the elbows of everyone in the room are black with the color of the cloth on which they are working. . . . Every floor has at least two, sometimes four, such shops.[10]

Sweatshop workers did not get a fixed salary or hourly wage. They were paid "by the piece" or "by the dozen"—so much money for so many items produced. For an eighty-four-hour workweek, they earned from $2.50 to $4. To make matters worse, having to work at top speed caused accidents. "Sometimes in my haste I get my finger caught and the needle goes right through it," said Sadie Frowne, whom we have already met. "I bind the finger tip with a piece of cotton and go on working. We all have accidents like that." Working in close quarters spread tuberculosis, a disease that destroys the lungs. Known as "the worker's disease," tuberculosis raged in the sweatshops. It spread so easily that infected parents dared not hug their children. Infected workers coughed constantly, spewing the disease-causing bacteria onto the garments they were making. In that way, tuberculosis spread from the worker to the consumer.[11]

The New-Model Factory

During the first years of the twentieth century, the number of sweatshops slowly began to fall for two reasons: changing women's fashions and improvements in garment-making technology.

For decades, the well-dressed woman had favored long, one-piece dresses that swept the ground. To give her the desired "hourglass" figure, she wore a corset, an undergarment stiffened with whalebone and tightly bound with laces to make her waist narrow. By the early 1900s, corsets, rightly called "cloth prisons," went out of fashion. Women began to wear looser-fitting, more comfortable clothing like the shirtwaist, or "waist" for short. This was a cotton blouse with a high collar

A 1906 advertisement for shirtwaist designs.

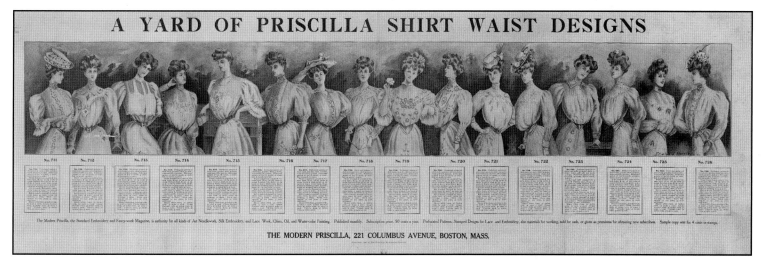

and wide sleeves worn with a separate ankle-length skirt. The shirtwaist became a symbol of women's liberation, suitable for every occasion. Wealthy women wore it to social events. College women wore it to class. Office workers wore it on the job.

Two men led in the manufacture of shirtwaists. Max Blanck and Isaac Harris had arrived at Ellis Island as poor immigrants. Like others, the partners began their careers in tenement sweatshops. Unlike most, however, they joined forces, becoming contractors and finally striking out on their own as manufacturers. Nicknamed the "Shirtwaist Kings," they built their Triangle Waist Company into the largest and most modern of its kind in New York, if not the nation. Although called a "shop," like other factories, it streamlined the manufacturing process, making the entire garment under one roof. By 1910, New York had about six hundred such "new-model factories."

The Triangle Waist Company occupied the top three floors of the Asch Building, a ten-story skyscraper at the corner of Washington Place and Greene Street, a half block east of Washington Square. Blanck and Harris used the most up-to-date technology that money could buy. Their machinery ran on electricity. To increase output, they replaced the cutter's handheld knife with a recent invention, the electric knife, which could cut over a hundred layers of cloth at once. Electric sewing machines, each able to sew three thousand stitches a minute, replaced the less expensive but slower foot-powered machines used in home-based sweatshops. The Asch Building's large rooms allowed the owners to attach rows of sewing machines to a single electric motor. Plate-glass windows flooded workrooms with natural light. Elevators sped people and goods to their destinations in seconds.

Workers in new-model factories

were nearly all Jewish (55 percent) and Italian (35 percent) immigrant women. There were fewer Italian women probably because they married early and stayed home to care for their young children. Jewish women tended to marry after they and their husbands-to-be had saved enough money to set up a household. Whether married or single, workers ranged in age from fourteen to thirty-five; about half were under twenty years old. The rest were American-born women, mostly of German and Irish heritage, and Jewish men. African Americans were all but absent from garment factories, due to racial discrimination.[12]

Employees saw factory work as a blessing and a curse. It was a blessing because the environment was healthier than tenement sweatshops. Factories had clothing lockers, toilets, and washing facilities. Electric lights and large windows made it easier on the eyes than gloomy apartments. Hours were long, but regular: work usually began at 7:00 a.m. and ended at 8:00 p.m., with a half-hour break for lunch. (Sweatshops might work around the clock to fill special orders.) Lunch was usually a sandwich brought from home. If not, vendors sold a piece of dry cake and a glass of water for two cents. Weekly pay ranged from about six dollars for sewing machine operators, both women and men, to twenty dollars for experienced cutters, all men.[13]

Workers disliked factories for several reasons. Time was money, for the more shirtwaists produced in a given time, the more owners had to sell, and the larger their profits. Thus, bosses sped up clocks at lunchtime to steal a few extra work minutes; wristwatches were too expensive for most workers. Toward quitting time, some bosses covered the clocks to gain a few more minutes of work time. If a worker went to the toilet, a forelady, or supervisor, followed, knocking on the door if she stayed more

A sewing room in a new-model factory, 1907.

than a minute or two. Workers described some of their grievances:

The forelady drives you. If you fix a pin in your hair or your collar, before you know it there is a forelady saying to you, "It isn't six o'clock yet. You have no right to fix your collar."

Once I wanted to go home because my mother was very sick. The boss said, "No favors here." I was afraid to lose my position so I stayed.

They locked the doors so you'd have to stay for night work.

You cannot be a free person. A smile from the boss makes you to live. They are dictators, czars, [it] really is not right.

There are no words to describe that shop. It was terrible. Slavery holds nothing worse.[14]

Work rules were humiliating. Talking, laughing, or singing wasted time, so anyone caught breaking the rule against "noise" paid a fine. Yet women had to put up with loudmouthed bosses. "The bosses in the shops are not what you would call educated men," said Clara Lemlich, a future strike leader. "They yell at the girls and they 'call them down' even worse than I imagine slaves were in the South. . . . They swear at us and sometimes they do worse—call us names that are not pretty to hear." As if insults were not enough, other abuses cost money. Employers charged workers for everything they used: needles, thread, chairs, electricity, lockers to store their hats. Workers said bosses who charged for these things had "one-cent souls." Some deducted a half day's pay for coming to work a half hour late. Failure to work fast enough, or to produce enough, brought instant dismissal, as did work that did not meet the owner's high standards.[15]

In the era of the new-model factory,

a frail toothpick of a man spoke for fellow workers as few others could. Morris Rosenfeld earned his daily bread as a garment worker, but his true "calling" was writing poetry. Every Yiddish speaker on the Lower East Side, it seemed, knew his poems. "Rosenfeld," one said, "is in the blood of every one of us."[16]

Rosenfeld had a magical way with words. In a few lines, he could express what others felt deep down, but could not put into words themselves. One of his finest poems, titled "In the Factory," goes like this:

Oh, here in the shop the machines
roar so wildly,
That I sink and am lost in the
terrible tumult;
And I am but a machine.
I work and I work and I work,
never ceasing. . . .
The clock in the workshop—it rests
not a moment;

It points on, and ticks on:
Eternity—Time. . . .
The tick of the clock is the Boss in
his anger!
The face of the clock has the eyes of
a foe;
The clock—Oh, I shudder—dost
hear how it drives me?
It calls me "Machine!" and it cries
to me "Sew!"[17]

What did Rosenfeld's readers want? To make a decent living and to live decently. Above all, to be treated with dignity, as human beings should, and not as mindless machines governed by clocks. But that would not come easily.

IV

AN OVERFLOW OF SUFFERING: THE UPRISING OF THE TWENTY THOUSAND

It was not…a woman's fancy that drove them to it, but an eruption of a long-smoldering volcano, an overflow of suffering, abuse and exhaustion.
—*Theresa Malkiel*, The Diary of a Shirtwaist Striker *(1910)*

A Gathering Storm

Any factory owner was always more powerful than any employee. Since owners hired workers and paid their wages, they made the rules, however unfair these might be. By themselves, then, individual workers were helpless. Employers could fire them at any time, for any reason or no reason at all, and the workers could do nothing about it. Thus, only by uniting in trade unions could workers use their combined power to balance the owners' power. A trade union's chief aims were (and are) to improve the wages, hours, and working conditions of its members through negotiations, also called "collective bargaining." In such negotiations, unions and employer representatives meet to work out agreements that each side can accept. If collective bargaining fails, unions may use their most potent weapon, the refusal to work—striking.

American workers formed their first unions in the late 1860s. Since then, powerful unions arose in industry after industry—steel, coal, and railroads, to name just a few. In 1881, Samuel Gompers, an English immigrant of Dutch descent, helped form the American Federation of Labor (AFL), serving as its president until his death in 1924. As its name tells us, the AFL was a federation—that is, an organization whose members control their own affairs. Since the AFL included unions in many trades, it was really a union of unions to help members with advice, publicity, funds, and negotiations with employers. A favorite AFL tactic was to use labels to identify goods manufactured by its member unions. Advertising campaigns urged consumers to "look for the union label"—that is, buy only products made by unionized workers.

The first step in forming a union was to get workers to join it. But that was easier said than done. While unions in each industry had their own unique history, they shared one thing: manufacturers despised unions, fearing they would limit their control of the workplace and raise production costs. Thus, they fought unionization with all their might. Employers fired workers who tried to organize or join unions, then exchanged blacklists to prevent such "troublemakers" from getting jobs in the industry. During strikes, employers often resorted to violence, hiring thugs and armed guards to break the strike.

At first, garment unions were impossible to form, thanks to the sweatshop system. There were thousands of these so-called cockroach operations scattered among Lower East Side tene-

Demonstrators protesting child labor, 1909. The signs say "Abolish Child Slavery!"

ments. With immigrants pouring ashore from Ellis Island every week, an owner could easily fire the entire shop if workers dared speak of unionizing. There was never a shortage of job-hungry greenhorns in the Pig-market to take their places. Besides, the men who led the AFL and its members did not regard women, the backbone of the garment industry, as equals. Female workers, they believed, were hardly worth organizing, because they lacked men's "drive" and "fighting spirit." Yet, on the other hand, they were "too emotional."

The new-model factory, however, did more than increase production; it made it easier to form unions. Firms like the Triangle Waist Company gathered hundreds of workers under their roof. With so many people so close together, they had the chance to share ideas, voice grievances, and discuss solutions.

A big change took place in 1900, the same year the Triangle Waist Company opened its doors, with the formation of the International Ladies' Garment Workers' Union (ILGWU). Open to all who made women's clothing, the ILGWU had various "locals," or branches, each specializing in certain tasks, throughout the country. In New York City, men alone—cutters and pressers—belonged to Local 10. Shirtwaist makers joined Local 25. While its

members were nearly all women, men controlled the executive board and made the key decisions. But this seemed meaningless, since, in 1909, Local 25 barely survived, with about a hundred members and four dollars in its bank account. While factory owners opposed all unions, they had no respect for, let alone fear of, this one. They should have.

In September 1909, workers' anger boiled over. Led by Local 25 members, workers in several shirtwaist factories—including the Triangle Waist Company—voted to strike for higher wages and shorter hours. Each shop struck on its own, without a unified plan or organization. Owners, however, united behind Max Blanck and Isaac Harris of the Triangle Waist Company. Their aim: do whatever it took to crush the strike.

The key to the owners' plan was hiring "scabs," slang for non-union workers who take strikers' places. Scabs might be poor themselves, but strikers saw them as villains, stealing bread from others' mouths. To get to work, scabs had to cross a union picket line—that is, a line of strikers called "pickets." The pickets walked in front of factory entrances with signs telling of their grievances and demands. Scabs often lost heart, turning back when pickets looked them in the eye and asked, "How would you feel if we stole *your* jobs?"

Owners decided to get rough. Nearby, the Bowery swarmed with "fancy ladies," slang for prostitutes.

Women garment workers on picket duty, circa 1909.

These often-desperate women sold their bodies to escape what one called "the biting, grinding poverty" of the tenements. Owners hired them to break the picket lines, allowing scabs to enter without having to face strikers. Groups of fancy ladies stormed out of the Bowery. Screaming and cursing, they scratched pickets' faces with their nails, jabbed them with hat pins, and clubbed them with lead-weighted umbrellas.[1]

Some strikers, however, encouraged the others to stand fast. To raise their spirits, they led them in Russian folk songs about resistance to oppression. A favorite, "Ekh, Dubinushka" ("Hey, Little Club"), was about the club that landowners used to beat peasants and about the coming revolution.

Hey, oaken club, come on!
Hey, the green club moves
by itself!
Let's pull, let's pull
together!

But the time has come,
and the people rose,
and it straightened its
mighty spine,
and it shook off from its
shoulders
the heavy yoke that had
been there
the heavy yoke that had
been there for centuries,
and now it raised the club
against its enemies.[2]

Owners saw such people and such songs as dangerous, because they inspired resistance in others. So they turned to the *shtarkers,* Yiddish for "sluggers" or "tough guys," gangsters who beat up anyone, even committed murder, for a few dollars. For example, they charged four dollars to blacken a person's eyes, ten dollars for breaking a nose, twenty-five dollars for a stabbing, and one hundred dollars and up for murder.[3]

Shtarkers *lounging on a tenement stoop, 1909.*

One day, Clara Lemlich set out for home after picket duty at the Leiserson Company. Like many immigrant women, Lemlich, twenty-three, had quit school and gone to work to help support her family. At first glance, she did not seem like a threat to anyone. Short and slim, she was five feet tall, with a round face, curly hair, and dark eyes. Oh, those eyes! When she felt wronged, they blazed with fury, and then the words came like a firestorm. "Ah—then I had fire in my mouth!" she said many years later. A natural leader,

Clara Lemlich helped to found Local 25.

she helped found Local 25. Lemlich, then, was what a sister worker called a "pint of trouble for the bosses." They wanted to shut her up and set an example for other troublemakers.[4]

As Lemlich walked home, two *shtarkers,* one an ex-prizefighter, attacked her with their fists. "Like rain, the blows fell on me," she recalled. When they finished, she lay on the side-walk bleeding, with six broken ribs. "Clara was so badly hurt," said a friend, "that she was laid up for several days." Though bruised and aching for weeks afterward, she soon returned to the picket line but did not tell her parents, not wanting to worry them. Meanwhile, the fancy ladies and sluggers terrorized the strikers.[5]

The police did nothing, for at this time the New York Police Department was riddled with corruption. Law enforcement, and much else in the city, was under the thumb of "the Hall." This was the popular name for Tammany Hall, or Democratic Party headquarters. Each election district had a Tammany club run by a leader called a "boss." A typical boss, like Timothy "Big Tim" Sullivan of the Lower East Side, cared for his district as if it were his family. People counted on Big Tim for free coal in a blizzard, free shelter after a tenement fire, and free turkeys and shoes on holidays. Yet the boss was no Santa Claus. He expected repayment with votes on Election Day.

A paddy wagon unloading strikers.

Victory at the polls allowed Tammany bosses to turn city government into their private cash register. Contracts to build bridges, sewers, and elevated railroads went to the highest bidder. Want a job as a city clerk or judge, or a promotion from patrolman to sergeant or captain? Pay up! Street-smart tenement kids knew the score. "What're pennies made of?" one would yell behind an officer's back, referring to his copper badge. "Dirty copper," the other shouted as they ran away laughing.

Since Tammany sided with the factory owners, the police did, too. Despite their efforts, the strikers were getting

"Big Tim" Sullivan (right), Tammany boss of the Lower East Side, 1913.

nowhere. Clearly, shop-by-shop strikes were not the answer. The public hardly noticed, or cared, about their plight. Time was against them. For without public support, they must admit defeat soon, leaving the owners stronger than ever. What to do?

Cooper Union

Local 25 gave out thousands of circulars in Yiddish, Italian, and English announcing a meeting at Cooper Union to discuss the situation. This sprawling redbrick building had great historic and symbolic meaning. Located a few blocks east of the Triangle Waist Company, Cooper Union offered free courses in art, science, and engineering. Fifty years earlier, Abraham Lincoln had denounced slavery in its Great Hall, a vast basement auditorium. People were not property, the future president said. No one had the right to own another person. As president, in 1863, at the height of the Civil War, Lincoln is-

sued the Emancipation Proclamation, freeing the slaves. Garment workers identified with the old-time slaves, calling themselves "wage slaves."

On the evening of November 22, some three thousand union and non-union workers packed the Great Hall. While the weather was cold outside, the

American Federation of Labor president Samuel Gompers, 1915.

crowd made the hall hot and stuffy. Celebrities, nearly all well-dressed and well-groomed men, sat on the stage: ILGWU leaders, columnists from Yiddish newspapers, guest of honor AFL president Samuel Gompers. For two hours, they droned on in Yiddish. Instead of discussing practical answers, they came across as uncertain. Gompers seemed weak. On the one hand, he warned, strikes were costly and to be avoided if possible. On the other hand, not striking might "rivet the chains of slavery upon our wrists." With each speech, the audience grew more restless.[6]

Suddenly a woman stood up. "I want to say a few words," she cried. A buzz of excitement went through the audience; everyone knew, or knew of, Clara Lemlich. "Get up on the platform," people shouted. When she got there, hands reached down to lift her.[7]

Those in the crowd would always remember Lemlich's few words. "I am a working girl, one of those striking against intolerable conditions," she said in Yiddish. "I am tired of listening to speakers who talk in generalities. . . . I offer a resolution that a general strike be declared. Now!" A general strike was the riskiest move imaginable. For it would shut down not merely some shops, but the entire shirtwaist industry, raising the stakes for both sides. Surely, it would demand huge sacrifices, but might also win a huge victory.[8]

Some Italians knew enough Yiddish to get Lemlich's meaning; others had it explained by those who spoke broken Italian with a Yiddish accent. The effect was electrical. A wave of excitement swept the Great Hall. Everyone rose, cheering. Chairman Benjamin Feigenbaum, of the *Jewish Daily Forward,* got carried away, too. "Do you mean it in good faith? Will you take the old Jewish oath?" he cried, raising his right hand. Thousands of hands shot up: "If I turn traitor to the cause I now pledge, may this hand wither from the arm I raise." With that pledge, a strike became an uprising.[9]

The Uprising of the Twenty Thousand

Next morning, November 23, every-one came to work as usual. But this day was different. You could feel the tension in the air. Most had never been on strike. Last night's enthusiasm had worn off and been replaced by fear. It was not the sluggers or the beatings; Clara Lemlich had come through all right. So would they—probably. These young women faced

The women of Local 25 voting to strike.

a harsher test. Although they might have saved a few dollars, these would not last through a long strike. How would they eat, or keep a roof over their heads, or help support their families without the weekly pay envelope? Did they have the inner stuff, the courage, to go on if things really got bad? Only time would tell.

Many shared the experience of Natalya Urosova, a sewing machine operator. "We all sat at the machines with our hats and coats beside us, ready to leave," she recalled. "Shall we wait like this?" they whispered, remembering the silence rule. "There is a general strike. Who will get up first?" It went like this for two hours, each debating with herself, each gathering her courage. Finally, Natalya got up. Just then, "we all got up together, in one second."[10]

The same scene was repeated in one factory after another. By evening, more than twenty thousand workers had left their sewing machines, thus the name "Uprising of the Twenty Thousand." By week's end, another ten thousand had walked off the job, including some of those princes, the cutters. So began the largest strike by women ever seen in the United States until then.

The sheer number of strikers forced the public to take notice and choose sides. If the owners had Tammany bosses, the police, and sluggers in their corner, the strikers found allies, too. Around the year 1900, a reform movement called "progressivism" set out to change America. Progressives believed in progress, the idea that society could, and must, be improved. While drawn from the well-to-do, the movement did not have one set of leaders or program. Instead, progressives formed many groups that aimed to create a "good society" by, among other things, eradicating slums, ending child labor, and furthering women's rights. To do that, however, they first had to fight political corruption and reduce the power of big business.

The Women's Trade Union League (WTUL) was a progressive group with branches in every major city. Composed largely of upper-middle-class and college-educated women,

the WTUL aimed at bettering the lives of working women by helping them organize trade unions. When the Uprising of the Twenty Thousand began, Mary Dreier, a wealthy person in her own right and president of the organization's New York chapter, offered to help.

Local 25 and the WTUL divided

Local 25, on strike.

their tasks. Local 25 officials negotiated with the owners for higher wages, a fifty-two-hour workweek, and a "closed shop." The last demand meant that a worker must join the union to get a job, in effect giving it control of the labor supply. That way, the union could set uniform work rules rather than have each owner set them for himself.

Meanwhile, the WTUL helped with the strikers' everyday problems. It rented meeting halls and set up telephone networks to keep strikers at various shops in touch. That was not as simple as it sounds, because many immigrant women did not know how to use a telephone. The WTUL also got reform-minded lawyers to defend, free of charge, arrested strikers in court. In these and other ways, as a striker put it, "the league women are the goodest of the good."[11]

Best of all, the WTUL helped strik-

Mary Dreier, head of the New York Women's Trade Union League.

ers outsmart factory owners and Tammany bosses. Mary Dreier and her aides believed the strike could not succeed without the support of public opinion. In short, it was also a propaganda battle in which shame was as potent a weapon as picket lines and nightsticks. The idea was to win the public's sympathy by embarrassing opponents. This, in turn, meant using the media to tell the strikers' story in the most favorable ways. Today, there are many media outlets: radio, television, the Internet, Twitter, YouTube. In 1911, however, only newspapers could reach a large audience quickly. America's leading newspapers were based in Manhattan. Stories in them flashed around the nation within hours by telegraph, then were picked up by countless other papers, which often printed them word for word.

To gain a "good press," the WTUL advised strikers to wear their best clothes on the picket lines. Always be polite. Never call anyone a "scab" or provoke them in any way. Acting like "ladies" would not only increase strikers' own self-respect, but show the public that immigrant women were responsible people who wanted only fair treatment.

To counter police brutality, WTUL members joined the picket lines, along with volunteers from the top women's colleges: Vassar, Bryn Mawr, Barnard, Wellesley. Police officers had a nasty habit. They would raise their nightsticks, promising to crack strikers' skulls if they so much as looked at them the wrong way. Russian Jews cringed; they remembered the czar's Cossacks. Knowing that WTUL members were on the picket lines and that pickets dressed very much alike made Tammany's "Cossacks" think twice about using their nightsticks. For how could you tell a "lady" from a common worker?

Going after the "wrong" woman could cause a scandal. One day, for example, a supervisor at the Triangle Waist Company heard Mary Dreier speak to a worker. "You are a dirty liar," he shouted. She turned to an officer and said, "You heard the language that man addressed to me. Am I not entitled to your protection?" The

*A group of striking
shirtwaist workers, 1909.*

officer arrested her for "disturbing the peace." When the judge learned her identity, he freed her on the spot. The officer stammered, "Why didn't you tell me you was a rich lady? I'd never have arrested you." Too late! Local newspapers pounced on the story. Not only did it embarrass the police and shop owners, it aroused sympathy for the strikers nation-wide.[12]

Despite WTUL help, the workers bore the brunt of their strike. The police arrested dozens each day, hauling them away in horse-drawn vans. Usually, they took them to the Tombs, the city prison, a grimy building with tiny barred windows and thick walls. Later, police took the prisoners to night court. There, Tammany judges fined them either three dollars or five dollars, a large sum in the best of times, a fortune to a striker. Sometimes, a lecture went with the fine, free of charge. Judge Olmstead, for example, confused factory owners with the Almighty: "You are on strike against God and nature, whose firm law is that man shall earn his bread in the sweat of his brow. You are on strike against God."[13]

Judges sentenced repeat offenders to the women's workhouse on Blackwell's Island (now Roosevelt Island) in the East River. They expected five days among prostitutes, thieves, and drug addicts to make strikers see the error of their ways. (For some unknown reason, though arrested seventeen times, Clara Lemlich was never sent to Blackwell's Island.)

One repeat offender, Rose Perr, was small and thin, with a child's voice and her hair in a braid down her back. Rose looked ten years old, not sixteen, her true age. Like any workhouse prisoner, she did hard labor. Wearing a scratchy woolen dress and heavy shoes, she scrubbed floors on her knees, with a brush, and washed mounds of dirty clothes. Washing exhausted healthy, well-fed, adult housewives; prisoners ate moldy bread and watery soup. Washing involved scrubbing wet clothes on a washboard with lye soap, which burned Rose's hands. Next, she placed the clothes in a vat of boiling water and stirred them with a wooden pole. Finally, she lifted them out with a stick, rinsed them (twice) in cold water, and hung them up to dry. Failure to finish on time, or breaking the silence rule, meant a sleepless night in the "dark room," a pitch-black dungeon teeming with rats and cockroaches.[14]

Sending strikers to the workhouse backfired, though. Instead of breaking their will, it toughened them. More, it made them martyrs, admired examples of people who would rather suffer than betray their cause. Having served their time, Rose Perr, Lena Lapido, and five other ex-prisoners were brought by boat to Manhattan. Upon their landing, WTUL greeters handed each a bouquet of American Beauty roses. The Lower East Side filled with pride. *Unzere vunderbare farbrente meydlekh,*" people called them in Yiddish. "Our wonderful fiery little girls."[15]

Their courage stiffened strikers' resolve, winning more allies. Race prejudice, we recall, all but barred African American women from the garment industry. The strike, however, gave them a chance to work

An illustration of the workhouse on Blackwell's Island, 1866.

in large numbers—as scabs. That set off a debate within the black community. Black women owed white strikers nothing, many said. Yet many more admired the strikers' grit and willingness to stand up for their rights. A mass meeting held in a black church had the last word on strike-breaking. It voted to urge "the colored girl" to "refrain from injuring other working women, and whenever possible, to ally herself with the cause of union labor." Black women honored the picket lines.[16]

Enter the Mink Coat Brigade

Still others saw the Uprising of the Twenty Thousand as more than a struggle over wages and working conditions. Called "feminists," they believed the Chinese proverb "Women hold up half the sky"—that women are just as important to the world as men. It followed that women should have equality with men and the same rights as they did, especially the vote. Women could not vote because, opponents said, politics would take away their charm, making them

unfit wives and mothers. (In 1920, the United States adopted the Nineteenth Amendment to the Constitution, giving women the right to vote.)

Alva Belmont disagreed. She was the widow of a millionaire banker, and her family owned New York City's major subway lines. An ardent feminist, too, she urged women: "Pray to God. She will help you." Belmont wanted women priests, women judges, women athletes—women everything. But none of that could happen unless women won the right to vote. A feminist poem titled "Why?" explained her reasoning.

Why are you paid less than
*   a man?*
Why do you work in a fire-trap?
Why are your hours so
*   long? . . .*
BECAUSE YOU ARE A
*   WOMAN AND HAVE NO*

VOTE.
VOTES MAKE THE LAW.
VOTES ENFORCE THE LAW.
THE LAW CONTROLS
   CONDITIONS.
WOMEN WHO WANT
   BETTER CONDITIONS
   MUST VOTE.[17]

In the 1950s and 1960s, the same reasoning, that votes mean power, drove the civil rights movement in its campaign for equality for African Americans. Alva Belmont supported the strike as a battle in the wider war for the vote. Doing so, she believed, educated strikers and the public about the link between working conditions and the ballot. She spent night after night in the Jefferson Market Court with her lawyer. When the police brought in strikers, often at 3:00 a.m., she posted their bail. "Mrs. Belmont has enough money," said an admirer. One night, however, she ran

Alva Belmont.

out of cash. Would Judge Butts, please, accept her Madison Avenue mansion as security? He would, and the strikers went home.[18]

Alva Belmont's example inspired the "Mink Coat Brigade," a group of wealthy women, to aid the strikers. Among them was Anne Morgan, thirty-six, the youngest child of banker J. Pierpont Morgan, among the richest men on the planet. The strike touched her deeply. For her, it was as much about human decency as votes for women. Strikers, she said, worked under such dreadful conditions that "we can't live our lives without doing something to help them." She joined the WTUL.[19]

Anything the Mink Coat Brigade did automatically made headlines. The idea was to barrage the public with dramatic events to win sympathy for the strikers—and eventually votes for women. In one event after another, strikers, WTUL members,

college students, champions of the vote for women, and clergy joined to focus attention on the strike. These events featured speeches by community leaders, followed by emotional "human interest" stories told in broken English with Yiddish and Italian accents. Reporters gobbled them up.

Alva Belmont began by sponsoring the largest meeting in New York labor history at the Hippodrome, an enormous arena used for sports events and circus performances. On December 6, speakers linked low wages to prostitution and both to women's lack of the vote. Yetta Ruth, seventeen, then told how arresting police officers called her things "a girl is ashamed to talk about."[20]

Next, Anne Morgan held a meeting at the Colony Club, a lavish social club she had founded. On December 15, some 150 ladies, the highest of high society, heard ten strikers tell their life stories. A girl explained that she had to quit school to support her parents and three small children on $3.50 a week. "My mother can't see good out of her eyes. That's all I've got to say. I am fifteen years old." The audience gasped when an Italian girl, who earned six dollars a week as a finisher, said her employer got a priest to denounce the strike. "A priest came to our shop and told us girls that if we struck we should go—excuse me, please, ladies—to hell." After the meeting, the ladies took their guests to tea and gave $1,300, a fortune, to the Local 25 strike fund.[21]

On December 21, the Mink Coat Brigade held a "motor parade." A line of fifteen chauffeur-driven automobiles moved down Fifth Avenue and through the Lower East Side. Alva Belmont and Anne Morgan rode in the lead autos. Each auto was decked with posters saying THE WORKHOUSE IS NO ANSWER TO THE DEMANDS FOR JUSTICE and VOTES FOR WOMEN. Strik-

Anne Morgan.

ers sat next to socialites. Since immigrant factory workers did not get to ride in an auto often, if ever, this was a thrilling experience. As they drove past the picket lines, Rose

Perr and other workhouse veterans smiled and waved, while strikers cheered.[22]

On January 2, 1910, strikers and their allies held an all-out rally in Carnegie Hall, the city's most famous concert hall, built by steel tycoon Andrew Carnegie. The rally's theme was the abuse of power by police and courts. In the front row of the stage, beside the speakers, sat twenty ex-workhouse inmates, and behind them 350 women who had been arrested, hauled into court, and fined. Each wore a sash with the message WORK-HOUSE PRISONER or ARRESTED. Overhead, banners declared THE WORK-HOUSE IS NO ANSWER TO A DEMAND FOR JUSTICE and PEACEFUL PICKETING IS THE RIGHT OF EVERY WORKER.[23]

The January 2 rally at Carnegie Hall, with strikers and their allies protesting the abuse of power.

Rose Perr moved the audience to tears, telling how she had been sent to Blackwell's Island because she had asked non-union workers "not to take the bread out of their sisters' mouths."[24]

Morris Hillquit gave the main speech. A prominent lawyer, Hillquit was also a leader of the Socialist Party. Socialists believed that society should own all factories, railroads, power plants, and banks, running them not for the benefit of the wealthy few, but for everyone. Hillquit stressed the importance of unions and the closed shop. Then he denounced greedy owners, brutal police officers, and corrupt judges. "Be of good cheer, sisters," he said, pointing to the workhouse veterans. "You are not alone in your fight. Your victory will be glorious."[25]

Anne Morgan was not pleased; she was, after all, a banker's daughter. Next morning, she blasted

Morris Hillquit.

Hillquit for trying to turn strikers into fanatical socialists. Apparently, she did not realize that socialism was deeply ingrained on the Lower East Side; many had brought the idea with them from Russia and Italy. Democratic socialists, the majority, wanted to bring change peacefully, through

Strikers taking a break from the picket line.

End

The strike dragged on. Both sides suffered. Unable to fill customers' orders for shirtwaists, owners of smaller shops could not pay their bills. Several closed their doors. As many as 350 other firms accepted the union's terms, took back their workers, and resumed production. The dozen largest firms, led by the Triangle Waist Company, held fast. Although willing to raise wages and reduce hours, they rejected the closed shop because they feared that having to hire only union members would make them lose control of their factories.

Meanwhile, it grew harder for the remaining strikers to keep going. Help from their allies could only go so far. Beyond that, they must make do as best they could. That was a lot to expect in the dead of winter. Wind-

the ballot box. While Anne Morgan and Alva Belmont still supported the strikers' cause, objections to socialism made some of their wealthy friends lose interest in the strike.

driven rain chilled pickets to the bone. Snow fell, then melted to slush. Many got sick but could not afford to see a doctor. Landlords evicted strikers for missing rent payments, tossing their belongings into the street. Credit at neighborhood grocery stores ran out. On December 25, the *New York Times* published an article titled "Facing Starvation to Keep Up the Strike," because it had come to that—starvation. "In this charitable city," the author said, "every homeless man may have turkey on Christmas Day, but there will be no turkey tomorrow for most of the striking shirtwaist makers. There is no charitable organization to provide a Christmas meal for poor women. . . . The girl who was [evicted] had only an apple for breakfast, she said, but she is still doing picket duty." She and others walked the picket line in lightweight over-coats and shoes with holes in their thin soles.[26]

Should they go back on their oaths, abandoning the strike? Some did, out of misery and concern for their families. Most did not. When, for example, Sarah Rozner thought she ought to return to work, her mother would not hear of it. Strike-breaking, she insisted, was a sin. "Sarah, we'll all die before [I will let] you go back to work."[27]

Nobody died. On February 15, 1910, the strike ended after more than twelve weeks. A day or two earlier, Max Blanck, of the Triangle Waist Company, met secretly with strike leaders. Mary Dreier recalled that he pleaded with them, saying "that he didn't want it to seem that we had beaten him into making changes." He added that if "we would only help him save his face and let the girls go

Women discussing the strike on the Bowery, 1910. What do you suppose the woman pointing her finger is saying?

back," he would meet their demands.[28]

Blanck's cave-in allowed both sides to claim victory. Local 25 and the holdout firms agreed on a 12 percent pay raise, a fifty-two-hour workweek, and an end to petty abuses like charging for needles and chairs. Although the major firms "accepted" the union, they agreed only not to dismiss workers who joined, but rejected the closed shop.

The ordeal proved that immigrant women could, and would, stand up for their rights. By the strike's end, 85 percent of all shirtwaist makers in New York had joined the ILGWU. Local 25 grew from a hundred members before the strike to at least twenty thousand after it. Most of all, said Morris Hillquit, it touched the conscience of New Yorkers. "The people of this city began to realize that society owes some duties" to those who struggle for a living. Yet the people's conscience would soon face another test. This time by fire.[29]

V

THE THIRD GATE: FIRE AT THE TRIANGLE

Hell has three gates: lust, anger, and greed.
—Bhagavad Gita, or Song of the Lord,
Hindu holy book (c. 200 BCE)

An Evil Omen

On the evening of Friday, March 24, 1911, two sisters, Becky and Gussie Kappelman, ages eighteen and twenty-two, came home from work at the Triangle Waist Company. Exhausted from their long day, they sat at a table in the three-room tenement apartment where they boarded. They sat silently, picking at their food, clearly upset. Finally, their landlady asked what was wrong. "Oh," Becky cried, "I wish we could quit the shop! This place is going to kill us someday."

Gussie explained that things had gotten worse since the end of the great uprising. Not only at their company, but at most shops, employers had broken their agreement with Local 25. They still fined workers for petty offenses. Experienced workers (who were paid more) had to teach six others all they knew, then were dismissed and replaced by the learners.

Strike leaders like Clara Lemlich were blacklisted, barred from working in the garment industry.

But what worried the sisters most was the threat of fire. Almost exactly four months earlier, on November 26, 1910, a blaze had trapped young immigrant women in a cotton underwear factory in nearby Newark, New Jersey. Next day, the lead article in the *New York Times* had these headlines:

23 DIE, 40 HURT IN NEWARK FIRE

Many Other Women and Girls Caught in a Flame-Swept Factory Missing

BUILDING WAS A FIRE TRAP

Two Fire Escapes on It Useless, and Victims, Ablaze, Leaped Out of High Windows

SOME IMPALED ON PICKETS

Firemen's Nets Smashed to the Ground with the Weight of Plunging Women

The thought of dying in a fire made Becky tremble with fear. "Since that factory in Newark where so many girls were burnt up," she said, "there's not a day when I don't wonder what would happen if a fire started in our shop." Little did she know that history was about to repeat itself, and practically just as described in the *New York Times* article, only on a larger scale. By evening of the next day, she would be among the victims of a disaster known to history simply as the Triangle Fire.[1]

A Disaster Waiting to Happen

At first glance, the sisters' fears did not seem reasonable. The Newark blaze happened in a rickety four-story

The Asch Building, on the corner of Greene Street and Washington Place.

wooden building dating back to the Civil War. The ten-story Asch Building, where they worked, was a modern, fireproof skyscraper. Built in 1901 of steel and concrete, nothing short of a powerful internal explosion could bring it down. Each stairway landing had a standpipe, a large, upright pipe connected to a 5,500-gallon water tank on the roof. The standpipe allowed a fire hose kept on a nearby rack to release water at high pressure. Every floor had buckets filled with water placed at key points. Should a fire break out, hallways also had an alarm box; pulling the lever in any box set bells clanging in firehouses across the Lower East Side.

The Fire Department of the City of New York (FDNY) had a highly trained, professional force. Admired for their courage, firefighters would one day earn the nickname "New York's Bravest."

Their equipment was top-notch, by 1911 standards, but not perfect. Aerial ladders and portable towers lifted firefighters and water high above the ground. Unfortunately, no ladder could reach above the sixth floor of a building. (A modern ladder can reach the twelfth floor.) Horses drew firefighters and their equipment to the scene of a fire. While factories turned out automobiles and trucks in ever larger numbers, the FDNY did not get its first motorized vehicles until later in the year. (The FDNY retired its last horse-drawn vehicles in 1922.) Water came from a maze of pipes, called mains, buried under the city's streets. Mains fed thousands of hydrants, large upright pipes with hose connections for drawing water. A system of cutoffs allowed area pumping stations to shut down certain mains to increase water pressure in hydrants along a selected street.

The science of fire prevention was as advanced as that of firefighting, proof that necessity is the mother of invention. New England's cotton mills in the 1880s had been dangerous places. Spinning thread and weaving cloth filled the air with cotton dust. When inhaled over

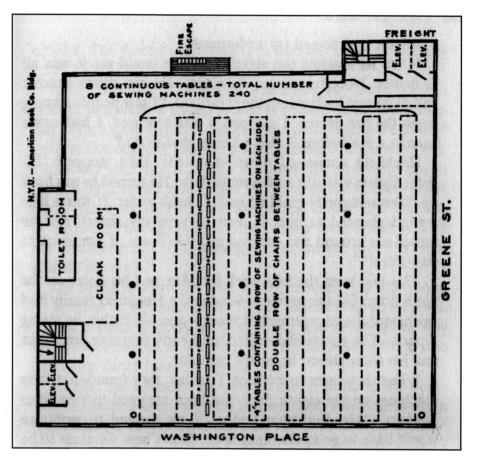

a long period, the dust irritated lung tissue, even destroyed it, causing a lingering death. Worse, dust built up like "snowdrifts" on mill floors and machinery. Any spark could ignite the

A diagram showing the ninth floor of the Asch Building, which had eight long tables that stretched across the length of the room.

particles, causing a terrific explosion. Hundreds died every year in cotton mill fires and explosions.

By the 1890s, however, such disasters lay in the past for two reasons. First, the invention of the sprinkler made it possible to drown a fire in seconds. Sprinklers, attached to ceilings, had sensitive fuses. Heat rising from a fire triggered the fuses, which automatically released a deluge of water stored in overhead sprinkler pipes. Second, cotton mills adopted fire drills. In these, employees rehearsed what to do at the sound of an alarm or the sight of fire. Thus, if a fire broke out, they could reach safety quickly and without panic, a major cause of death in fires. Schools adopted fire drills, too. Each year, depending on the state, every school had to have a set number of fire drills.

These precautions, though well known, were almost totally absent in New York City, because fire safety did not "pay." It did not pay the insurance industry, since safer buildings lowered insurance costs, reducing the earnings of insurance sellers, called brokers. They made their living by keeping a percentage of the cost of a policy sold to a client. High-risk clients paid higher rates, raising agents' incomes.[2]

Safety did not "pay" factory owners, either. Let's say an owner had many unsold garments at the end of the summer season. A fire might be a good business move, ridding him of extra stock while allowing him to collect its value from his insurance company. Arson was a big business in New York. Certain gangsters specialized in torching garment shops—for a price. The insurance companies seldom made a fuss, because their total profits were still greater than the claims they paid to individual owners. Owners did not install sprinklers because that cost money; they also thought they might have to burn their shops later. Fire drills, owners feared, might raise suspicions about their intentions. Besides, time spent on a fire drill took away from work time. No laws required owners to have sprinklers or hold fire drills.[3]

And the workers? What of them? "The neglect of factory owners in the matter of safety of their employees is absolutely criminal," said H. F. J. Porter, New York's leading safety engineer. "One man whom I advised to install a fire drill replied to me: 'Let 'em burn. They're a lot of cattle, anyway.'" Workers could easily be replaced.[4]

The Asch Building had recently had four small fires of unknown cause, but at night when nobody was around. City inspectors reported that the building, though fireproof, did not have enough exits. There were two concrete stairways leading from the tenth floor to exits on Washington Place and Greene Street, around the corner. The stairways were narrow, just thirty-three inches wide, meaning that people would have to walk single file to get out. Exit doors swung inward, because the stairways were too narrow for them to swing outward without hitting a wall and blocking the way. This meant that panicky workers might bunch up at a door, shutting it by the weight of their own bodies. There was also a fire escape, or series of steel ladders, bolted to the building's outer wall. It led to a rear courtyard, ending six feet above a glass skylight. A six-foot iron rail fence, topped with four-inch spikes, enclosed the skylight to deter burglars. Two elevators on opposite sides of the building carried passengers and freight.

FDNY chief Edward F. Croker was among the bravest of the Bravest. He had always had one ambition in life: to be a firefighter. Saving lives, he said, was "a noble profession." The chief would not hesitate to charge into a burning building as the roof seemed about to collapse to see if it was safe to let his men enter. Like the Kappelman sisters, Croker feared the worst.

Fireproof construction, he knew, would save a building from collapse, but fire would consume those who worked inside it. "This city may have a fire as deadly as the one in Newark at any time," he warned. "A fire in the daytime would be accompanied by a terrible loss of life."[5]

And so it was.

Holocaust

As we saw, the Triangle Waist Company occupied the top three floors of the Asch Building. On the eighth floor, forty cutters, all men, worked at long wooden tables. Nearby, about a hundred women did basting and other tasks. Paper patterns hung from lines of string over the tables. Although cutters wasted as little fabric as possible, there were always scraps, which they threw into bins under the tables. Every two months or so, a rag dealer took away about a ton of scraps, paying about seven cents a pound. He then sold them back to cotton mills to remake into new cloth. The last pickup was in January.

On March 25, the cutters prepared for their next day's work. Since it was Saturday, everyone would leave early, at 4:45 p.m. Workers from other firms had already left; Triangle employees had to stay longer to fill back orders. Carefully, cutters spread "lawn" (from the French word *lingerie*) on their tables 120 layers thick. Lawn was not just *any* cotton fabric. Sheer and lightweight, it was beautiful and comfortable—and burned as easily as gasoline. Each layer was separated from the others by a sheet of equally flammable tissue paper.

After cutting, the various pieces would go by freight elevator to the ninth floor for sewing and finishing. There, eight rows of sewing machine tables, holding 288 machines in all, occupied the entire width of the room. Only a narrow aisle separated one row from another; the tables were so close together that chairs touched back to back between the rows. From time to time, workers would take the finished shirt-waists to the tenth floor for inspection, packing, and shipping. This floor also held the showroom and owners' offices.

By 4:40 p.m., the cutters had finished their work. With five minutes to go, they stood around, talking until the quitting bell rang. Although it was against the rules, some lit cigarettes, hiding the smoke by blowing it up their jacket sleeves. On the floor above, workers had begun to walk toward the lockers to get their coats and hats. They looked forward to Sunday and family visits, boyfriends, dances, and nickelodeons. Although they had no inkling of what was about to happen, many had only minutes to live.

We will never know for sure what started the Triangle Fire. Most likely, a cutter flicked a hot ash or tossed a live cigarette butt into a scrap bin. Whatever the cause, survivors said the first sign of trouble was smoke pouring from beneath a cutting table.

Cutters flung buckets of water at the smoking spot, without effect. Flames shot up, igniting the line of hanging paper patterns. "They began to fall on the layers of thin goods underneath them," recalled cutter Max Rothen. "Every time another piece dropped, light scraps of burning fabric began to fly around the room. They came down on the other tables and they fell on the machines. Then the line broke and the whole string of burning patterns fell down." A foreman ran for the hose on the stairway wall. Nothing! No water came. The hose had not been connected to the standpipe. Seconds later, the fire leaped out of control.[6]

Yet help was already on the way. At exactly 4:45 p.m., someone pulled the eighth-floor fire alarm. In less than two minutes, the horse-drawn vehicles of Engine Company 72 arrived from a firehouse six blocks away. The moment

Fire engines racing to the burning building.

a fire. Heat can easily damage their machinery, leaving trapped passengers dangling in space, to burn or suffocate. Despite the danger, the operators made several trips, saving scores of workers before heat bent the elevators' tracks and put them out of action.

Those who could not board elevators rushed the stairway door. They caused a pileup, so that those in front could not open the door. Whenever someone tried to get it open, the crowd pinned her against it. "All the girls were falling on me and they squeezed me to the door," Ida Willensky recalled. "Three times I said to the girls, 'Please, girls, let me open the door. Please!' But they would not listen to me." Finally, cutter Louis Brown barged through the crowd and forced the door open.[7]

Workers, shouting, crying, and gasping for air, slowly made their way downstairs. There were no lights in the stairway, so they had to grope their way in darkness. A girl fell; others fell on top

they arrived, the firefighters unloaded their equipment and prepared to swing into action. As they did, the area pumping station raised water pressure in the hydrants near the Asch Building. Other units soon arrived from across the Lower East Side with more equipment.

Meanwhile, workers on the eighth floor rang furiously for the two passenger elevators. Safety experts have always advised against using elevators in of her, blocking the stairs until firefighters arrived moments later. Yet everyone who took the strairway from the eighth floor got out alive, exiting through the Washington Place doors. Those on the ninth floor were not so lucky.

New Yorkers say that March comes in like a lion (with cold wind) and leaves like a lamb (with April's warm showers). Now, as fire raged on the eighth floor, the elevator shafts became wind tunnels. Wind gusts made eerie sounds, like the howling of great beasts in pain, while sucking flaming embers upward. On the ninth floor, embers landed on piles of finished shirtwaists and cans of oil used to make the sewing machines run smoothly. Instantly, the air itself seemed to catch fire.

Had there been fire drills, surely more would have survived. Unfortunately, confusion reigned. Workers had to make life-and-death decisions in split seconds amid fire, smoke, and panic. It was everyone for themselves. "I was throwing them out of the way," Mary Bucelli said of the women near her. "No matter whether they were in front of me or coming from in back of me, I was pushing them down. I was only looking out for my own life." Mary joined others who ran to the Greene Street stairway. They made it down to the street or up to the tenth floor and the roof, before flames blocked this escape route.[8]

Others headed for the elevators and stairway on the Washington Place side of the building. Forcing open the doors to the elevator shaft, they looked down and saw an elevator starting what would be its last trip from the eighth floor. "I reached out and grabbed the cables, wrapped my legs around them, and started to slide down," recalled Samuel Levine, a sewing machine operator. "While on my way down, as slow as I could let myself drop, the bodies of six girls went falling past me. One of them struck me, and I fell on top of the elevator. I fell on the dead body of a girl.

Finally I heard the firemen cutting their way into the elevator shaft, and they came and let me out."[9]

Those who reached the ninth-floor stairway door found it locked. This was not unusual, as employers often locked doors to discourage latecomers and keep out union organizers. "My God, I am lost!" cried Margaret Schwartz as her hair caught fire. Nobody who went to that door survived, nor any who reached the windows.[10]

With a wave of fire rolling across the room, workers rushed to the windows, only to meet more fire. Hot air expands. Unless it escapes, pressure will keep building, eventually blowing a hole even in a heavy iron container like a boiler. Heat and pressure blew out the eighth-floor windows. Firefighters call the result "lapping in"—that is, sucking flames into open windows above. That is why you see black scorch marks on the wall above the window of a burnt-out room.

With fire advancing from behind and flames rising before them, people knew they were doomed. Whatever they did meant certain death. By remaining in the room, they chose death by fire or suffocation. Jumping ninety-five feet to the ground meant death on the sidewalk. We cannot know what passed through the minds of those who decided to jump. Yet their thinking, in those last moments of life, may have gone like this: If I jump, my family will have a body to identify and bury, but if I stay in this room, there will be nothing left.

A girl clung to a window frame until flames from the eighth floor lapped in, burning her face and setting fire to her hair and clothing. She let go. Just then, Frances Perkins reached the scene from her friend's town house on the north side of Washington Square. "Here they come," onlookers shouted as Engine Company 72 reined in their horses. "Don't jump; stay there." Seconds later,

Hook and Ladder Company 20 arrived.[11]

Firefighters charged into the building, stretching a hose up the stairways as they went. At the sixth-floor landing, they connected it to the standpipe. Reaching the eighth floor, they crawled into the inferno on their bellies, under the rising smoke, with their hose. Yet nothing they did could save those at the windows. Photos of the portable towers show streams of water playing on the three top floors. (A modern high-pressure pumper can send water as high as one thousand feet.) Plenty of water got through the windows, but not those with people standing in them. A burst of water under high pressure would have hurled them backward, into the flames.

Firefighters attempt to extinguish the fire, but ladders only reach the sixth floor.

Hoping to catch jumpers before they hit the ground, firefighters held up life nets, sturdy ten-foot-square nets made of rope. It was useless. A person falling from the ninth floor struck with a force equal to eleven thousand pounds. Some jumpers bounced off nets, dying when they hit the ground; others tore the nets, crashing through to the pavement. "The force was so great it took men off their feet," said Captain Howard Ruch of Engine Company 18. "Trying to hold the nets, the men turned somersaults. The men's hands were bleeding, the nets were torn and some caught fire" from burning clothing. Officers, fearing their men would be struck by falling bodies, ordered the nets removed. The aerial ladders failed, too, reaching only to the sixth floor. Desperate jumpers tried to grab hold of a rung on the way down, missed, and landed on the sidewalk.[12]

People began to jump singly or in groups of two or three, holding hands as they stepped out the windows.

William G. Shepherd, a reporter for United Press, watched the "shower of bodies" in horror.

I saw every feature of the tragedy visible from outside the building. I learned a new sound—a more horrible sound than any description can picture. It was the sound of a speeding, living body on a stone sidewalk.

Thud—dead, thud—dead, thud—dead, thud—dead. Sixty-two thud—dead. I call them that, because the sound and the thought of death came to me each time, at the same instant. . . . Down came the bodies in a shower, burning, smoking—flaming bodies, with the disheveled hair trailing upward. . . .

On the sidewalk lay heaps of broken bodies. A policeman later went about with tags, which he fastened with wires to the wrists of the dead girls. . . . The floods of water from the firemen's hose that ran into the gutter was actually stained red with blood.[13]

Onlookers saw many dreadful sights, none more so than the end of a love affair. A young man appeared at a window. Gently, he helped a young woman step onto the windowsill, held her away from the building—and let go. He helped another young woman onto the windowsill. "Those of us who were looking saw her put her arms around him and kiss him," Shepherd wrote. "Then he held her out into space and dropped her. But quick as a flash he was on the windowsill himself. . . . He was brave enough to help the girl he loved to a quicker death, after she had given him a goodbye kiss."[14]

Meanwhile, others managed to reach the fire escape. It had not been designed for a quick exit. FDNY experts later declared that those on the three top floors of the Asch Building could not have made it to the ground in under three hours. In reality, they had only minutes.

People crowded onto the fire escape. As they walked single file, flames lapped at them through broken windows. Worse, the human load became too heavy for the device to bear. Bolts that fastened it to the building became loose. It began to sway, then collapsed at the eighth floor, tumbling dozens into

The collapsed fire escape.

the courtyard. "As the fire-crazed victims were thrown by the collapse of the fire escape, several struck the sharp-tipped palings," the New York *Herald* reported. "The body of one woman was found with several iron spikes driven entirely through it." Others crashed through the skylight into the room below, where they died on the cement floor.[15]

The tenth floor was the best place to be. Those who worked there, or reached it from the floor below, survived by dashing up the stairs to the roof. When they arrived, they found the roof fifteen feet lower than its Washington Place neighbor's, a building shared by New York University and the American Book Company.

Luckily, Professor Frank Sommer was teaching his law class in a room that overlooked the Asch Building. When Sommer realized what was happening, he led his class to the roof of their building. There they found two ladders left by painters during the week. Students lowered the ladders, climbed down, and helped survivors to safety. For some women, said Sommer, "it was necessary to beat out the flames that had caught their clothing, and many of them had blackened faces and singed hair and eyebrows." Yet only one person from the tenth floor died. Seeing flames licking up from the ninth floor, she panicked and jumped out a window.[16]

By 5:15 p.m., exactly thirty-five minutes after flames burst from beneath a cutting table, firefighters had brought the blaze under control. An hour later, Chief Croker made his inspection. He found that the Asch Building had no damage to its structure. Its walls were in good shape; so were the floors. It had passed the test. It was fireproof.

The woodwork, furniture, cotton goods, and people who worked in it were not. Of the 500 Triangle employees who reported for work that day, 146

The decimated ninth floor of the Asch Building. The structure itself was fireproof, though everything inside was destroyed.

died. Of these, sixteen men were identified. The rest were women or bodies and body parts listed as "unidentified."

The Triangle Fire was New York's worst workplace disaster up to that time. Only the September 11, 2001, terrorist

In the wake of the fire, doctors examine victims, hoping for survivors.

FDNY chief Edward Croker, 1910.

attacks on the twin towers of the World Trade Center took more (about 2,500) lives.

Chief Croker was no softie; he was used to the horrors that came with his job. But this was different. As he explored the top three floors of the Asch Building, he saw sights "that utterly staggered him," the New York *World* reported. "In the drifting smoke, he had seen bodies burned to bare bones, skeletons bending over sewing machines." Those sights sent him down to the street with quivering lips.[17]

Next morning, March 26, Chief Croker returned for another look. The only creatures he found alive were some half-drowned mice. He picked one up, stroked it gently, and put it in his pocket. The chief would take it home, he said. "It's alive. At least it's alive."[18]

VI

A STRICKEN CONSCIENCE

There was a stricken conscience of public guilt and we all felt that we had been
wrong, that something was wrong with that building which we had accepted or the
tragedy never would have happened. Moved by this sense of stricken guilt, we banded
ourselves together to find a way by law to prevent this kind of disaster.
—*Frances Perkins, March 25, 1961*

Shock and Mourning

New Yorkers' first reaction to the Triangle Fire was shock. The tragedy deeply affected police officers at the scene, some of whom, surely, had bullied strikers during the Uprising of the Twenty Thousand. These tough street cops took pride in having "seen everything" in the line of duty. But they had not. Horrible sights, of falling bodies and bodies burned beyond recognition, left them shaken. In a typical exchange, a newspaper reporter pointed to charred remains on the sidewalk. "Is that a man or a woman?" he asked. The stunned officer turned pale as a sheet of paper. "It's human, that's all you can tell," he said with trembling lips.[1]

Somehow, dazed survivors found their way home. Most lived close enough to the Asch Building to go on

Firefighters at the scene.

foot. Josephine Nicolosi and a friend walked back to Little Italy. Both were dirty and in tears; Josephine's face was also streaked with blood. When her mother saw her from their tenement window, she ran downstairs. Josephine grabbed hold of her—tight. *"Tutti morti, Mamma, tutti morti,"* she sobbed over and over. "All dead, Mama, all dead." We do not know about Josephine's life after the fire. We can be sure, however, that she never forgot her experience.[2]

"Time heals all wounds," the saying goes. It does not. Fire survivors, and survivors of other life-threatening events such as wars and natural disasters, may not have visible wounds.

Certain wounds do not bleed, nor can they be bandaged or treated with medicine. For they are wounds to the spirit, invisible scars carried for the rest of the survivors' lives. They may constantly remember and relive the experience. Nightmares may jolt them awake, shaking, sweating, and screaming. Everyday noises—sirens, clanging bells, thunder—can make them panic.

So it was with those who lived through the Triangle Fire. Two examples tell their story. "I couldn't stop crying for hours, for days," Rose Cohen recalled at the time. "Afterwards, I used to dream I was falling from a window, screaming. I remember I would holler to my mother in the dark, waking everybody up, 'Mama! I just jumped out of a window!' Then I would start crying and I couldn't stop." Rose Freedman, the last survivor of the fire, died peacefully at the age of 107 in the year 2001. The memory of the fire stayed with her to the end. "I have always tears in my eyes when I think" of it, she said. "I feel it. Still."[3]

After putting out the blaze, firefighters gathered the victims' remains. That night, horse-drawn ambulances took them to a temporary morgue at "Misery Lane," a large shed on a nearby East River pier. At midnight, police officers allowed the anxious crowd to file in slowly. "Everywhere," a *New York Times* reporter wrote, "burst anguished cries for sister, mother, and wife, and a dozen pet names in Italian and Yiddish rising in shrill agony above the deeper moan of the throng." Most bodies were too badly burned and broken for easy identification. Families found their own by recognizing a ring, a locket, the heel of a shoe. Esther Rosen touched the hair of a woman in a coffin. "It's mamma's hair. I braided it for her," she said.[4]

The fire sent ripples of misery in all directions. The greatest hurt, of course, was the loss of a loved one, a profound

The temporary morgue at "Misery Lane," where people searched for their loved ones.

emotional shock. Yet that loved one had also played a practical role. Victims, usually daughters, had been family breadwinners. Often, too, they supported aged parents in Russia and Italy. How could these people live now?

In response to the tragedy, New Yorkers gave generously. The American Red Cross, the WTUL, the ILGWU, and many civic organizations took up collections. Individuals, rich and poor alike, opened their purses. Alva Belmont, Anne Morgan, and Andrew Carnegie gave on their own and got their friends to give. Donations arrived at newspaper offices. A letter from a young boy reached the *New York Times* with a ten-dollar bill. It came with instructions to "please give it to the right one to use it for somebody whose little girl jumped out of a window." In all, some $150,000 was collected, worth about $3,411,000 in 2009 dollars.[5]

During the week after the fire, funeral processions wound through the streets of the Lower East Side and Little Italy. On March 27, a reporter for the *New York Evening Post* wrote, "One could scarcely walk a distance of two blocks in certain . . . neighborhoods without coming upon a hearse." In Little Italy, he added, "up narrow, twisting flights of stairs in many a tenement, one came upon [a] funeral in progress." The Maltese family had three funerals: for Catherine, the mother, and her two daughters, Rosaria, fourteen, and Lucia, twenty.

By the first week in April, all that remained was to bury seven unclaimed and unidentified bodies in a Brooklyn cemetery. As the day approached, sadness mixed with anger in the city's immigrant neighborhoods. Morris Rosenfeld, the Yiddish poet, expressed the mood in a poem that filled the entire front page of the *Jewish Daily Forward*. He damned "you golden princes," you greedy factory owners, for making such a tragedy possible. A few lines:

Over whom shall we weep first?
Over the burned ones?
Over those beyond recognition?
Over those who have been crippled?
Or driven senseless?
Or smashed?
I weep for them all.

Let us light the holy candles
And mark the sorrow. . . .

This is our funeral,
These our graves,
Our children,
The beautiful, beautiful flowers
destroyed,
Our lovely ones burned,
Their ashes buried under a
mountain of caskets.[6]

April 5, 1911. Funeral procession moves up Fifth Avenue through Washington Arch, at the north end of Washington Square Park.

April 5, 1911. The day matched the mood. It dawned gray and rainy. New York had not seen anything like it since Abraham Lincoln's funeral procession almost forty-six years earlier that month. The route led from Washington Square, up Fifth Avenue, to a ferry dock on the East River. According to the police department, 400,000 people turned out, of whom no fewer than 120,000 joined the line of marchers, led by horse-drawn hearses draped in black. Despite the

Horse-drawn hearses lead a procession for unidentified victims of the fire.

crowd's size, the only sound was the pitter-patter of raindrops and rumbling of hearse wheels over cobblestones; otherwise, it was so quiet you could hear a pin drop.

Martha Bruere, a wealthy reformer, watched the procession go past her window for six hours. "Never have seen a military pageant or triumphant ovation so impressive," she wrote in her diary. "It is dawning on these thousands on thousands that such things do not have to be!"[7]

From time to time, gusts of wind-blown rain lashed the onlookers, the marchers, and the banners they carried. Some carried trade union banners, others black-bordered banners with the inscription WE MOURN OUR LOSS. A group of women garment workers carried a banner reading WE DEMAND FIRE PROTECTION.[8]

Never Again!

Three days earlier (April 2), civic and religious leaders, progressive reformers, members of the Mink Coat Brigade, and workers had attended a mass meeting at the Metropolitan Opera House. Anne Morgan had rented the building for the Women's Trade Union League to discuss action on fire safety in the workplace. Speakers called for a resolution asking the city to create a Bureau of Fire Prevention. Suddenly shouts came from the upper galleries, filled with workers. For *this*, 146 young people had died! No, they wanted something stronger than a scrap of paper that officials tied to Tammany Hall would pretend to welcome, then ignore. The meeting seemed about to break up in anger and disgust when a woman sitting onstage near Frances Perkins stood to have her say.[9]

Rose Schneiderman, twenty-nine, stepped forward. Nicknamed Little Rose, she stood four feet eight inches and had flaming-red hair. The daughter of a widowed Polish immigrant mother, she went to work at thirteen and quickly got involved in union

A 1911 gathering of union workers and sympathizers to mourn those lost in the fire and to protest dangerous working conditions.

organizing. During the Uprising of the Twenty Thousand, she led the workers out of the Triangle factory. A forceful speaker, she was never at a loss for words.

Schneiderman now gave a speech that became an American classic. Here is some of what she said:

> I would be a traitor to these poor burned bodies if I came here to talk good fellowship. We have tried you good people of the public and we have found you wanting. The old [Spanish] Inquisition had its rack and its thumbscrews and its instruments of torture with iron teeth. We know what these things are today; the iron teeth are our necessities, the thumbscrews are the high-powered and swift machinery close to which we must work, and the rack is here in the firetrap structures that will destroy us the minute they catch on fire. . . . The life of men and women is so cheap and property is so sacred. There are so many of us for one job it matters little if 146 of us are burned to death. . . .

> We have tried you citizens; we are trying you now, and you have a couple of dollars for the sorrowing mothers, brothers and sisters by way of a charity gift. . . . Public officials have only words of warning to us— warning that we must be intensely peaceable, and they have the workhouse just back of their warnings. The strong hand of the law beats us back, when we rise, into the conditions that make life unbearable.

> I can't talk fellowship to you who are gathered here. Too much blood has been spilled. I know from my experience it is up to the

*working people to save
themselves.*[10]

Little Rose's emotional speech changed the tone of the meeting. Catcalls from the galleries stopped. Those onstage pledged to form a blue-ribbon citizens' committee to demand reforms from the New York State legislature. Anne Morgan and Mary Dreier of the WTUL were among its members. Frances Perkins joined as committee secretary and contact person with the lawmakers. Her job was to persuade them to pass the laws the committee asked for statewide. She would soon learn how things were done in politics.

Enter Al Smith

In Albany, the state capital, lawmakers listened to Perkins's ideas, nodded agreement, smiled, and did nothing. She was getting nowhere—fast. Then she met Al Smith, "the gorgeous knight of the brown derby and the cocked cigar."[11]

Bread and Roses

Little Rose Schneiderman continued her efforts to improve the lives of working people. In the August 1912 issue of the WTUL magazine *Life and Labor*, she wrote: "What the woman who labors wants is to live, not simply exist—the right to life as the rich woman has it, the right to life, and the sun, and music, and art. You have nothing that the humblest worker has not a right to have also. The worker must have bread, but she must have roses too."

Bread and roses! By "bread," Schneiderman meant material things: higher wages, shorter hours, safer workplaces, health care. "Roses" stood for the things of the spirit: educational opportunities, recreation, the chance to develop one's mind to the fullest extent possible—in short, the right to become a complete person.

In that same year, 1912, women led a massive strike in Lawrence, Massachusetts, the largest cloth-manufacturing town on earth. "We must have bread—and roses too," was their rallying cry.

Schneiderman became president of the New York chapter of the WTUL and head of the New York State Department of Labor. She also became friends with Eleanor Roosevelt. When Eleanor's husband, Franklin D. Roosevelt, became president in 1933, Little Rose helped shape major laws. The Social Security Act provided pensions for the elderly. The National Labor Relations Act guaranteed workers the right to organize unions. The Fair Labor Standards Act set the national minimum wage, required overtime pay after forty hours a week, and forbid child labor and factory work at home—that is, in sweatshops.

Schneiderman died in 1972, at the age of eighty-eight.

Alfred E. Smith was a child of the Lower East Side. "Al," as everyone called him, stood five feet seven inches and had a pink face and a large "pickle" nose. Born to an Irish mother and Italian-German father, he identified most with his Irish heritage. Growing up in the shadow of the Brooklyn Bridge, he, like other boys, pitched pennies, played stickball, and, in summer, dove off piers into the East River. That took a strong stomach, as an old-timer explained: "The only recreation was to go down to the East River where the barges were. The people would swim in it, but they also moved their bowels there." Al spoke in the accent of the streets. "Woids" like "woik," "foist," "poisonally," and "avenoo" tumbled off his tongue as he strolled the "sidewauks" of "Noo Yawk." And he talked with food in his mouth, spraying bystanders.[12]

Forced to quit school and find a job after his father's death, the eighth-grade dropout boasted that he held degrees, with honors, from two of the world's finest schools: the Fulton Fish Market and the College of Hard Knocks. Starting as a shlepper in the Fulton Fish Market, no place for sissies, Al graduated to running errands for local Tam-

Al Smith's tenement neighborhood, in the shadow of the Brooklyn Bridge (drawing circa 1909).

many Hall bigwigs. They liked the brash teenager, who told hilarious jokes and spat on the floor between puffs of a huge cigar that seemed glued to the corner of his mouth. Yet he was also a go-getter, an organizer with a gift for making friends.

Smith rose through Tammany's ranks. A shrewd political operator, he became majority leader in the New York State Assembly. (Eventually, he would serve four terms as governor.) Unlike corrupt bosses, however, he had real sympathy for the poor. Al understood how doctors' bills could burn up a family's savings, forcing it deeper into poverty, and how children became adults without ever having a pair of new shoes. Immigrant Jews called him *"ein Irisher mensch,"* literally "an Irish man." But *mensch* means more than "man" in Yiddish; it also means "real man," a "good guy," with a heart of gold. When, for example, he saw bullies throw rocks at a peddler, Al said nothing. Instead, he put his arm around the old fellow as if he were a brother. That was a signal to the bullies: Leave him alone, or Tammany will "fix" you.[13]

Tragedy brought out the best in Al Smith. Many Triangle Fire victims lived in his district. That night, he told Frances Perkins, he visited the tenements where they had lived to tell their families "of his sympathy and grief." Toward midnight, he went to the morgue to help grieving relatives identify their loved ones' remains. "It was a human, natural, decent thing to do," Perkins recalled, "and it was a sight he never forgot." He did not want to go through such an ordeal ever again.[14]

Smith gave Perkins some advice. Bringing about reform requires more than fine speeches by well-meaning people. It requires *politics.* And that means getting the state legislature to set up its own commission. "If the legislature does it," he said, "the legislature will be proud of it, the legislature will listen to their report, and the legislature will do something about it." Otherwise, reform will just get "the cold shoulder."[15]

Although eager to set up a commission, Smith could do nothing without the consent of Tammany Hall. And that meant winning over "Silent Charlie" Murphy. Nothing important happened in New York City or New York State government without the approval of Charles F. Murphy, Tammany's supreme boss of bosses. An unsmiling, quiet man, he believed it better to say nothing than risk saying too much. True to his belief, he spoke little, sometimes waiting minutes between sentences, then saying "Maybe." Murphy was a political calculating machine. For him, any problem boiled down to two questions: What is in it for Tammany Hall? How can we get votes at election time?

Until the Triangle Fire, Tammany Hall had been a largely Irish affair. Although "the Hall" originated in the 1790s, it really gained power in the 1850s. In the 1840s, the potato crop, Ireland's chief food, failed for several years running. Tens of thousands starved to death; entire villages lay deserted, their roofs collapsed and their streets covered with weeds. As the

*"Silent Charlie" Murphy,
the Tammany chief, circa 1924.*

Fate of Max Blanck and Isaac Harris

On March 30, 1911, five days after the fire, the partners reopened their business at another location near Washington Place. They began an advertising campaign to restore the Triangle name's image. It failed; nothing could clear its name, or theirs.

On April 11, the Manhattan district attorney indicted them for manslaughter—that is, the unintended but unlawful killing of a person. The charge grew out of survivors' testimony about the locked door on the ninth floor. In December, the jury returned a verdict of not guilty. It reasoned that, while Blanck and Harris had locked the door in the past, no one could prove they had done so on the day of the fire. If it was locked, someone may have done it without the owners' knowledge or consent. When the judge read the verdict, victims' family members in court fainted. "Murderers!" a young man cried. "Murderers! Not guilty! *Not guilty?* Where is the justice?" The title of a magazine article said it all: "147 Dead, Nobody Guilty."[16] (There were slight discrepancies in numbers due to early reporting.)

Blanck and Harris filed insurance claims larger than their losses. Their insurance company decided not to fight; it paid two hundred thousand dollars, or sixty thousand dollars above the proven value of the partners' losses. Seen another way, the settlement was a profit of $410.95 for each fire victim. Eventually, the partners paid victims' families seventy-five dollars for each life lost. The Triangle Waist Company soon fell on hard times. Competitors took away customers. Styles changed. In 1914, Blanck and Harris were caught faking union labels, proof that a garment was made under decent conditions. The company disappeared around the year 1918.

Governor Alfred E. Smith.

famine spread, a tidal wave of Irish immigrants headed for America aboard "coffin ships," poorly built, dangerous sailing vessels that offered cheap fares. Many settled in Boston and many others in parts of Manhattan's Lower East Side and West Side, in a section called Hell's Kitchen. There they met with discrimination; employers refused to hire the newcomers simply because they were Irish. "No Irish need apply" was a popular slogan at the time. Yet Irish people had an important thing going for them in America: the right for men to vote. They put that right to good use, electing their own political leaders to help them get housing and jobs.

The new immigrants, however, outnumbered the Irish, upon whom Tammany Hall depended. During the meeting at the Metropolitan Opera House, outraged workers insisted conditions would not improve until they united for change "at the polls." At the polls! Voting! That was language a Tammany boss could understand. The fire affected Italian and Jewish immigrants, the very people Tammany needed to keep its power. Clearly, it must reach out to them, do something for them—something big. So, Silent Charlie Murphy gave his blessing to the creation of a factory-investigating commission.[17]

Reform

The New York Factory Investigating Commission began work on June 30, 1911, under the "Tammany Twins," Al Smith and Robert F. Wagner. Like Smith, Wagner was a child of the East Side, the son of a German-born janitor. The youngest of six children, he alone went to public school, then put himself through law school. Like Smith, he caught the eye of Tammany bosses, who got him elected to the state legislature, where he became speaker of the Senate (and later a U.S. senator). Although Wagner chaired the commission, Smith, the vice chair, was its powerhouse.

Smith insisted on taking control. "We can't have mistakes here," he said, "we can't make any blunders and I am going to sit here myself, I am not going to turn this over to somebody else."[18]

The legislature gave the commission

Clara Lemlich's Later Life

Blackballed after the Uprising of the Twenty Thousand, Clara Lemlich could not get another job in the New York garment industry. Instead, she became what we call today a "community organizer." She founded the Wage Earners' League, a group devoted to winning the right to vote for women. In 1913, she married Joe Shavelson, a printer, and had three children with him. As a homemaker, she spent all her free time organizing other homemakers to demand tenants' rights. In 1917, she led a boycott of butcher shops against high meat prices. During the Great Depression of the 1930s, she helped the wives of unemployed workers raise money for community kitchens and nursery schools. When landlords evicted tenants for failure to pay rent, she held rallies to prevent evictions. In the 1960s, she protested against the spread of nuclear weapons and the Vietnam War. She also supported Sojourners for Truth, an African American civil rights group, named for Sojourner Truth, a former slave and the first black woman orator to denounce slavery. Meanwhile, she lost her husband and moved to California to be near her married children. There, the widow entered an old-age home. Always an organizer, she helped the orderlies form a union. She died in 1982, at the age of ninety-six.

great power. It was to carry out the state's, if not the nation's, most thorough study of worker safety and health done until then. Not only must it study fire hazards, but sweatshops, sanitary conditions, work-related diseases, and child labor in factories. Better yet, it could call witnesses and have them testify under oath. Lying at a commission hearing could bring a fine and a jail term.

To avoid slipups, the commission planned to move in two stages. First, it would collect accurate, hard-hitting facts. After that, it would use these facts as a basis for drafting laws to solve the problems it found. Smith named Frances Perkins the chief investigator, charged with naming her assistants. She chose well. Her staff included women with wide labor-organizing and workplace experience: Mary Dreier, Rose Schneiderman, and Clara Lemlich, among others.

Perkins was the driving force behind the investigating team. A can't-say-no-to sort of person, she insisted, she demanded, she ordered, she bullied. She got her way. On one inspection tour, she made Robert Wagner crawl through a tiny hole in a wall that led to an ice-covered "fire escape" ending twelve feet above the ground. Another time, she took Al Smith to see hundreds of women coming off an all-night shift in a rope-making factory.

Commissioners also saw laundry workers standing ankle-deep in filthy water, bakery workers covered with body lice, candy makers wearing dresses smeared with chocolate, with gobs of chocolate hanging from their hair. They found child cannery workers—five-, six-, seven-year-olds—shelling peas at 4 a.m., their bleeding fingers bound with bits of rag. "We made sure that they saw the machinery that would scalp a girl or cut off a man's arm. Hours so long that both men and women were depleted and exhausted became realities to them through seeing for themselves the dirty little factories," said Perkins. Visiting a sweatshop, they asked a boy how long he had worked at hand-rolling cigarettes. The little fellow answered, "Ever since I was."[19]

Garment factories seemed almost heavenly compared to chemical plants. Every day, all day, workers handled poisons such as lead, arsenic, phosphorus, and mercury, used in making paint and matches. Plants lacked ventilating systems, so workers inhaled chemical fumes and dust. Wherever one turned, there was danger. In a plant near Niagara Falls, a world-famous vacation resort, inspectors saw a worker "in a dark corner passing under an iron trough clumsily supported on wooden blocks and filled with hot caustic soda, every drop of which . . . would produce a painful and permanent injury." Falling into such a trough from an overhead catwalk would dissolve a person in seconds, leaving only a few bones.[20]

The Fate of Tammany Hall

Reformers constantly battled Tammany Hall. In 1933, it suffered a stunning defeat when President Franklin D. Roosevelt, a Democrat, helped Fiorello La Guardia, a Republican, become mayor; he served from 1934 to 1945. Born to a Jewish mother and an Italian father, "the Little Flower," the translation of his Italian first name, spoke three languages fluently. La Guardia would begin a speech in English, switch to perfect Italian, switch again to flawless Yiddish, ending in English. A crusader against corruption, he was bold and fearless against Tammany Hall. "It makes no difference if I burn my bridges behind me—I never retreat," he said. True to his word, the Little Flower stripped the bosses of their power to award government contracts and give jobs to supporters. He cleared slums, built parks, and weeded corruption out of the police department. Corrupt bosses went to jail. Tammany never recovered. In 1943, it sold its East Seventeenth Street headquarters—to the ILGWU.

Factory visits upset the commissioners, as Perkins intended they should, particularly Al Smith. But there is nothing like seeing things for oneself. Those visits, she said, changed Smith's "life, his outlook, the whole direction of his career." They made him more of a mensch than ever before.[21]

During hearings, he left no doubt about where his sympathies lay. Once, a lawyer for building owners challenged the right of Perkins, only "a *girl*," to testify. Al declared her an expert on real estate, winked, and whispered, "Now give 'em the best you've got." Another time, a witness argued that night work for women was not so bad. That did it! Al bit down on his cigar and hissed, "You can't tell me. I've seen these women. I've seen their faces. I've seen them."[22]

The commission served four years, from 1911 to 1915. During that time, it investigated 3,385 workplaces, questioned 472 witnesses—owners, managers, workers—and took over 7,000 pages of testimony. Its findings advanced a new idea about the role of government in American life. The Founding Fathers had wanted government to keep out of people's affairs as much as possible. As Thomas Jefferson said, "That government is best which governs least." This was because the founders, having fought a revolution against British oppression, feared that a too-powerful, too-active government might lead to tyranny.

Al Smith and his fellow commissioners saw things differently. Government, they believed, could be a force for good. Safe, healthy working conditions were basic human rights that society should guarantee through government and laws. America was a democracy, though women could not yet vote. Even

so, it was the duty of the *people's* government to look after their well-being. "How is it wrong for the State to intervene with regard to the working conditions of people who work in the factories and mills?" Smith asked. "What did we set up the government for?"[23]

Information collected by the commission led to the drafting of laws. In all, the legislature passed thirty-four laws based on its findings. Those laws changed how we live today, in ways we seldom realize, because they seem so sensible. All you need do to see their results is to look around any factory, workshop, office building, school, or theater. New laws ordered lifesaving measures like fire drills, fire extinguishers, and automatic sprinklers. Doors must swing outward and stay unlocked during the workday. To prevent pileups, exit doors must have panic bars that open them outward with a hand or shoulder blow. Doors and windows leading to fire escapes have to be painted bright red and marked EXIT in large letters; a red light must be placed over all exits. To avoid overcrowding, room capacities are limited to a certain number of people per square foot.[24]

Other laws ordered safety guards and automatic shutoff devices on machinery, suitable lighting, and ventilation in factories. Proper sanitary conditions, such as toilets and washing facilities, became the rule. A compensation scheme paid benefits to workers injured or disabled on the job. Laws applying to women limited work hours (fifty-two hours a week), abolished night shifts, and banned working for a month after giving birth to a child. Children under fourteen were barred from working in canneries and tenements— that is, sweatshops. To enforce the laws, the state hired 123 full-time inspectors. Silent Charlie Murphy supported these laws; they helped Tammany Hall. "It is my observation," he told Frances Perkins, that a certain law "made us many votes. I will tell the boys to give all the help they can." If women ever won the right to vote, he added, "I hope you will remember that you would make a good Democrat."[25]

While working for the commission, Frances Perkins met a young state senator named Franklin D. Roosevelt. No Tammany man, "FDR," as friends called him, came from a different back-

Frances Perkins as secretary of labor in the 1930s, the first female cabinet member in U.S. history.

ground than Al Smith. Born into a wealthy family, and a relative of former president Theodore Roosevelt, FDR got his education at a private high school and Harvard College. Yet, like the knight of the brown derby and the cocked cigar, he was a reformer. Perkins and FDR respected each other, becoming allies in the cause of reform. When FDR was elected governor in 1929, he made Perkins state commissioner of industry. He became president in 1933, during the Great Depression, the worst economic downturn in American

Names of the victims of the Triangle Fire are inscribed in chalk each year in front of their homes.

history. Upon taking office, he named Perkins secretary of labor and the first woman to serve in a cabinet post.

Perkins had come a long way since death cast its shadow over that bright spring afternoon in 1911. The Triangle Fire set her on a path she would follow the rest of her life. From then on, she devoted her talents to bettering the lives of working people and children. Thanks to her efforts, the reforms that followed the Triangle Fire became models for national policies.

On the fiftieth anniversary of the fire, in 1961, Perkins dedicated a plaque in memory of the Triangle victims. New York University had bought the Asch Building years before for science classes, renaming it the Brown Building. Other than that, the building had changed little since the fire; today, it is a National Historic Landmark. The victims' ordeal, she said, had ignited a movement for reform that benefited future generations. "They did not die in vain and we will never forget them."[26]

She was right. On each anniversary of the fire, people gather at the Brown Building to pay their respects. Groups from neighborhood elementary schools wear red plastic firefighters' hats. A fire truck raises its ladder in tribute, but not fully, to remind visitors of those who jumped to their deaths. In 2009, filmmaker Ruth Sergel formed a group called Chalk. On March 25, group members visit the places fire victims once lived. At each place, they chalk the person's name on the sidewalk. "It's not permanent," said Sergel. "It washes away, but you know what? It's going to come back next year."[27]

THE PRICE OF LIBERTY

Eternal vigilance is the price of liberty.... Only by continual oversight can a people be kept sufficiently awake to principle not to let liberty be smothered in material prosperity.

—Wendell Phillips, Speeches Before the Massachusetts Anti-Slavery Society (1853)

Of Rags and Gangsters

Nothing in this world stays the same forever. Sure as day follows night, time brings change. Generation follows generation. People age and pass from the scene, making way for others. New problems arise, calling for new solutions. The only way to preserve past gains is by eternal vigilance and the good sense to make needed changes in time. To understand what this means, we must look beyond the Triangle Fire and the reforms that followed it.

In the 1920s, workers who made clothing for both men and women split into two opposing camps. Each New York garment union fought its own civil war. Radical workers, favoring drastic changes, felt that past gains were no longer enough. Wage increases had failed to keep up with rising prices for food, clothing, and housing. Nor had factory owners yet made all the safety improvements required by law. To win further gains, radicals favored a general strike. Moderates, however, were cautious, not inclined to take unnecessary risks.

In June 1926, radicals gained the upper hand, shutting down the entire New York garment industry. For twenty-six weeks, fifty thousand strikers walked picket lines. The unions' joint strike committee spent $3.5 million, a huge sum, equal to over $420 million in 2009 dollars. Lost sales cost manufacturers millions more. The settlement left both sides broke.

The strike was nothing like the Uprising of the Twenty Thousand in 1909. This time it was total war. There was nothing noble about it, no uplifting speeches, no heroes defying brutal police officers and corrupt Tammany judges. Both sides turned to the underworld for help. Employers hired Jack "Legs" Diamond and his goons to protect them and their scabs, and beat up strikers and union leaders. The unions paid the "king of the East Side gunmen," Jacob "Little Augie" Orgen, and his thugs to protect picketers and union leaders, and batter employers and scabs.[1]

As the violence grew, union leaders came to Abraham Rothstein for advice. Called "Abe the Just" by Governor Al Smith, he was a highly respected textile dealer who gave generously to charity. Although he could not help the union

Gangster "Legs" Diamond (far right), alongside his two attorneys, 1931.

leaders, he sent them to an unnamed garment manufacturer he knew. This man said they had gone to the wrong Rothstein. They should speak to Abe the Just's disgraced son, Arnold, otherwise known as the "Great Brain."[2]

Arnold Rothstein had not crossed the Atlantic Ocean in steerage or gone through Ellis Island. American-born, he grew up in a town house on the Upper East Side. In his early teens, the thrills of the Bowery drew him downtown like a magnet; it was only a short ride on the elevated railway. He began to visit pool halls and gambling dens. "Big Tim" Sullivan, Tammany's boss of the Lower East Side, liked the scrawny kid. "Rothstein's a good boy, and smart," he said. Closely tied to gangsters, the boss had an eye for criminal talent.[3]

Big Tim helped Rothstein, advising and opening doors for him. Like any gangster, the youngster believed that people were either hunters or prey, jerks or wiseguys, and thought himself better than "crumbs," who worked for a living. Starting as a gambler, he expanded his activities into loan-sharking (lending money at high interest rates) and the narcotics trade. Rothstein sent agents to Europe and Asia to buy and smuggle opium into the United States. After being refined into heroin, a highly addictive drug, raw opium that cost Rothstein $1,000 a pound brought a profit of $150,000. Always a "gentleman," he never soiled his hands, never beat or shot anyone, but paid others to do his dirty work. By 1926, he had become the father of organized crime, large-scale criminal activities by groups of gangsters, in America. In effect, the Great Brain was the first "godfather."[4]

Rothstein made two telephone calls. As if by magic, Legs Diamond and Little Augie Orgen withdrew their thugs. What did he tell them? Surely not "Be nice, fellows, and don't hurt anyone." Most likely, he told them not to pass up the chance of a lifetime. Although they

Arnold Rothstein, aka the "Great Brain" of the New York underworld, in 1928.

had withdrawn before the strike ended, they still had their contacts with union leaders and manufacturers. With the end of the strike, they could use these contacts to worm their way into the industry. Hiring them in the first place, therefore, was the worst mistake each side could have made. For it bears out the proverb "He needs a long spoon who sups with the devil." Translation: Do not get too close to certain people, as keeping bad company will get you into trouble. Not only the garment industry, but every industry that called in gangsters to settle labor disputes eventually found itself in deep trouble. For, after the strike, the gangsters could keep their hooks buried in the unions and the manufacturers. So, while a gunman killed the Great Brain over a gambling debt in 1928, he had guaranteed that the garment industry would have no peace.

In the decade after the Triangle Fire, the industry began to leave the Lower East Side. It found quarters in modern, low-rent buildings in the Garment District on the West Side of Manhattan, from Thirty-Fourth Street to Fortieth Street, between Broadway and Ninth Avenue. The Garment District was hard hit during the Great Depression of the 1930s. Then, in 1941, after Japan attacked the U.S. naval base at Pearl Harbor in the Hawaiian Islands, the country entered the Second World War. With vast armies to supply, the United States needed mountains of uniforms, underwear, socks, backpacks, tents, parachutes, and other cloth items. High-paying jobs became plentiful. These boom-time conditions lasted throughout the 1950s and 1960s. In the 1970s, however, signs of serious trouble appeared in the garment industry.

That trouble grew from seeds sown in the days of Arnold Rothstein. Organized crime found new opportunities after the 1926 strike. Gangsters began to muscle their way into unions through bribery, threats, and violence. Officials who refused to go along got visits from hard-faced men demanding cooperation—or else. That "or else" spelled a beating, a smashed kneecap, or a bullet. Cooperation, in turn, opened a union's purse wide. Organized crime collected a monthly "fee" for each member. Burrowing deeper, it looted welfare and pension funds, even

put its own men into union posts. Some officials were outright crooks, stealing from their own members.

Meanwhile, gangsters gained control of garment companies themselves. Manufacturers had lost a fortune

Organized crime was rampant in New York in the 1920s and 1930s. This police department photo shows three New York City gangsters.

"Dutch" Schultz, posing for the camera after a brief stay in jail, in 1935.

during the 1926 strike. Hungry for cash to restart their businesses, they turned to the loan sharks. Those loans allowed the likes of Arthur "Dutch" Schultz, a brutal gunman, to gain a foothold in the industry. Gangsters offered "insurance" against strikes by gang-controlled unions. For a price, they promised "protection" against "accidents," like factory fires after midnight and acid spills on bolts of expensive cloth. The racket paid well. At the height of his power in the 1930s, Dutch Schultz made ten million dollars a year—until a bullet ended his career in a restaurant toilet. The shooter was from Murder Inc., a group of hired killers from Brooklyn.

In 1957, Carlo Gambino became the most powerful man in the Garment District. Gambino was a *mafioso*—that is, a member of the Mafia, a secret criminal society that began in Sicily centuries ago. The Gambino crime "family," the country's largest, used its hold on unions to take over the trucking companies that served the Garment District. In doing so, they prevented manufacturers from getting deliveries of raw materials or shipping finished goods to dealers and stores. Any trucking company that refused to share its business with them had an unexpected strike, a rash of slashed tires, or bombings. Once they gained the upper hand, gangsters demanded kickbacks, part of the value of the goods shipped, from manufacturers and truckers alike. This placed a huge, illegal "tax" on the garment industry. For example, a dress that should have cost fifteen cents to ship cost forty cents. To put it another way, the consumer paid an extra $3.50 on every $100 clothing purchase.[5]

In the early 1990s, the New York Police Department, Manhattan district attorney, and Federal Bureau of Investigation went all out to defeat organized crime in the Garment District. To get evidence, detectives posed as union officials and garment company executives. Police technicians got court orders allowing them to break into suspects' homes and offices. Once inside, they planted wiretaps, electronic devices attached to telephones, and "bugs," tiny hidden microphones, to overhear and record conversations. Eventually, they gathered enough evidence to convict corrupt union leaders and organized crime bosses. With gangsters driven from the Garment District, workers could get what they deserved from their unions, while shipping costs fell. By then, however, the damage had been done. The industry, already weakened, was suffering from deeper problems that continue to this very day.

Return of the New York Sweatshop

The numbers tell a sad tale. In 1950, over 95 percent of America's clothing was made in the States, chiefly in New York City. By 1980, foreign imports made up half the clothing sold in this country. In 2009, only 5 percent of our clothing was American-made. What happened?[6]

If organized crime drove many companies from New York, foreign competition threatened their very existence. Over the years, the United States had lowered or ended most tariffs—that is, the taxes a government charges on imported goods. As a result, foreign-made

The Garment District in the 1950s, when most of America's clothing was produced at home.

clothing began to flood into the country. While strong American unions tried to keep wages high, foreign producers had to deal with only weak unions or none at all. Thus, their labor costs stayed low. This was a key advantage, for it allowed them to charge lower prices than those for American-made goods of equal quality. For example, in the year 2000, New York gave the contract to make police uniforms to a Chinese company. Uniforms made on the other side of the globe were cheaper than those made right there, in the city.[7]

Unable to compete, American firms closed their doors or moved their manufacturing operations overseas to take advantage of lower labor costs. Inevitably, their employees felt the pinch. In 1990, New York had 139,000 workers making men's, women's, and children's clothes. Ten years later, its garment factories employed fewer than fifty thousand workers—a number that keeps falling. New York is now a fashion center, where more people design and market clothes than make them.[8]

Meanwhile, small firms unable or unwilling to move their operations overseas had to cut costs to survive. The best way to do that was to have a large labor force willing to accept low wages. Luckily for small firms, history is repeating itself.

A Chinese proverb says, "First comes the bitterness, then there is sweetness and wealth and honor." In other words, bearing hardships today can pay off tomorrow. So it had been with the new immigrants of the early 1900s. Eventually, better wages and working conditions created opportunities for them and, more important, their children. By the 1960s, most Italian and Jewish families had left Little Italy and the Lower East Side for other neighborhoods. Once the backbone of the garment industry, these families also moved upward in society, into the middle class. They achieved the American dream, educating their children, producing scientists, doctors, lawyers, members of Congress, even justices of the U.S. Supreme Court.

From the 1960s onward, America experienced a "new" new immigration. Unlike the earlier southern and eastern Europeans, these newcomers were Asians—Chinese, South Koreans, Pakistanis, Vietnamese—Puerto Ricans, Hispanics from Central America, and blacks from the Caribbean islands. Between 1966 and 1979, over one million legal immigrants entered New York alone, and possibly an equal number illegally. It was a perfect fit: their need for jobs matched small garment manufacturers' need for low-wage workers. The result was a rebirth of the underground sweatshop in New York.

According to the U.S. Department of Labor, 4,500 of the city's 7,000 garment factories are sweatshops. It is easy to open a sweatshop. "The equipment is really just a few sewing machines," says Ginny Coughlin, a labor rights activist. "Just rent space, pay the electric bill, and you're in business." Sweatshop workers always earn less than the minimum wage set by law. Often they work in the same Lower East Side buildings that housed sweatshops a century ago. Chinese sewing machine operators in the Chinatown section, just south of Little Italy, work from sixty to one hundred hours a week. Sweatshops are hard to eliminate. No sooner do inspectors close one than it reopens at another address. Luckily, we have not seen anything like the Triangle Fire. So far.[9]

Sweatshops in the Developing World

Sweatshop conditions in the developing world differ little from those at the Triangle Waist Company a century ago. That tragedy awakened America's conscience, leading to improvements in factory safety. Today, private groups—the National Labor Committee, United

Asian women in a New York City sweatshop, 1981.

Students Against Sweatshops, International Labor Rights Fund—try to raise American awareness about sweatshops overseas. Labor rights activists denounce these as harsh and cruel, a sin upon the heads of the greedy, who gain by exploiting the weak.

Congress has passed laws against importing goods made by low-paid workers in unsafe and unsanitary conditions. Boycotts and bad publicity have hurt American firms that make garments in foreign factories, some of which are really large sweatshops. In 1996, for example, activists embarrassed television talk show host Kathie Lee Gifford. They revealed that factories in Honduras were making her "Kathie Lee" clothing line, featured at Wal-Mart stores across the country. These factories, supposedly, paid thirty-one cents an hour for fifteen-hour days in poorly ventilated buildings surrounded by barbed wire and armed guards. Shocked at the news, Gifford became a foe of such factories, especially their use of young children.[10]

Others have a kinder view of the role of sweatshops in the developing world. Economists Jeffrey D. Sachs of Harvard University and Paul Krugman, winner of a Nobel Prize in economics, argue that they serve a useful purpose. "My concern," says Sachs, "is not that there are too many sweatshops but that there are too few." For, he insists, they are the price a nation must pay for economic development and a higher standard of living. He also argues that labor rights activists may harm the very people they want to help. Banning child labor or closing sweatshops throws poor people out of work. When, for example, garment factory owners in Bangladesh, a South Asian nation, were forced to fire child workers, the children had no place to go. To survive, many lived on the streets as beggars. Many others became prostitutes or starved.[11]

Life is such that we cannot always

choose between the good and the bad. Sometimes, we must choose between the awful, the bad, and the less bad. In India, Paul Krugman notes, poor farm families may face slow starvation, an awful death. Out of desperation, parents may decide to sell a child to a gang of beggars, who blind him or injure him in other ways to gain sympathy from passersby in the streets. "If this is the alternative," Krugman says, "it is not so easy to say that children should not be working in factories."[12]

Hourly wages in garment factories in developing countries vary: Bangladesh ($0.13), Vietnam ($0.26), Indonesia ($0.34), China ($0.44), Haiti ($0.49), Dominican Republic ($1.62). Yet that is not as bad as it may seem, because workers in other fields, the majority, often earn far less. In Haiti, Vietnam, and the Dominican Republic, for example, garment workers earn three to seven times the national average. While the wages are low by standards in the United States (where the minimum hourly wage is $7.25), the cost of living is lower in developing countries, so earnings often go further than they would here.[13]

Conditions in sweatshops are usually better than workers had ever known, economists note. They are less strenuous than planting rice, where farmers work knee-deep in water from sunup to sundown, bending down to place each seedling in the mud. Thus, for many in developing countries, factory work is highly desirable.

While visiting a garbage dump on the outskirts of Phnom Penh, Cambodia, *New York Times* reporter Nicholas D. Kristof saw vast fields of rotting, burning filth. Barefoot children ran about, gathering old plastic cups to sell to recyclers for five cents a pound. "I'd love to get a job in a factory," said Pim Srey Rath, a nineteen-year-old woman. "At least there, work is in the shade. Here is where it's hot." In other words, a sweatshop, bad as it might be by American standards, is less bad than a garbage dump.[14]

Another example. In a village in Thailand, newspaper reporters asked Mongkol Latlakorn, a farm laborer, if he had any children. He did—daughter Darin, fifteen, a bright, pretty girl who quit school to work in a garment factory in Bangkok, the nation's capital. She earned two dollars a day for a nine-hour shift, six days a week. "It's dangerous work," Mongkol said. "Twice the needles went right through her hands. But the managers bandaged her hands, and both times she got better again and went back to work."

"How terrible," the reporters said, shocked.

Mongkol disagreed. "It's good pay," he said. "I hope she can keep that job," as it was better than any she could get in the village. For Darin, a factory job was a great improvement in her life and that of her family, whom she helped support.

"Asian workers," the reporters note,

A garbage dump in Cambodia, with a youngster scavenging, 2005.

"would be aghast at the idea of American consumers boycotting certain toys or clothing in protest" against sweatshop conditions. "The simplest way to help the poorest Asians would be to buy more from sweatshops, not less."[15]

Still, too many factory workers in developing countries endure conditions not unlike those Frances Perkins's investigators found after the Triangle Fire. Even so, hard, low-paying jobs may offer a "step up," a way of improving one's life or the life of future generations. In America, unions, the right to vote, reformers, and sympathetic politicians like Al Smith gave force to the immigrants' cry for change. But change did not come quickly, or easily, or without a tragedy to awaken public outrage. Sadly, this history may be repeating itself in the developing world.

To illustrate this, we will focus on Bangladesh, though realizing that other developing nations face similar problems. Bangladesh is a South Asian nation of 162 million people bordered almost entirely by India. With an average yearly income of about $520 a year in 2008, Bangladesh is one of the poorest countries in the world. Having few natural resources, it depends heavily on farming. However, industry is growing rapidly, due to its large low-wage labor force. This is especially true of the manufacture of clothing and textiles, the country's most valuable export.

Bangladesh's garment industry employs over three million people, 90 percent of them young women, in more than four thousand factories. Overcrowded factories have poor ventilation and inadequate toilet facilities. Petty fines cheat workers of earnings, there is no extra pay for overtime, and workers seldom get their pay on time. Hired thugs beat up union organizers and terrorize workers who speak out against abuses. Garment workers have been clubbed, even killed, for stealing a T-shirt.[16]

The Triangle Fire has replayed itself in another way, too. Bangladesh's garment factories have an awful fire safety record. Between 1990 and 2005, some three hundred workers died and two thousand were injured in garment factory fires there. This is because many plants lack sprinklers and never hold fire drills. In some, employers lock exit doors or block them with boxes, barrels, and crates.[17]

Bangladesh's deadliest factory fire was almost a mirror image of the Triangle disaster. It happened at the KTS Textile Mill in the city of Chittagong, a seaport on the Bay of Bengal. On February 23, 2006, some five hundred workers were on the night shift when an electrical generator exploded on the first floor of the three-story building. Seconds later, fire spread to barrels of chemical dyes and stacks of yarn. Flames lapped out of windows, igniting fires on the floors above.

Security guards had locked exit gates to prevent workers from coming late and leaving early. "When the fire erupted," a survivor said, "I was working on the second floor. Of the two gates on the floor, one was padlocked. Finding it impossible to come out through the milling crowd at the other gate, I jumped out through a window on the roof of a nearby two-story building. Some local people standing on the rooftop of that building broke open the window and helped us out."

Panic spread. Trapped by a rolling wall of fire, many leaped from windows, their hair and clothes burning. In all, ninety-one died, suffocated, burned, or smashed against the pavement. Most were teenage girls, some as young as twelve, thirteen, and fourteen. Outraged workers held protest rallies to demand improvements in factory safety. Rallies and pressure from Bangladesh's overseas trading partners, particularly the United States, persuaded the government to order safety improvements.[18]

However, these still have a long way to go. People still lose their lives in fires in Bangladeshi garment factories. On February 26, 2010, flames engulfed the Garib and Garib Sweater Factory near Dhaka, the capital, killing twenty-one and injuring forty workers. It was the same old story. "Everyone working on the factory's top floor died because exit gates were locked; they were all women, they were all trapped and they all suffocated," said a report.[19]

If the Bangladeshi experience teaches anything, it is that short memories and greed are a deadly mixture. When things are going well, we are likely to forget the past. Short memories are dangerous, because they allow greed to take control. The result is disaster. Thus, eternal vigilance truly is the price of liberty *and* safety.

That is the lasting lesson of the Triangle Fire.

BIBLIOGRAPHY

Alland, Alexander. *Jacob A. Riis: Photographer and Citizen*. Millerton, NY: Aperture, 1993.

American Social History Project. *Who Built America? Working People and the Nation's Economy, Politics, Culture, and Society*. Vol. 1, *From the Gilded Age to the Present*. New York: Pantheon, 1992.

Baron, Salo W. *The Russian Jew Under Tsars and Soviets*. New York: Macmillan, 1976.

Boorstin, Daniel. *The Americans: The Democratic Experience*. New York: Random House, 1973.

Brands, H. W. *The Reckless Decade: America in the 1890s*. New York: St. Martin's, 1995.

Burns, Ric, and James Sanders. *New York*. New York: Knopf, 1999.

Burrows, Edwin G., and Mike Wallace. *Gotham: A History of New York City to 1898*. New York: Oxford University Press, 1999.

Collier, Christopher, and James Lincoln Collier. *The Rise of the Cities, 1820–1920*. New York: Benchmark Books, 2001.

Dash, Joan. *We Shall Not Be Moved: The Women's Factory Strike of 1909*. New York: Scholastic, 1996. A book for young readers.

Dye, Nancy S. *As Equals and as Sisters: Feminism, the Labor Movement, and the Women's Trade Union League of New York*. Columbia, MO: University of Missouri Press, 1980.

Foner, Philip S. *Women and the American Labor Movement: From Colonial Times to the Eve of World War I*. New York: Free Press, 1979.

Fried, Albert. *The Rise and Fall of the Jewish Gangster in America.* New York: Columbia University Press, 1993.

Gay, Ruth. *Unfinished People: Eastern European Jews Encounter America.* New York: Norton, 1996.

Glenn, Susan A. *Daughters of the Shtetl: Life and Labor in the Immigrant Generation.* Ithaca, NY: Cornell University Press, 1990.

Handlin, Oscar. *The Uprooted: The Epic Story of the Great Migrations That Made the American People.* Boston: Little, Brown, 1952.

Howe, Irving. *World of Our Fathers.* New York: Harcourt Brace Jovanovich, 1976.

Jackson, Kenneth T., and David S. Dunbar, eds. *Empire City: New York Through the Centuries.* New York: Columbia University Press, 2002.

Jensen, Joan M. "The Great Uprisings: 1900–1920." In *A Needle, a Bobbin, a Strike: Women Needleworkers in America,* edited by Joan M. Jensen and Sue Davidson.

Philadelphia: Temple University Press, 1984, 83–182.

Josephson, Matthew, and Hannah Josephson. *Al Smith: Hero of the Cities.* New York: Houghton Mifflin, 1969.

Kisseloff, Jeff. *You Must Remember This: An Oral History of Manhattan from the 1890s to World War II.* New York: Harcourt Brace Jovanovich, 1989.

Kraut, Alan M. *The Huddled Masses: The Immigrant in American Society, 1880–1921.* Wheeling, IL: Harlan Davidson, 1982.

Malkiel, Theresa S. *The Diary of a Shirtwaist Striker.* Ithaca, NY: Cornell University Press, 1990. A true-to-life novel first published in 1910.

McFarlane, Arthur E. "Fire and the Skyscraper." *McClure's Magazine,* September 1911, 467–83.

Metzker, Isaac, ed. *A Bintel Brief: Sixty Years of Letters from the Lower East Side to the* Jewish Daily Forward. Garden City, NY: Doubleday, 1971.

Morrison, Joan, and Charlotte Fox Zabusky, eds. *American Mosaic: The Immigrant Experience in the Words of Those Who Lived It.* New York: Dutton, 1980.

Orleck, Annelise. *Common Sense and a Little Fire: Women and Working-Class Politics in the United States, 1900–1965.* Chapel Hill: University of North Carolina Press, 1995.

Rasenberger, Jim. *America, 1908.* New York: Scribner, 2007.

Reppetto, Thomas. *American Mafia: A History of Its Rise to Power.* New York: Holt, 2004.

Riis, Jacob A. *How the Other Half Lives.* 1890; reprint, New York: Hill and Wang, 1957.

Riis, Jacob A. *The Making of an American.* New York: Macmillan, 1901.

Rischin, Moses. *The Promised City: New York Jews, 1870–1914.* Cambridge, MA: Harvard University Press, 1977.

Schoener, Allon, ed. *Portal to America: The Lower East Side, 1870–1920.* New York: Holt, Rinehart and Winston, 1967.

Slayton, Robert A. *Empire Statesman: The Rise and Redemption of Al Smith.* New York: Free Press, 2001.

Sorin, Gerald. *The Jewish People in America: A Time for Building, the Third Migration, 1880–1920.* Baltimore, MD: Johns Hopkins University Press, 1992.

Stein, Leon, ed. *Out of the Sweatshop: The Struggle for Industrial Democracy.* New York: Quadrangle, 1977.

Stein, Leon. *The Triangle Fire.* New York: Carroll & Graf, 1962.

Still, Bayrd. *Mirror of Gotham: New York as Seen by Contemporaries from Dutch Days to the Present.* New York: New York University Press, 1956.

Tax, Meredith. *The Rising of the Women: Feminist Solidarity and Class Conflict, 1880–1917.* New York: Monthly Review Press, 1980.

Von Drehle, David. *Triangle: The Fire That Changed America.* New York: Grove Press, 2003.

Wertheimer, Barbara M. *We Were There: The Story of Working Women in America.* New York: Pantheon, 1997.

Internet Sources

New Deal Network
Photographs of the Triangle Fire and a dramatic colored mural
http://newdeal.feri.org/library/d_4m.htm

The Triangle Factory Fire: Online Exhibit from Cornell University's Kheel Center
A marvelous collection of photographs and documents
www.ilr.cornell.edu/trianglefire

Uprising of 20,000 (1909) | Jewish Women's Archive
A collection of documents and pictures on the 1909 strike
jwa.org/encyclopedia/article/uprising-of-20000-1909

NOTES

Prelude:
From the Ashes

1. Leon Stein, *The Triangle Fire* (New York: Carroll & Graf, 1962), 211.

I. Huddled Masses

1. Hamilton Holt, ed., *The Life Stories of (Undistinguished) Americans as Told by Themselves* (New York: Routledge, 1990), 22.

2. Laurence Bergreen, *Capone: The Man and the Era* (New York: Simon & Schuster, 1994), 24; Thomas Reppetto, *American Mafia: A History of Its Rise to Power* (New York: Holt, 2004), 3.

3. "Pompeii in Peril," *The New York Times*, April 11, 1906; "The Last Days of Bosco Tre Case," *The New York Times*, April 29, 1906.

4. "Four Days Among the Ruins of Messina and Reggio," *The New York Times*, June 5, 1908.

5. Alan M. Kraut, *The Huddled Masses: The Immigrant in American Society, 1880–1921* (Wheeling, IL: Harlan Davidson, 1982), 19.

6. Irving Howe, *World of Our Fathers* (New York: Harcourt Brace Jovanovich, 1976), 10.

7. Susan A. Glenn, *Daughters of the Shtetl: Life and Labor in the Immigrant Generation* (Ithaca, NY: Cornell University Press, 1990), 14.

8. Paul Johnson, *A History of the Jews* (New York: Harper & Row, 1987), 359, 362.

9. Gerald Sorin, *The Jewish People in America: A Time for Building, the Third Migration, 1880–1920* (Baltimore, MD: Johns Hopkins University Press, 1992), 14.

10. "Jewish Massacre Denounced," *The New York Times*, April 28, 1903.

11. Johnson, *History of the Jews*, 365–66; Moses Rischin, *The Promised City: New York Jews, 1870–1914* (Cambridge, MA: Harvard University Press, 1977), 20; Howe, *World of Our Fathers*, 30.

12. Glenn, *Daughters of the Shtetl*, 414.

13. Mary Antin, *From Plotzk to Boston* (Boston: W. B. Clarke & Co., 1899), 11–12.

14. Howe, *World of Our Fathers*, 42.

15. Ibid., 41.

II. Into the Magic Cauldron

1. Howe, *World of Our Fathers*, 43–44.

2. Bayrd Still, *Mirror of Gotham: New York as Seen by Contemporaries from Dutch Days to the Present* (New York: New York University Press, 1956), 206.

3. Ibid., 279.

4. Ibid., 231.

5. William Archer, *America To-day: Observations and Reflections* (London: William Heinemann, 1900), 18.

6. Still, *Mirror of Gotham*, 220, 231–32.

7. Ibid., 211.

8. Sorin, *Jewish People in America*, 71.

9. Ibid.

10. Jeff Kisseloff, *You Must Remember This: An Oral History of Manhattan from the 1890s to World War II* (New York: Harcourt Brace Jovanovich, 1989), 29.

11. Rischin, *Promised City*, 83; Kisseloff, *You Must Remember This*, 31.

12. Sorin, *Jewish People in America*, 72; Theresa S. Malkiel, *The Diary of a Shirtwaist Striker* (Ithaca, NY: Cornell University Press, 1990), 6.

13. Jacob A. Riis, *How the Other Half Lives* (New York: Hill and Wang, 1957), 84–85.

14. Glenn, *Daughters of the Shtetl*, 54.

15. Still, *Mirror of Gotham*, 247.

16. Howe, *World of Our Fathers*, 537.

17. Edwin G. Burrows and Mike Wallace, *Gotham: A History of New York City to 1898* (New York: Oxford University Press, 1999), 1139; Rischin, *Promised City*, 199.

18. ashp.cuny.edu/ashp.-documentaries/heaven-will-protect-the-working-girl/.

19. Charles H. Hoyt and Percy Gaunt, "The Bowery," 1891.

20. Kisseloff, *You Must Remember This*, 29.

21. Mary Antin, *The Promised Land* (Boston: Houghton Mifflin, 1912), 198; Isaac Metzker, ed., *A Bintel Brief: Sixty Years of Letters from the Lower East Side to the* Jewish Daily Forward (Garden City, NY: Doubleday, 1971), 71.

22. Kraut, *Huddled Masses*, 139.

III. Flesh and Blood So Cheap

1. *The Bulletin of the General Contractors Association*, vol. 5 (1914), 842.

2. Reppetto, *American Mafia*, 19.

3. Rischin, *Promised City*, 55.

4. Riis, *How the Other Half Lives*, 85–86.

5. Glenn, *Daughters of the Shtetl*, 91–92.

6. Daniel Boorstin, *The Americans: The Democratic Experience* (New York: Random House, 1973), 92.

7. Ibid., 100.

8. Glenn, *Daughters of the Shtetl*, 89.

9. Ibid., 87.

10. Riis, *How the Other Half Lives*, 91–92.

11. Sadie Frowne, "Days and Dreams," *Independent*, September 25, 1902, in *Out of the*

Sweatshop: The Struggle for Industrial Democracy, edited by Leon Stein (New York: Quadrangle, 1977), 61; Metzker, *Bintel Brief*, 87–88.

12. Meredith Tax, *The Rising of the Women: Feminist Solidarity and Class Conflict, 1880–1917* (New York: Monthly Review Press, 1980), 211.

13. Stein, *Out of the Sweatshop*, 66.

14. Mary van Kleeck, "The Shirtwaist Strike and Its Significance," unpublished lecture, 1910, Mary van Kleeck Papers, Box 29, Sophia Smith Collection, Smith College, Northampton, MA.

15. Glenn, *Daughters of the Shtetl*, 175.

16. Howe, *World of Our Fathers*, 423.

17. Morris Rosenfeld, "In the Factory," from *Songs of Labor and Other Poems* (Boston: Richard G. Badger, 1914), 7–8.

IV. An Overflow of Suffering: The Uprising of the Twenty Thousand

1. Albert Fried, *The Rise and Fall of the Jewish Gangster in America* (New York: Columbia University Press, 1993), 9.

2. www.kaikracht.de/balalaika/english/songs/dubi_not.htm.

3. Herbert Asbury, *The Gangs of New York* (New York: Thunder's Mouth Press, 1998), 211.

4. David Von Drehle, *Triangle: The Fire That Changed America* (New York: Grove Press, 2003), 9; Howe, *World of Our Fathers*, 299.

5. Annelise Orleck, *Common Sense and a Little Fire: Women and Working-Class Politics in the United States, 1900–1965* (Chapel Hill: University of North Carolina Press, 1995), 49, 59.

6. Stein, *Out of the Sweatshop*, 69.

7. Ibid.

8. Howe, *World of Our Fathers*, 298.

9. Ibid., 299.

10. Stein, *Out of the Sweatshop*, 71.

11. Malkiel, *Diary of a Shirtwaist Striker*, 88.

12. Philip S. Foner, *Women and the American Labor Movement: From Colonial Times to the Eve of World War I* (New York: Free Press, 1979), 327; Tax, *Rising of the Women*, 215–16.

13. Tax, *Rising of the Women*, 220.

14. Malkiel, *Diary of a Shirtwaist Striker*, 180–85.

15. "Pickets from Prison Are Guests of Honor," *The New York Times*, Dec. 23, 1909; Howe, *World of Our Fathers*, 300.

16. Tax, *Rising of the Women*, 225.

17. Von Drehle, *Triangle*, 67; Tax, *Rising of the Women*, 173–74.

18. *The New York Times*, Dec. 23, 1909; "Mrs. Belmont to the Aid of Girl Strikers," *The New York Times*, Dec. 20, 1909.

19. "Miss Morgan Aids Girl Waist Strikers," *The New York Times*, Dec. 14, 1909.

20. Von Drehle, *Triangle*, 68–69.

21. "Girl Strikers Tell the Rich Their Woes," *The New York Times*, Dec. 16, 1909; "Rich Women's Aide Gives Strikers Hope," *The New York Times*, December 19, 1909.

22. "Autos for Strikers in Shirtwaist War," *The New York Times*, Dec. 21, 1909; "Police Break Up Strikers' Meeting," *The New York Times*, Dec. 22, 1909.

23. "The Rich Out to Aid Girl Waistmakers," *The New York Times*, Jan. 3, 1910.

24. Malkiel, *Diary of a Shirtwaist Striker*, 46; *The New York Times*, Jan. 3, 1910.

25. *The New York Times*, Jan. 3, 1910.

26. "Facing Starvation to Keep Up the Strike," *The New York Times*, Dec. 25, 1909.

27. Glenn, *Daughters of the Shtetl*, 197.

28. "Doors Were Locked, Say Rescued Girls," *The New York Times*, March 27, 1910.

29. Foner, *Women and the American Labor Movement*, 344.

V. The Third Gate: Fire at the Triangle

1. Miriam Finn Scott, "The Factory Girl's Danger," *The Outlook*, April 15, 1911, at www.ilr.cornell.edu/trianglefire/texts/.

2. Von Drehle, *Triangle*, 160; Stein, *Triangle Fire*, 24.

3. Von Drehle, *Triangle*, 160–62.

4. Stein, *Triangle Fire*, 28.

5. Von Drehle, *Triangle*, 179; Stein, *Triangle Fire*, 27.

6. Stein, *Triangle Fire*, 34.

7. Ibid., 38.

8. Ibid., 57.

9. "Stories of Survivors," *The New York Times*, March 26, 1911.

10. Von Drehle, *Triangle*, 153.

11. William G. Shepherd, "Eyewitness at the Triangle," *Milwaukee Journal*, March 27, 1911, in Stein, *Out of the Sweatshop*, 189.

12. Stein, *Triangle Fire*, 17.

13. Shepherd, in Stein, *Out of the Sweatshop*, 188–89.

14. Ibid., 192.

15. Stein, *Triangle Fire*, 80–81.

16. "Rescues by Law Students," *The New York Times*, March 27, 1911.

17. Stein, *Triangle Fire*, 77.

18. "Crowd of 50,000 Watches the Ruins," *The New York Times*, March 27, 1911; Stein, *Triangle Fire*, 88.

VI. A Stricken Conscience

1. "141 Men and Girls Die in Waist Factory Fire," *The New York Times*, March 26, 1911. Some reports give the number of dead as 171 and 147; the actual number was 146.

2. Stein, *Triangle Fire*, 70.

3. Stein, *Triangle Fire*, 69; "Rose Freedman," www.injuredworker.org/Letters/ Rose_Freedman.htm.

4. "141 Dead in Waist Factory Fire Here," *The New York Times*, March 26, 1911; "Sad All-Day March to Morgue Gates," *The New York Times*, March 27, 1911; Stein, *Triangle Fire*, 105.

5. Stein, *Triangle Fire*, 124–25.

6. Ibid., 145–46.

7. "The New York Factory Investigating Commission," www.dol.gov/oasam/ programs/history/mono-regsafepart07.htm.

8. "120,000 Pay Tribute to the Fire Victims," *The New York Times*, April 6, 1911; Stein, *Triangle Fire*, 154.

9. "Mass Meeting Calls for New Fire Laws," *The New York Times*, April 3, 1911.

10. Ibid.

11. John Gunther, *Roosevelt in Retrospect: A Profile in History* (New York: Harper & Brothers, 1950), 244.

12. Kisseloff, *You Must Remember This*, 19; Von Drehle, *Triangle*, 200–204.

13. Von Drehle, *Triangle*, 212; Howe, *World of Our Fathers*, 385–86.

14. "Lecture by Frances Perkins," Sept. 30, 1964, www.ilr.cornell.edu/trianglefire/ texts/lectures/perkins.html.

15. Ibid.

16. Von Drehle, *Triangle*, 258; *Literary Digest*, Jan. 6, 1912.

17. "Mass Meeting Calls for New Fire Laws," *The New York Times*, April 3, 1911.

18. "Lecture by Frances Perkins."

19. Frances Perkins, *The Roosevelt I Knew* (New York: Viking, 1946), 22–23; Robert A. Slayton, *Empire Statesman: The Rise and Redemption of Al Smith* (New York: Free Press, 2001), 94–95.

20. "The New York Factory Investigating Commission."

21. Matthew and Hannah Josephson, *Al Smith: Hero of the Cities* (New York: Houghton Mifflin, 1969), 135.

22. H. Paul Jeffers, *The Napoleon of New York: Mayor Fiorello La Guardia* (New York: Wiley, 2002), 41; Slayton, *Empire Statesman*, 97.

23. George Martin, *Madam Secretary: Frances Perkins* (Boston: Houghton Mifflin, 1976), 120.

24. Slayton, *Empire Statesman*, 98–99.

25. Stein, *Triangle Fire*, 209; Slayton, *Empire Statesman*, 98–99; Perkins, *Roosevelt I Knew*, 25; Martin, *Madam Secretary*, 99–100.

26. Stein, *Triangle Fire*, 212.

27. Clyde Haberman, "Choosing Not to Forget What Is Painful to Recall," *The New York Times*, March 26, 2010.

VII. The Price of Liberty

1. Jenna Weissman Joselit, *Our Gang: Jewish Crime and the New York Jewish Community, 1900–1940* (Bloomington: University of Indiana Press, 1983), 118; Fried, *Rise and Fall of the Jewish Gangster*, 138–39.

2. David Pietrusza, *Rothstein: The Life, Times, and Murder of the Criminal Genius Who Fixed the 1919 World Series* (New York: Carroll & Graf, 2003), 216.

3. Pietrusza, *Rothstein*, 56.

4. Reppetto, *American Mafia*, 189; Joselit, *Our Gang*, 148–49.

5. Steven Malanga, "How to Run the Mob Out of Gotham," *City Journal*, Winter 2001, www.city-journal.org/printable.php?id=523; Selwyn Raab, *Five Families: The Rise, Decline, and Resurgence of America's Most Powerful Mafia Empires* (New York: St. Martin's, 2005), 314–15.

See also John H. Davis, *Mafia Dynasty: The Rise and Fall of the Gambino Crime Family* (New York: HarperCollins, 1993).

6. "New York City Seeks to Consolidate Its Garment District," *The New York Times,* Aug. 10, 2009.

7. Kevin Strouse, "The Fraying of the Garment Industry," *Gotham Gazette,* Sept. 18, 2000, www.gothamgazette.com/iotw/garments/.

8. Ibid.

9. "Sweatshops: Harsh Conditions Create Public Support for Reform," www.heartsand minds.org/articles/sweat.htm; "Garment Industry," www.tenement.org/encyclopedia/garment_sweat.htm.

10. "Sweatshops: Worse Than Ever; Top US Companies Exposed," www.hartford-hwp .com/archives/47/266.html; "Kathie Lee's Latest Sweatshop Scandal," E! Online, Sept. 22, 1999, www.eonline.com/uberblog/b38744_Kathie_Lee_s_Latest_Sweatshop _Scandal.html.

11. Sachs quoted in Allen R. Myerson, "In Principle, a Case for More 'Sweatshops,'" *The New York Times,* June 22, 1997; "The Case for Sweatshops," *Hoover Daily Report,* Feb. 7, 2000, Hoover Institution, Stanford University, www.hoover.org/pubaffairs/dailyreport/archive/2864991.html.

12. Myerson, "In Principle, a Case for More 'Sweatshops.'"

13. Benjamin Powell and David Skarbek, "Sweatshops and Third World Living Standards: Are the Jobs Worth the Sweat?" Independent Institute, September 27, 2004, www.independent.org/publications/working_papers/article.asp?id=1369.

14. Nicholas D. Kristof, "Where Sweatshops Are a Dream," *The New York Times,* Jan. 12, 2009.

15. Nicholas D. Kristof and Sheryl WuDunn, "Two Cheers for Sweatshops: They're Dirty and Dangerous. They're Also a Major Reason Asia Is Back on Track," www.nytimes.com/library/magazine/home/20000924mag-sweatshops.html.

16. Nasrin Siraj Annie, "Workers Dying in Garment Factories: Some Questions," www.meghbarta.org/nws/nw_main_p01b .php?issueId=6&sectionId=20&articleId=123.

17. "Death Toll in Bangladesh Garment Factory Fire Rises to 23," *Pakistan Times,* Jan. 5, 2005, http://pakistantimes.net/2005/01/ 09/top15.htm.

18. Jake Skeers, "Bangladesh: 54 Workers Killed in Textile Factory Fire," www.wsws.org/articles/2006/mar2006/ bang-m02.shtml; Arifa Akter Shumi, "Fire Safety in Garments Industry: Design Matters," *The Daily Star,* June 28, 2008, www.thedaily star.net/story.php?nid=43117.

19. Cat Barton, "Suspicion, Anger After Deadly Bangladesh Factory Fire," www.industry week.com/ReadArticle.aspx?ArticleID=21196; "21 Garment Workers Die as Bangladesh Government Fails to Learn from Mistakes of the Past," International Textile, Garment and Leather Workers' Federation, www.itglwf .org/lang/en/press/press-releases26022010 .html.

PICTURE CREDITS

INDEX

RUSSIAN HILL PRESS®
~~PROUDLY~~ PRESENTS:

BIG-ASS MOCHA

A SAN FRANCISCO COMIC STRIP®
BOOK.

BY DON ASMUSSEN AND
NO ONE ELSE 'CAUSE HE'S DIFFICULT
TO WORK WITH.

RussianHillPress
SanFrancisco

Russian Hill Press • San Francisco
www.russianhill.com
© 1997 by Don Asmussen
All previously published material is © 1997 by
The San Francisco Examiner and used by permission

All rights reserved. Published October 1997
Printed in the United States of America
00 99 98 97 5 4 3 2 1

Book and jacket design by Don Asmussen and Kirk Franklin
This book is set in Be Gothic and Asmussen Crap Handwriting

Library of Congress Cataloging-in-Publication Data
Asmussen, Don
San Francisco Comic Strip Book of Big-Ass Mocha / by Don Asmussen
-1st ed.
[97-066721]
CIP
ISBN 0-9653524-6-3

ONE OF THOSE BLANK PAGES
AT THE BEGINNING OF BOOKS.

ONE OF THOSE BLANK PAGES
AT THE BEGINNING OF BOOKS.

SOME OFFICIAL STUFF ABOUT WHO CURRENTLY OWNS MY ASS

"THE SAN FRANCISCO COMIC STRIP®" IS THE PROPERTY OF THE SAN FRANCISCO EXAMINER (IN WHICH IT RUNS WEEKLY ON SUNDAYS) AND DON ASMUSSEN, FROM WHICH IT SPEWS FORTH.

MANY THANKS TO THE HEARST BOYS FOR GRANTING PERMISSION TO USE MATERIAL FOR THIS BOOK, AND TO BIG CHEESE PHIL BRONSTEIN FOR INSTIGATING THE PAINFUL BIRTH OF THIS STRIP IN THE FIRST PLACE.

KISS-ASS.

THIS BOOK IS DEDICATED
TO ANYONE WHO HAS EVER
GOTTEN A POLITE LAUGH.

A MESSAGE FROM THE AUTHOR

DEAR READERS,
I'D LIKE TO SAY THAT THIS
BOOK IS THE FULFILLMENT OF
A LIFE-LONG DREAM, BUT IN TRUTH
IT IS MERELY SOMETHING I SLAPPED
TOGETHER IN ABOUT A WEEK. AN
EASY WEEK. BLAME RUSSIAN HILL
PRESS.® THEIR ADVANCE WASN'T EVEN
ENOUGH TO PAY FOR A TAXI BACK HOME
FROM THEIR OFFICES...
JERKS.

DON ASMUSSEN
DON ASMUSSEN

Contents

Yet Even More Contents

Special Supplementary Section: S.F. Comix Big-Ass Mocha Criterion Edition 171

CHAPTER ONE

AN S.F. COMIC STRIP HISTORY OF COMPLETE INACCURACY

The Beginnings

"The San Francisco Comic Strip," currently beloved by millions of readers across the map, and for good reason, can be traced back to the night of September 14th, 1850.

"Olde Mutton Chops" Asmussen
1822-1906 Creator of "Ye Olde San Francisco Comic Strip"

Legend has it that "Ye Olde San Francisco Strip," as it was called then, was the product of a late Muni stagecoach. A man known as "Olde Mutton Chops" Asmussen, current artist Don Asmussen's great grandfather (though dismissed as average by the S.F. Bay Guardian) set out from Rhode Island to California on a Muni stagecoach in 1848 to join in the famed "Gold Rush," but did not arrive in San Francisco until 1850 because the driver kept taking breaks. By this time, no gold was left, but Asmussen did find endless deposits of irony.

Asmussen's "Great Irony Rush" of 1850 failed to cause a stir, and in history books he is often unfairly overshadowed by the S.F. Gold Rush's chief benefactor, enterpriser Samuel Brannan. Brannan used his riches to build The City's first school, and is often called "San Francisco's Founding Father," though some blame this on the times' archaic DNA testing.

Enterpriser Samuel Brannan 1673-1965
(actually a picture of Rene Descartes because Brannan photo was misplaced at press time. Whaddya want for $11.95?)

"Olde Spackle" 1836-1837
Asmussen's trusty dog and his favorite toy. "It took a 'man' to play fetch with that fella," Asmussen would brag.

YE OLDE DIARY

Meanwhile, "Mutton Chops" Asmussen did something of far greater impact than the stupid gold rush; he drew the first "Ye Olde San Francisco Comic Strip," in hopes of publishing it in the S.F. Examiner. His pursuit was in vain, for the Examiner was not to exist for several more years. He would have to bide his time. In the meantime, he published solely in his personal diary. The first diary comic appeared on September 14th, 1850 to a circulation of one (himself.) Shockingly, he still managed to receive hate mail.

Things could only get better, but they got worse anyway. Focus groups voted "Ye Olde San Francisco Comic Strip" as their least favorite comic ever, leading to Asmussen's embarrassment of his being dropped from his own diary. Asmussen retreated into a funk that would last fifty-six years. Below is a rare reproduction of that first "Ye Olde San Francisco Comic Strip," reprinted here for the first time.

Comic strip historians feel that the world was not ready for such biting, satirical humor. In fact, comedian Gallagher's great great grandfather was quite the rage at the time. Asmussen, like most geniuses, would never see the rewards of his art. Experts point to this first Asmussen strip as the official start of the "Golden Age of Comics." All comics from that point on would be directly influenced by Asmussen's choice of using "drawn lines and words to say stuff," though few would admit the debt.

Bad timing

Asmussen finally ended his 50-year funk in 1906. Rejuvinated by the sudden popularity of ironic detachment, he finally sat down to start "Ye Olde San Francisco Comic Strip" #2. Legend has it that this strip was his crowning masterpiece, but

First "Ye Olde San Francisco Comic Strip" Sept. 14th, 1850
Considered pretty sucky at the time.

we'll never know because at the exact moment he finished it, the 1906 earthquake finished him. The strip, and Asmussen, were never found. A funeral was held the next Sunday, but only Gallagher's great great grandfather showed up. Fortunately, "Olde Mutton Chops" Asmussen had passed on his seed. A two-year-old son, named "Stu," was already showing great promise. The best was yet to come.

A rebirth

By 1962, Stu Asmussen was tapping into the zeitgeist with a new, revolutionary vision called "San Francisco Groovy Comic Strip." It consisted of large buttocks talking and arguing about current events. Asmussen's catchy phrase, "Hey, my buttocks begs to differ," became a battle cry for a generation. Below is an example of a typical "S.F. Groovy Comix," circa 1968. In fact, it's the only one he ever drew, and he just constantly reran it. Everyone was so stoned, nobody noticed.

The Muni Stagecoach Disaster of 1850
Muni workers pick up the remains of commuters who've been waiting for "Line 1" since 1849. Asmussen was one of the lucky ones.

"San Francisco Groovy Comic Strip" 1968
Considered pretty sucky at the time.

Like too many from those heady times, Stu didn't live long enough to realize his full potential. Although a press release proudly stated that Stu had died at 27 of a drug overdose, the truth was much less glamorous. On September 14th, 1971, Asmussen devoured sixteen ounces of a wall-plaster called "Spackle," which had been erroneously poured into a nearby sourdough bowl. Mistaking it for a hearty bowl of New England clam chowder, Stu sealed himself shut for good. According to witnesses, Asmussen's last words were, "It's a bit thick, but there's a nice hint of bacon." Then he was gone.

Yet another paragraph

Fortunately for San Francisco, Stu had also passed on his seed. Only two years old when his father's cracks were forever sealed, Li'l Donni Asmussen took over the strip in 1972. He put his stamp on it immediately. The strip quickly tackled the concerns of two-year-olds everywhere. There was nothing this strip wouldn't take on: lead paint, eating marbles, cats sucking your breath out, etc. Young readers were hooked and Asmussen never let them go.

A strip as a "love letter" to a city

Nowadays, "The San Francisco Comic Strip" has become an institution, a little older, a little mellower, but still occasionally grouchy when the need is there. Cartoonist Don Asmussen, known worldwide as "Mr. San Francisco," is still looked to as the final word on anything in the Bay Area. Although now 85 years old and counting, Asmussen says he still gets out to see a Pavement show now and then. He even says he likes some of those newer "weird" comic strips so popular these days. So read this book and celebrate the last 150 years of "The San Francisco Comic Strip," and think back to when this city was a little less complicated, a little less crowded. Sit in a coffee house, open this book and ask, "Has this strip ever been funny?" And after reading it, calmly reassure yourself, "No, it hasn't." Heaven.

Li'l Donni Asmussen
1978
His love of flags was second only to that of the "S.F. Comic Strip"

Downtown San Francisco
"No city compares," says booster Asmussen

A strange dream Asmussen had in 1992
This image of two men wrestling in a strangly-shaped bathtub has always haunted Asmussen

San Francisco's "Space Needle"

Built in 1849 to announce Gold Rush

CHAPTER TWO

SOME S.F. STUFF

BIG FONTS!

SOME READER FAVORITES

"Fanaticism consists in redoubling your efforts when you have forgotten your aim." — George Santayana

Adventure at Kabuki 8 Cinemas

"Movies are rarely so great that if we cannot appreciate great trash we have little reason to be interested in them."
— Pauline Kael

I WAS LUCKY. I HAVE A FRIEND WHO ACTUALLY GOT IN KABUKI ROOM "8.5", WHERE A GUY ACTS OUT THE MOVIES WITH HAND PUPPETS..

DON'T LEAVE YET! THE BIG SEX SCENE IS COMING! IT'S HOT!

BUTTER

LAST TANGO IN PARIS 🗙

ANYWAY, I ENTER THE "HEE-HAW" ROOM. AS USUAL, ALTHOUGH THE ROOM IS COMPLETELY EMPTY, A PERSON COMES IN AND SITS RIGHT ON MY HEAD..

IS THIS ALL RIGHT?

THE MOVIE FINALLY STARTS. I SUDDENLY REALIZE SOME IDIOT'S SHADOW IS BLOCKING THE SCREEN..

☆◇#☆ MELON-HEAD!

BECAUSE OF HIGH CANDY PRICES, PEOPLE TEND TO SNEAK FOOD INTO THE THEATER. ONE GUY BEHIND ME BROUGHT IN A NOISY BREAD-MAKING MACHINE. ANOTHER ACTUALLY CARVED UP A LIVE COW DURING SOME CRUCIAL DIALOGUE..

SHHHHHHH...

Moooooooo! Moo

WA WA WA

THE WORST THING DURING A MOVIE IS HAVING YOUR CHAIR KICKED. HERE'S A LIST OF GOOD AND BAD PEOPLE TO SIT IN FRONT OF DURING A MOVIE..

BAD PEOPLE TO SIT IN FRONT OF IN A THEATER:

- SOCCER STAR PELE
- SASQUATCHES (BIG FEET)

GOOD PEOPLE TO SIT IN FRONT OF IN A THEATER:

- MATHEMATICIAN STEPHEN HAWKING
- 19TH CENTURY CHINESE WOMEN (TINY BOUND FEET)

ONE THING TO REMEMBER IF YOU WANNA MEET ANY WOMEN AT THE THEATER, DON'T EAT "JUJUBES" CANDY. THEY STICK TO EVERYTHING..

HI, I'M DON. WANT SOME JUJUBES? I'M FULL.

"It is better to waste one's youth than to do nothing with it at all." — Georges Courteline

17

"...human kind. Cannot bear very much reality." — T.S. Eliot

I WENT UNDERCOVER TO AN S.F. **STAR TREK** CONVENTION!

EXAMINER BUDGET RESTRAINTS FORCED ME TO CLEVERLY CREATE A CHEAP KLINGON COSTUME WITH A STAPLE GUN AND SOURDOUGH...

RONCO KLINGON COSTUME

CHA CHUNK

CONVENTION ATTENDANCE HAS BEEN STUNNING AS PEOPLE FROM ALL OVER HAVE BEEN COMING TO SEE **"THE WEEPING SHATNER,"** DECLARED A MIRACLE RECENTLY BY A GREEK ORTHODOX PRIEST...

KINDA PUTS EVERYTHING IN PERSPECTIVE, DOESN'T IT?

AT THE "STAR TREK" AUCTION I FOUND LOTS OF COOL CHRISTMAS GIFTS..

WORF ON GOLF

LAUGH ALONG WITH THE KLINGON KLUNTZ

VHS

ASSIMILATE ME ELMO

RESISTANCE IS FLUFFY!

ON SALE: "CAPTAIN JEAN-LUC PICARD" ROLL-ON ANTI-PERSPIRANT ®

"TV, a medium, so called because it is neither rare nor well done." — Ernie Kovacs

"If there is technological advance without social advance, there is, almost automatically, an increase in human misery." — Michael Harrington

THEY CAUGHT THE

UNABOMBER!

MANY OF THE UNABOMBER'S FORMER STUDENTS HAVE COME OUT WITH STORIES ABOUT HIS STRANGE TEACHING HABITS...

I REMEMBER THAT IF YOU GOT UNDER A "B" HE'D BLOW YOU UP. IT SOUNDS BAD, BUT HE JUST WANTED US TO DO WELL.

WHEN I FINALLY BLEW UP AT MY FIRST JOB, I WAS READY 'CAUSE OF HIM. I LOVE THAT BASTARD.

UNABOMBER SUSPECT TED KACZYNSKI'S NEIGHBORS SPEAK OF HIS TOTAL LACK OF MECHANICAL ABILITY. HE WAS SEEN ATTEMPTING TO MOW HIS LAWN WITH A 1947 ROYAL TYPEWRITER LATE LAST YEAR...

BLADES MUST BE DULL. TECHNOLOGY BAD!

UP WITH PEOPLE

THE FBI WAS CLOSE TO CATCHING HIM LAST YEAR AT A RARE "UNABOMBER MANIFESTO" BOOK SIGNING AT BARNES & NOBLE. UNFORTUNATELY, THE LINE WAS LONG AND THE FBI HAD A MOVIE TO CATCH AT 7:45 P.M...

WE GOTTA GO, ITS 7:44.

DAMN. WE WERE NEXT. HE'S ELUDED US AGAIN!

DRUNK WITH PUBLICITY, BROTHER DAVID KACZYNSKI STARTS TURNING IN FAMILY MEMBERS LEFT AND RIGHT..

CHIEF, IT'S DAVID AGAIN. SAYS HIS MOTHER IS JACK THE RIPPER AND HIS DOG HAS NO ALIBI FOR NOVEMBER 22ND, 1963. DO YOU KNOW WHAT THIS MEANS?

GOLDMINE!

TED KACZYNSKI HAS NOT YET BEEN CHARGED FOR ANY BOMBINGS. HE IS BEING HELD FOR ONE COUNT OF "BAD HAIR," FOR WHICH THE FBI CAN HOLD HIM FOR 10 DAYS.

CHIEF, KACZYNSKI'S MOM WANTED TO GIVE HIM THIS CAKE, BUT WE FOUND A COMB HIDDEN IN IT...

CHECK HIS ORIFICES FOR CURLERS!

THE FBI BELIEVES IT HAS FOUND THE BOMBER'S "FUTURE TARGET LIST" IN HIS CABIN...

HIS NEXT TARGET APPEARED TO BE A "MR. EGGS." WE WARN "MR. EGGS" THAT THIS BOMB MAY ALREADY BE IN THE MAIL.

LIST
EGGS ✓
MILK
PRINGLES

THE UNABOMBER TRIAL'S JURY IS DOMINATED BY HERMITS WHO WANT PAYBACK. KACZYNSKI GOES FREE...

EXAMINER
UNABOMBER NOT GUILTY!
LAWYERS PLAY "HERMIT CARD"
VERDICT DIVIDES HERMITS & NON-HERMITS

FINI

"In the matters of the heart, nothing is true except the improbable." — Madam De Stael

SAN FRANCISCO WOULD NOT SOON FORGET THE EXAMINER'S JULY 7, 1997 HEADLINE.

S.F. EXAMINER 25¢

WRECKAGE OF ALLEGED MUNI BUS FOUND NEAR "LINE 51"

SHY RANCH HAND SHYLY DISCOVERS CRASH SITE, FINDS FIRST KNOWN PROOF THAT MUNI BUSES DO INDEED EXIST P. 3

MORE MUNI WRECKAGE NEWS P. 4

EXPERTS SAY NO HUMAN COULD HAVE DESIGNED LOGO FOUND ON WRECKAGE.

CURE FOR CANCER FOUND P. 327

BEFORE THIS DISCOVERY, MUNI SIGHTINGS WERE SO RARE THAT FEW PEOPLE BELIEVED MUNI EXISTED.

THOSE WHO DID WERE CONSIDERED "KOOKS."

YEAH, I SAW ME ONE. RIGHT HERE, LAST NIGHT. LONG OBJECT, ORANGE STRIPE. I ENTERED THE CRAFT. THEY DID THINGS TO ME. UNSPEAKABLE THINGS.

THE LEADER NEVER CALLED OUT THE CROSS STREET NAMES. I ASSUMED HE WAS COMMUNICATING TELEPATHICALLY.

THE GOVERNMENT QUICKLY DISMISSED THE ALLEGED "MUNI WRECKAGE" AS THE REMAINS OF A TOP SECRET PROJECT IN WHICH ENORMOUS ACCORDIANS (SIMILAR IN SHAPE TO MUNI DOUBLE-SIZE BUSES) WERE DROPPED FROM HIGH ALTITUDES TO SEE WHAT NOISE THEY'D MAKE. CASE CLOSED. OUR ATTEMPTS TO OBTAIN BRIEFING DOCUMENTS PROVE "HEAVILY CENSORED."

TOP SECRET
EYES ONLY   COPY 1 OF 1
ALLEGED MUNI CRASH SITE
TOP SECRET BRIEFING

THE ████████
████ AND ████
████ HOM BABY
████ SCHWAG.

DESPITE THE GOVERNMENT'S EFFORTS, THE MUNI CRASH CAPTIVATED THE NATION. AUTHOR WHITLEY STRIEBER WROTE A BEST-SELLER ABOUT HIS "ALLEGED" VISIT ABOARD A "MUNI VESSEL."

COMMUNION
A TRUE STORY, REALLY. I SWEAR.
EXACT CHANGE OR I'LL GIVE YOU AN ANAL PROBE.
MUNI
BY WHITLEY STRIEBER, REALLY. I SWEAR.

ALSO, FOX'S "THE M-FILES," IN WHICH TWO FBI AGENTS WAIT FOR MUNI, ONE A BELIEVER, ONE NOT.

IT'S COMING. IS NOT.

"THE TRUTH WILL BE HERE ANY MINUTE."

RUMORS WERE FLYING THAT BODIES WERE RECOVERED FROM THE ALLEGED MUNI WRECKAGE. PROOF APPEARED TO BE AT HAND WITH THE DISCOVERY OF THE INFAMOUS **"TOP SECRET MUNI AUTOPSY FILM,"** BUT IT WAS INCONCLUSIVE...

ACCURATE DETAIL: MUNI DRIVERS OFTEN APPEAR TO BE DEAD.

INACCURATE DETAIL: THICK SKIN-FLAP IS FAKE; MUNI DRIVERS COMMONLY KNOWN TO BE THIN-SKINNED.

SOME BELIEVERS GO AS FAR AS SAYING OUR MODERN COMPUTER TECHNOLOGY IS BASED ON INFORMATION FOUND FROM THE "MUNI INCIDENT." SCIENTISTS DISMISS THIS NOTION...

RIDICULOUS! HOW DO PEOPLE COME UP WITH THIS STUFF?!

NEW APPLE LINE!

TOP SECRET

"Safe upon the solid rock the ugly houses stand: Come and see my shining palace built upon the sand!" — Edna St. Vincent Milay

SPECIAL REPORT!

PEOPLE HAVE BEEN CAMPING OUT ALL NIGHT IN FRONT OF EXAMINER NEWSPAPER BOXES IN HOPES OF GETTING THE FIRST COPIES OF "THE SAN FRANCISCO COMIC STRIP: THE SPECIAL EDITION," WITH NEW DIGITALLY-ENHANCED JOKES.

S.F. COMiX®
SPECIAL EDITION
READ IT AGAIN, FOR THE FIRST TIME

S.F. COMIX CREATOR DON ASMUSSEN HAS GONE BACK AND REWORKED HIS OLD STRIPS TO SHOWCASE THE BEST IN NEW, DIGITAL CARTOON TECHNOLOGY! NOW, IN ALL ITS RESTORED GLORY:

THE LOST HINCKLE THE HUT SCENE!

EWWW

"S.F. COMiX" LASTING APPEAL IS BASED ON ITS "GOOD VS. EVIL" MYTHIC QUALITY BORROWED HEAVILY FROM LEGENDARY AKIRA KUROSAWA'S JAPANESE COMIC STRIP "RASHOMON ALLEY.®" ASMUSSEN'S FANS HATE HIS EPITOME OF EVIL:

DA VADER!

YOU PROMISED TO FIX MUNI!

I AM ALTERING THE DEAL. PRAY I DO NOT ALTER IT FURTHER!

*SOURDOUGH-SABERS

THE CARTOON PANEL THAT ASMUSSEN MOST WANTED TO DIGITALLY REWORK WAS THE CLIMACTIC BATTLE AGAINST THE DARK SIDE, WHICH INCLUDES THE SPECTACULAR DESTRUCTION OF DAVADER'S HOME BASE OF ALL EVIL:

"THE DEATH STARS RESTAURANT"®

DEATH STARS

FOR THE "S.F. COMIX" COLLECTOR, AVAILABLE FOR ONLY $9.95 IS THE DOCUMENTARY..

THE MAKING OF "S.F. COMIX" SPECIAL EDITION
ASMUSSEN: THE MAN, THE DREAM

AND FOR THE POST-POST MODERNIST:

THE MAKING OF THE MAKING OF "S.F. COMIX" SPECIAL EDITION
SEE HOW THE DOCUMENTARY WAS MADE

"S.F. COMIX" CHANGED THE FACE OF COMIX FOREVER. CHARACTER-DRIVEN STRIPS LIKE BIL KEANE'S "FAMILY CIRCUS"® WERE FORCED INTO EFFECTS-LADEN EXCESS..

FAMILY CIRCUS SPECIAL EDITION

UNSATISFIED WITH JUST CHANGING HIS PAST STRIPS, ASMUSSEN BEGINS USING TECHNOLOGY TO CHANGE HIS PAST MISTAKES..

OKAY, NOW MAKE THE BIG MONSTER KILL MY EX-WIFE BEFORE SHE ASKS FOR ALIMONY!

FINI

"The car has become a secular sanctuary for the individual, his shrine to the self, his mobile Walden Pond." — Edward McDonagh

BAD DRIVING IN S.F.

RECENT ACCIDENTS HAVE RENEWED DEBATE ABOUT AUTO SAFETY AND RESPONSIBILITY IN THE BAY AREA. WHY CAN'T WE DRIVE SAFELY?

CALIFORNIA HAS ALWAYS PRIDED ITSELF ON ITS LACK OF BARRIERS. ONE LOOK AT S.F.'S ROAD SIGNS SHOWS AN ALARMING AVOIDANCE OF SELF·RESTRICTION...

STOP well, at least slow down, oh nevermind.

DO NOT PASS well, unless you really have to.

YIELD unless you had a bad childhood.

SELF·HELP HAS CREATED A SOCIETY OF HEDONISTIC BAD DRIVERS. THE PURSUIT OF SELF HAS CAUSED MILLIONS OF ACCIDENTS THROUGHOUT THE YEARS...

"BABY-STEPS, BABY LANE-CHANGES!" NO MORE BACK OF THE LINE! I DESERVE MORE! I DESERVE THIS!

EXPLOSIVES

THIS NEW AGE OF BLAME TRANSFERENCE HAS REDEFINED AUTO INSURANCE. ALONG WITH "NO FAULT," S.F. NOW OFFERS "PARENT'S FAULT" INSURANCE...

OH GOD! MY INNER-CHILD WASN'T PROPERLY STRAPPED DOWN!

THESE SELF-HELP ACCIDENT REPORTS CAN GET QUITE LENGTHY...

PLEASE DESCRIBE THE EVENTS LEADING UP TO THIS ACCIDENT ...

WELL, MY PARENTS NEVER HUGGED ME AS A CHILD, AND THEN MY UNCLE, WHO DRESSES LIKE A CLOWN, USED TO PLAY A GAME WITH ME CALLED "BAD BOZO" IN WHICH...

SNIFF, I HEAR YA, KID..

SCIENTISTS HAVE FOUND THAT CARS HAVE A STRANGE EFFECT ON AGGRESSIVE BEHAVIOR. IN A TEST, SCIENTISTS PUT SEXUALLY-TIMID PANDA BEARS IN SPORTS CARS TO RECORD BEHAVIORAL CHANGES...

EXPERIMENT #324B: PANDA IN SAAB

MALE PANDA CONSTANTLY REVS ENGINE. BURNS RUBBER. THE FEMALE PANDA BECOMES AROUSED.

EXPERIMENT RESULT: PANDA GETS POONTANG

RED LIGHT RUNNING IS SUCH AN EPIDEMIC THAT S.F. OFFICIALS HAVE PLACED RED LIGHTS IN FRONT OF CLIFFS IN HOPES OF LURING RUNNERS TO THEIR DEATHS...

I GOT IT, I GOT IT!

GOLDEN GATE BRIDGE COLLISIONS ARE SO FREQUENT, OFFICIALS ARE CONSIDERING NEW BARRIERS. THEY ARE CURRENTLY BEING TESTED IN THE SECOND MOST CROWDED TRAFFIC AREA IN S.F., CITY HALL'S EXITS...

NORTH
MAYOR WILLIE BROWN'S
HIRES

SOUTH
MAYOR WILLIE BROWN'S
FIRES

MOVABLE CONCRETE DIVIDER

CAUTION HEAD-ON TRAFFIC

MAYOR BROWN DECIDES TO SAVE MONEY BY USING YOUTH GANG MEMBERS AS GOLDEN GATE BRIDGE LANE-BARRIERS. IT WORKS WONDERS.

DON'T EVEN THINK ABOUT IT.

FINI

"Candy is dandy but liquor is quicker." — Ogden Nash

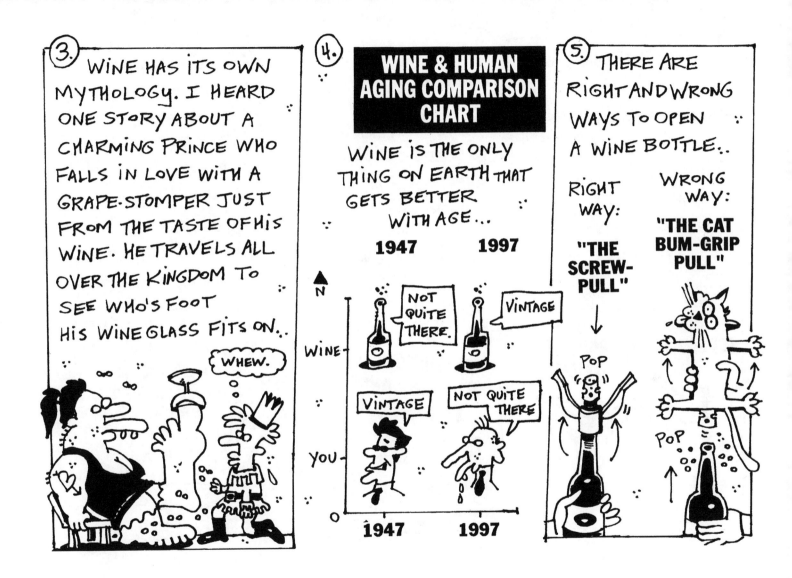

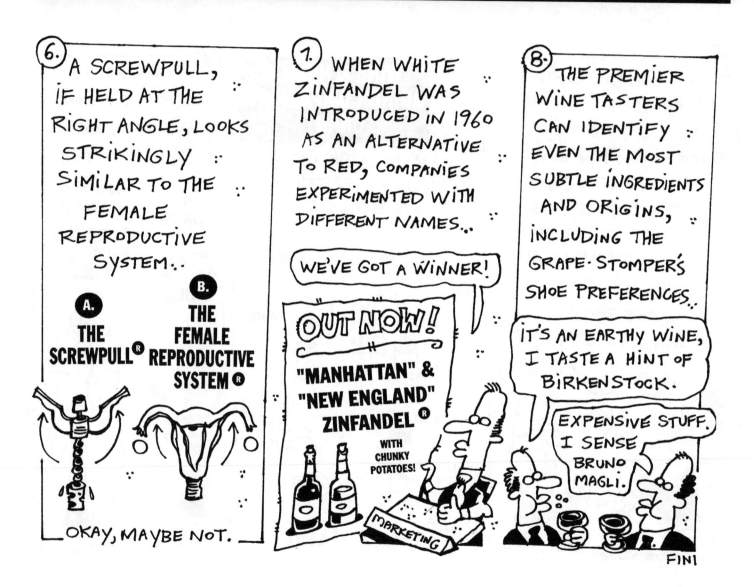

6. A SCREWPULL, IF HELD AT THE RIGHT ANGLE, LOOKS STRIKINGLY SIMILAR TO THE FEMALE REPRODUCTIVE SYSTEM..

A. THE SCREWPULL®

B. THE FEMALE REPRODUCTIVE SYSTEM®

OKAY, MAYBE NOT.

7. WHEN WHITE ZINFANDEL WAS INTRODUCED IN 1960 AS AN ALTERNATIVE TO RED, COMPANIES EXPERIMENTED WITH DIFFERENT NAMES..

WE'VE GOT A WINNER!

OUT NOW!

"MANHATTAN" & "NEW ENGLAND" ZINFANDEL®

WITH CHUNKY POTATOES!

MARKETING

8. THE PREMIER WINE TASTERS CAN IDENTIFY EVEN THE MOST SUBTLE INGREDIENTS AND ORIGINS, INCLUDING THE GRAPE-STOMPER'S SHOE PREFERENCES..

IT'S AN EARTHY WINE, I TASTE A HINT OF BIRKENSTOCK.

EXPENSIVE STUFF. I SENSE BRUNO MAGLI.

FINI

"Distrust all in whom the impulse to punish is powerful." — Friedrich Nietzche

ASKED WHY THE RAID NEEDED 100 AGENTS WITH WEAPONS AND RIOT GEAR TO TAKE ON ABOUT 10 OR SO MELLOW TOKERS, LOCAL HERO COP GREG CORRALES REPLIED:

CRITICS ACCUSED LUNGREN OF USING THE RIOT TO FURTHER HIS BID FOR CALIFORNIA GOVERNOR, BUT THE TRUTH IS MUCH DARKER. HE WAS AVENGING THE DEATH OF HIS BOYHOOD FRIEND "CHICO," KILLED BY A POWER MAD, POT-SMOKING WHEELCHAIR-BOUND CANCER PATIENT...

AT THE POST RAID PRESS CONFERENCE, CA. BUREAU OF NARC ENFORCEMENT'S JOE DOANE DENIED ANY POLITICAL MOTIVATIONS.

LISTEN, I LOST A PARTNER WHEN A SIMPLE "GIGGLE-FIT" ESCALATED INTO AN ALL-OUT "MUNCHIE-ATTACK."

CHICO, NOOOOOOOOOOO!

HAHAHAHA

VENGEANCE FOR CHICO!

IT WAS ANOTHER WACO! THEY WERE STOCKPILING AN ARSENAL OF COMFY COUCHES! ENOUGH TO RELAX THE WORLD THREE TIMES OVER! WE HAD TO GO IN BEFORE THEY WENT ON TO OTTOMANS!

THE ONLY LOCAL COP IN ON THE RAID WAS FAMED VENTRILOQUIST POLICE PUPPET BRENDAN O'SMARTY, MAKING UNDERCOVER PURCHASES FOR 2 YEARS...

HI, I'D LIKE SOME OF THAT GROOVY WEED, MAN.

OKAY. HEY WAIT, I JUST SAW THAT GUY'S LIPS MOVE, IS THIS A SET-UP?

WHO, HIM? HE'S DRINKING A GLASS OF WATER!

THE REAL TRAGEDY: S.F. AIDS SUFFERERS ARE LEFT WITHOUT POT DURING WHAT DOCTORS CONSIDER THE MOST PAINFUL STAGE OF THE AIDS DISEASE: THE REPUBLICAN CONVENTION.

NIGHT SWEATS!

AIDS?

NO, A DOLE SPEECH.

YOU'LL FEEL COLD, BUT IT'LL PASS AS YOU ENTER ETERNAL SLEEP.

S.F. COMIX QUIZ!!!

WHICH OF THE FOLLOWING IS A GROUP OF VERY SICK PEOPLE WHO USE ILLEGAL MEANS TO ESCAPE REALITY?

A. S.F. CANNABIS BUYERS CLUB

B. THE REPUBLICAN CONVENTION

PARTY ON, SUCKERS!

ALL CHARGES WERE DROPPED WHEN IT WAS DISCOVERED THE 150 POUNDS OF CONFISCATED CANNABIS WERE ACTUALLY THE LATE JERRY GARCIA'S ASHES...

NOTHING ELSE COULD BE THIS POTENT.

EVIDENCE

EVIDENCE

FBI

FINI

"The play's the thing, wherein we catch the conscience of the king." — William Shakespeare

BAY AREA THEATRE

LOCAL THEATRE PATRONS WERE SHOCKED A FEW MONTHS BACK WHEN BERKELEY REP'S ARTISTIC DIRECTOR, SHARON OTT, ANNOUNCED SHE WAS LEAVING FOR SEATTLE..

I'LL BE DEVELOPING THE SOFTWARE "PLAYMAKER 1.1" FOR MICROSOFT. GOOD LUCK, SUCKERS.

TONY TACCONE, OTT'S REPLACEMENT, DREW INSTANT CRITICISM WHEN HE CYNICALLY REPLACED **ANNA DEAVERE SMITH** WITH BIGGER BOX OFFICE DRAW **ANNA NICOLE SMITH** IN A VASTLY RETOOLED **"TWILIGHT LOS ANGELES, 1992: TRIPLE D-CUP."** STUNNINGLY, SHE WON OVER CRITICS WITH HER CHAMELEON-LIKE TRANSFORMATIONS...

TEE HEE, SO LIKE, NOW I'M A GUY, OKAY, AND, LIKE, UM, PREJUDICE IS, LIKE, BAD, OKAY?

TONY TACCONE IS ALSO REVIVING TONY KUSHNER'S POPULAR SOCIALISM DRAMA "SLAVS!", BUT IS COMBINING IT WITH THE UNPREDICTABLE MAGIC OF IMPROVISATION! CHECK OUT

¡IMPROVI-SLAVS!®

FORGET "THE BERLIN WALL.." THIS TIME THE "FOURTH WALL" IS COMING DOWN! THIS SEARCH FOR MUSE WILL MAKE YA SNOOZE!

UM, UH.. I'M A BUNNY RABBIT, AND I'M, UH, LOOKING FOR CARROTS.. UM...

SOMETIMES COMPLETE FREEDOM ISN'T SUCH A GOOD THING.

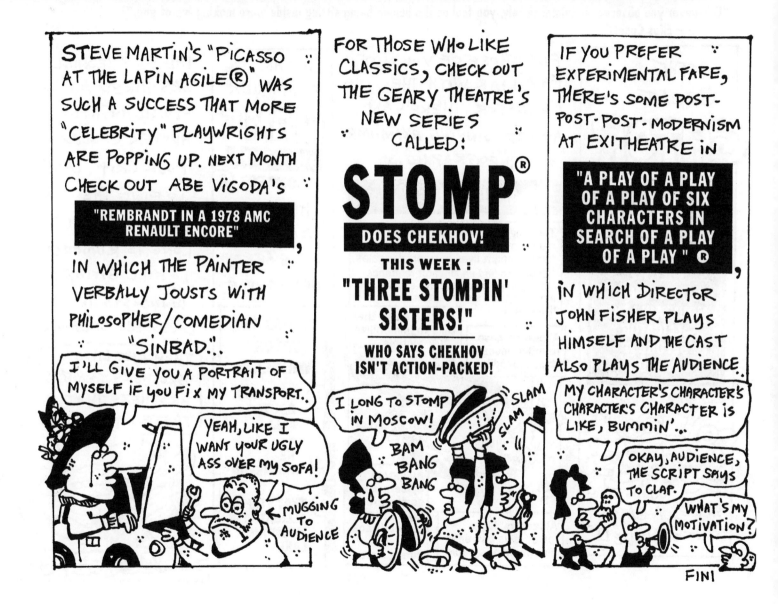

STEVE MARTIN'S "PICASSO AT THE LAPIN AGILE®" WAS SUCH A SUCCESS THAT MORE "CELEBRITY" PLAYWRIGHTS ARE POPPING UP. NEXT MONTH CHECK OUT ABE VIGODA'S

"REMBRANDT IN A 1978 AMC RENAULT ENCORE",

IN WHICH THE PAINTER VERBALLY JOUSTS WITH PHILOSOPHER/COMEDIAN "SINBAD."...

I'LL GIVE YOU A PORTRAIT OF MYSELF IF YOU FIX MY TRANSPORT..

YEAH, LIKE I WANT YOUR UGLY ASS OVER MY SOFA!

← MUGGING TO AUDIENCE

FOR THOSE WHO LIKE CLASSICS, CHECK OUT THE GEARY THEATRE'S NEW SERIES CALLED:

STOMP®

DOES CHEKHOV!

THIS WEEK:

"THREE STOMPIN' SISTERS!"

WHO SAYS CHEKHOV ISN'T ACTION-PACKED!

I LONG TO STOMP IN MOSCOW!

SLAM
SLAM

BAM BANG BANG

IF YOU PREFER EXPERIMENTAL FARE, THERE'S SOME POST-POST-POST-MODERNISM AT EXITHEATRE IN

"A PLAY OF A PLAY OF A PLAY OF SIX CHARACTERS IN SEARCH OF A PLAY OF A PLAY" ®,

IN WHICH DIRECTOR JOHN FISHER PLAYS HIMSELF AND THE CAST ALSO PLAYS THE AUDIENCE..

MY CHARACTER'S CHARACTER'S CHARACTER'S CHARACTER IS LIKE, BUMMIN'...

OKAY, AUDIENCE, THE SCRIPT SAYS TO CLAP.

WHAT'S MY MOTIVATION?

FINI

"Whenever you observe an animal closely, you feel as if a human being sitting inside were making fun of you."
— Elias Canetti

THE GREAT GATOR HUNT!

WILL WE FIND THE MOUNTAIN LAKE ALLIGATOR BEFORE IT FINDS US?

URP

HERE'S A GATOR INFO·GUIDE!

FOR THOSE OF YOU NOT FAMILIAR WITH THE ALLIGATOR, HERE'S AN AWARD-WINNING EXAMINER INFOGRAPHIC...

THE ALLIGATOR*

The alligator is one of the most dangerous of the reptile family. A fierce biter, it lives in tropical locales.
*Unable to find an alligator reference before press time, we have substituted a drawing of a subterranean flying squirrel.

Alligators have rounder noses than crocodiles.

Alligators use their tails to immobilize victims.

N

Alligators' large lower jaws can snap an opponent's neck.

Alligators' epidermal scales are layered to protect back and tail during battle.

SO FAR, THE EXAMINER **NAME THE GATOR CONTEST ®** HAS BEEN A HIT! HERE ARE THE BEST SO FAR.

"NAME THE GATOR" WINNERS:

1. **BOUTROS BOUTROS ALLI**

2. **THE CROCARENA**

3. **THAT STUPID ALLIGATOR IN MOUNTAIN LAKE**

THE S.F. CHRONICLE HAS HIRED A FLORIDA GATOR HUNTER CALLED AL "FOUR GRIT" LONG TO FIND THE BEASTY. ALTHOUGH LONG IS RUMORED TO KILL GATORS, HE INSISTS HE LOVES THE CREATURES.

THEY ARE LIKE BROTHERS TO ME, BROTHERS THAT TASTE LIKE CHICKEN.

"FOUR GRIT" LONG USED TO BE "SIX GRIT" LONG, BUT TRAGICALLY LOST TWO GRITS IN A GATOR ATTACK IN 1987...
DOCTOR, I CAN STILL FEEL MY MISSING TWO GRITS...
THAT'S GRIT GHOST PAIN.
DOWN TWO GRITS
THE RECOVERY TOOK YEARS. DOCTORS ATTEMPTED A CONTROVERSIAL "BABOON GRITS TRANSPLANT," BUT THE GRITS DIDN'T TAKE. HE WAS FOREVER "GRIT-CHALLENGED" AND SOUGHT REVENGE...
IT'S GATOR HARVESTIN' TIME!
THE EXAMINER REALIZED LONG'S INTENTIONS WEREN'T PEACEFUL WHEN, INSTEAD OF KILLING THE GATOR, HE SLOWLY TORTURED IT BY READING PAT STEGER'S SOCIETY COLUMN OUT LOUD...
CHARLOTTE MAILLIARD SWIG, LOOKING ABSOLUTELY RADIANT AFTER A MONTH AT TAHOE, GAVE A PARTY TO END ALL PARTIES...
GASP
AAK

A rescue team trying to save the gator, led by Examiner Executive Editor Phil Bronstein, was blocked by police. Here is a time line of the confrontation:

BRONSTEIN* ALLIGATOR RESCUE TIME LINE

Examiner Executive Editor Bronstein* attempts to enter lake, **1** but is blocked by police. Bronstein pleads for humanity. **2**

*Unable to find a Phil Bronstein reference before press time, we have substituted instead a drawing of a cute, fluffy little gerbil.

1 3:45 p.m.: Police block Bronstein from entering the lake.

2 3:46 p.m.: Bronstein pleads for humanity. Turned away, he resumes foraging for kibble.

N

THE HUNT CONTINUED. EXPERTS TRIED EVERYTHING INCLUDING USING MANNY THE HIPPIE AS BAIT, THE GATOR SWALLOWS MANNY, BUT ESCAPES. FORTUNATELY, THE GATOR IS NOW EASIER TO TRACK.

OUR SOUND EQUIPMENT HAS PICKED UP A SOUNDWAVE IN INTERVALS OF TWO SECONDS APART.

SCHWAG.. BEEP.. ..SCHWAG..

THE GATOR FINALLY DIES FROM SMOKE INHALATION CAUSED BY MANNY'S TOKING. THE GATOR MEAT SELLS FOR $200 A POUND, BUT CAN ONLY BE EATEN FOR MEDICAL PURPOSES..

WOW, HIPPIE TASTES JUST LIKE CHICKEN.

SCHWAG.

FINI

CHAPTER THREE

SOME MUNI STUFF

"All that is human must retrograde if it does not advance." — Edward Gibbon

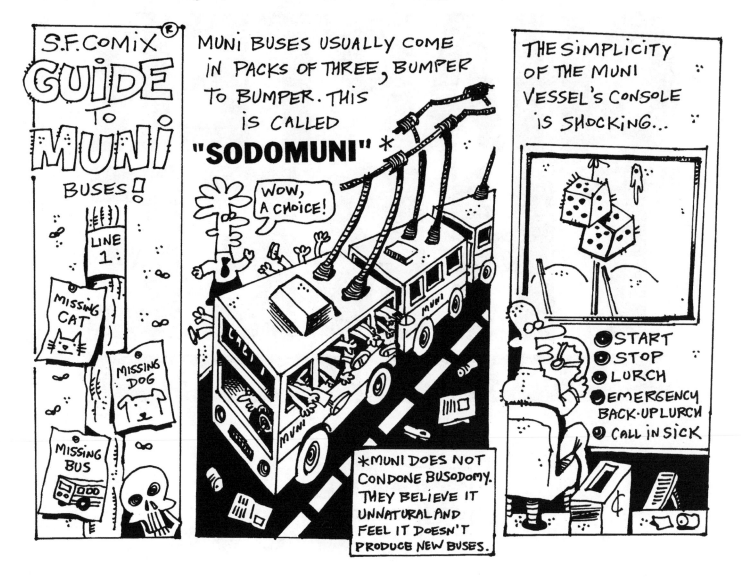

S.F. COMIX ®
GUIDE TO MUNI BUSES!

LINE 1

MISSING CAT

MISSING DOG

MISSING BUS

MUNI BUSES USUALLY COME IN PACKS OF THREE, BUMPER TO BUMPER. THIS IS CALLED **"SODOMUNI"** *

WOW, A CHOICE!

*MUNI DOES NOT CONDONE BUSODOMY. THEY BELIEVE IT UNNATURAL AND FEEL IT DOESN'T PRODUCE NEW BUSES.

THE SIMPLICITY OF THE MUNI VESSEL'S CONSOLE IS SHOCKING...

● START
● STOP
● LURCH
● EMERGENCY BACK-UP LURCH
● CALL IN SICK

SAFETY IS ALWAYS IMPORTANT! THERE HAVE BEEN THIRTY-SIX MUNI DEATHS THIS YEAR ATTRIBUTED TO **"MUNI BACKPACK ASPHYXIATION"**

DANGER CAN COME IN MANY FORMS. LAST YEAR FORTY-TWO RIDERS WERE INJURED WHEN A STREET MUSICIAN MISTOOK A DOUBLE-LENGTH MUNI BUS FOR AN ENORMOUS ACCORDIAN...

AAAAH!

AAAAH!

CRUNCH

CRUNCH

SECURITY DIDN'T ARRIVE UNTIL THE SECOND CHORUS OF "GREENSLEEVES."

ALWAYS AVOID SEATS WITH PUDDLES. THESE PUDDLES ARE BELIEVED TO BE THE "TEARS OF CHRIST," AND PEOPLE COME FROM ALL OVER TO SEE "THE CRYING BUSES OF SAN FRANCISCO."

THE STIGMUNI!

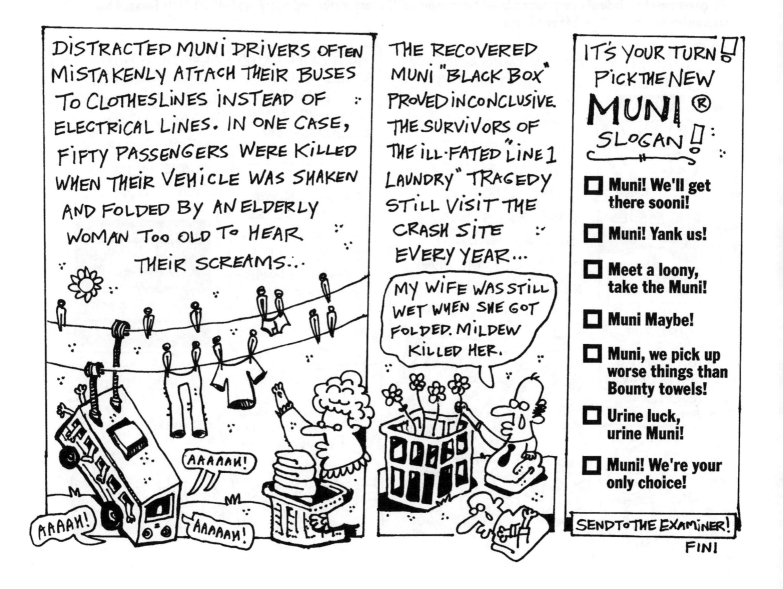

"All government — indeed every human benefit and enjoyment, every virtue and every prudent act — is founded on compromise and barter." — Edmund Burke

MUNI NEGOTIATIONS PART 2.

1. THIS IS A KNEELING BUS

MUNI CHIEF EMILIO CRUZ PLAYED REAL TOUGH DURING NEGOTIATIONS.

PLEASE, PLEASE GIVE SOMETHING UP!

NOPE

2. THIS IS A KNEELING MUNI CHIEF

AFTER GOING SMOOTHLY FOR ABOUT AN HOUR, NEGOTIATIONS SUDDENLY STALLED, THEN VIOLENTLY LURCHED FOWARD, SHOOK, LURCHED BACKWARDS AND STALLED AGAIN. IT TURNS OUT THE MUNI NEGOTIATOR HAD BECOME UNHITCHED...

MUNI CHIEF CRUZ REALLY HELD TOUGH AND CHANGED SOME DECADES-OLD UNION RULES...

RULE 342B: "A MUNI DRIVER MUST NOT CLOSE THE DOOR UNTIL AT LEAST "HALF" OF A PASSENGER'S LIMBS ARE IN THE BUS. THIS IS 1997, WE WANT A "MAJORITY OF LIMBS..."

THREE OUT OF FOUR LIMBS?! DO YOU KNOW HOW MUCH THAT WOULD DELAY SERVICE?

ALSO NEGOTIATED WAS A TRACKING DEVICE, LIKE THOSE IN "WILD KINGDOM," WHICH WOULD LOCATE MISSING MUNI DRIVERS...

SECRET TRACKING DEVICE CLIPPED TO DRIVER'S EAR ENABLES MUNI TO MONITOR DRIVER'S EATING, MATING & MIGRATING HABITS.

TO CHANGE MUNI'S IMAGE, CRUZ HAS HIRED THE ADVERTISING AGENCY FAMOUS FOR THE "GOT MILK?" CAMPAIGN TO TURN MUNI'S CONSTANT DELAYS INTO A POSITIVE "ANTICIPATORY EXPERIENCE."

LINE 1

got muni?

MUCH HAS BEEN MADE OF MUNI'S PROPOSED 800 COMPLAINT LINE, BUT EVEN MORE ALLURING ARE RUMORS OF A MUNI 900 SEX NUMBER...

HOT MUNI SEX TALK
1-900-HOT-MUNI
HOT MUNI DRIVERS WANNA TALK TO YOU!

I'LL DRIVE YOU CRAZY.

$1.00 FOR FIRST MINUTE, INCLUDES TWO TRANSFERS
1-900-LURCH-ME

AS AN EXPERIMENT, SCIENTISTS TOOK ASTRONAUT SHANNON LUCID, WHO'S USED TO LONG WAITS, AND HAD HER WAIT FOR MUNI LINE 1. MUNI BROKE HER...

ENOUGH ALREADY! GET ME BACK ON THE SHUTTLE!

LINE 1

FINI

49

"The winds and the waves are always on the side of the ablest navigators." — Edward Gibbon

"It is a bad plan that admits of no modification." — Publilius Syrus

THE DEFENSE OF MUNI ACT 99

MUNI CHIEF EMILIO CRUZ PLAYS HARDBALL WITH THE DRIVERS' NEGOTIATORS!

365 ALLOWED UNEXCUSED ABSENCES A YEAR IS UNACCEPTABLE!

HOW'S THIS, 364 ABSENCES AND A PERSONAL DAY.

DEAL! SORRY TO BE SO TOUGH.

TO PROMOTE A POSITIVE BUS ENVIRONMENT, MUNI DRIVERS MUST NOW KISS ALL BOARDING PASSENGERS FULL ON THE MOUTH...

SURRENDER TO MUNI!

SOME RIDERS PAY JUST FOR THE KISS...

UNDER THE NEW CONTRACT, MUNI DRIVERS WHO MISS MORE THAN FOUR SHIFTS IN EIGHT MONTHS WILL BE CHEMICALLY CASTRATED...

MAN, I JUST DON'T HAVE THAT "URGE TO LURCH" ANYMORE.

THOUGH STILL ABLE TO PERFORM, CASTRATED DRIVERS NOW FIND IT TAKES 30 MINUTES TO WORK UP A GOOD LURCH. REPORTS OF "HATE LURCHES" PLUMMET. BUT THE TESTOSTERONE REMOVAL HAS SOME SIDE EFFECTS...

MOVE TO THE BACK! WHADDYA ALL STARING AT?!

HEARING ABOUT THE CASTRATIONS, THE AMERICAN CIVIL LIBERTIES UNION CONDEMNS IT AS IN HUMANE...

EVEN THE WORST OF THE WORST DON'T DESERVE THIS! OH, IT'S FOR MUNI DRIVERS? NEVERMIND.

ACLU

IN A RELATED STORY, MUNI AUDITOR HARVEY ROSE IS ALSO CASTRATED BECAUSE OF A DISAGREEMENT WITH MAYOR BROWN, LEAVING HIM A BIT TOO "SUBMISSIVE."..

YOUR WISH IS MY COMMAND, MASTER. THIS ROSE HAS BLOOMED!

FINI

"Things are entirely as they appear to be — and behind them...there is nothing." — Jean-Paul Sartre

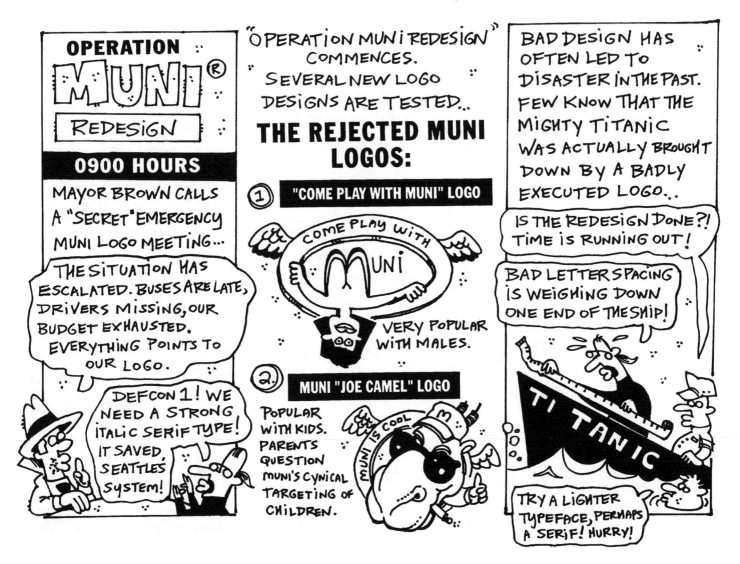

OPERATION MUNI® REDESIGN

0900 HOURS

MAYOR BROWN CALLS A "SECRET" EMERGENCY MUNI LOGO MEETING...

THE SITUATION HAS ESCALATED. BUSES ARE LATE, DRIVERS MISSING, OUR BUDGET EXHAUSTED. EVERYTHING POINTS TO OUR LOGO.

DEFCON 1! WE NEED A STRONG ITALIC SERIF TYPE! IT SAVED SEATTLE'S SYSTEM!

"OPERATION MUNI REDESIGN" COMMENCES. SEVERAL NEW LOGO DESIGNS ARE TESTED...

THE REJECTED MUNI LOGOS:

① "COME PLAY WITH MUNI" LOGO

COME PLAY WITH MUNI

VERY POPULAR WITH MALES.

② MUNI "JOE CAMEL" LOGO

POPULAR WITH KIDS. PARENTS QUESTION MUNI'S CYNICAL TARGETING OF CHILDREN.

MUNI IS COOL

BAD DESIGN HAS OFTEN LED TO DISASTER IN THE PAST. FEW KNOW THAT THE MIGHTY TITANIC WAS ACTUALLY BROUGHT DOWN BY A BADLY EXECUTED LOGO...

IS THE REDESIGN DONE?! TIME IS RUNNING OUT!

BAD LETTER SPACING IS WEIGHING DOWN ONE END OF THE SHIP!

TITANIC

TRY A LIGHTER TYPEFACE, PERHAPS A SERIF! HURRY!

A COLLEGE STUDENT'S LOGO IS FINALLY CHOSEN FOR MUNI. IT INSTANTLY FIXES ALL OF THE BUSES' PROBLEMS, AS EXPECTED. BUOYED BY THIS, MAYOR BROWN NEXT TACKLES THE S.F. HOMELESS PROBLEM, USING ONLY THE BEST DESIGNERS...

OKAY. I SEE "HOMELESS" IN HELVETICA. MAYBE SOME WINGS ON THE SIDE TO MAKE IT "SEXY." HELLO?!

HOMELESS
H

MUNI UNIFORMS ARE CHANGING, TOO! TO COMBAT CONSTANT ABUSE OF DRIVERS, THEIR UNIFORMS ARE BEING REDESIGNED TO RESEMBLE CUDDLY KOALA BEARS, CREATURES TOO SWEET TO YELL AT...

HEY, THE ☆&Q#☆ BUS IS THREE HOURS LATE, YOU.. CUDDLY KOALA BEAR? SUCH A FLUFFY TUMMY!

FOR HOMELESS PEOPLE, MAYOR BROWN HAS COMMISSIONED UNIFORMS WHICH RESEMBLE MAJESTIC REDWOOD TREES. HANDOUTS FROM TRENDY LIBERAL PASSERSBY QUADRUPLE..

SPARE CHANGE FOR A HOMELESS, UM.. I MEAN REDWOOD TREE?

OH LORD, A HOMELESS REDWOOD! WHAT HAVE WE DONE?

FINI

55

"Bureaucracy, the rule of no one, has become the modern form of despotism." — Mary McCarthy

THE MUNI AUDIT

BUDGET ANALYST HARVEY ROSE'S 237-PAGE MUNI AUDIT HAS REVEALED THIS SHOCKING NEWS:

MUNI SUCKS THE BIG ONE.

THE MUNI AUDIT

SHOCKING, HUH?! IN THESE PARTS, MUNI SIGHTINGS HAVE BECOME AS MYSTERIOUS AS U.F.O. SIGHTINGS. NO ONE BELIEVES MUNI EXISTS...

RIGHT HERE, LAST NIGHT. I SAW IT. LONG OBJECT, WITH AN ORANGE STRIPE. THE DOOR OPENED, AND I ENTERED THE CRAFT. THEY DID THINGS TO ME...

...UNSPEAKABLE THINGS.

INCONCLUSIVE BLURRY PHOTO

LINE 1

ROSE'S AUDIT EXPOSED MUNI'S WASTE. ROSE FOUND THAT WORKERS OFTEN STARTED UP MUNI CHIEF PHIL ADAMS AND LEFT HIM IDLING FOR UP TO THREE HOURS EVERY MORNING...

HE KEEPS STALLING!

PUTT PUTT SPUTTER PFFT

PUTT

EMISSIONS!

ADAMS

A SHOCKING DISCOVERY WAS MADE THAT 88 DRIVERS WERE BEING USED AT "CLERICAL DESK JOBS" INSTEAD OF ON BUSES. EVEN WORSE, THEY ALSO WERE OFTEN LATE AND ARRIVED IN THREES...

FOR THREE MONTHS IN 1995, BECAUSE OF A LACK OF WORKING BUSES, MUNI USED GARBAGE TRUCKS TO TRANSPORT RIDERS. NO ONE NOTICED THE DIFFERENCE...

CRUNCH

MUNI

BUT WORST OF ALL, LAYERS AND LAYERS OF MUNI MANAGEMENT HAVE MADE EVEN THE SIMPLEST OF REPAIRS TAKE FOREVER...

BUS DOWN ON LINE 1!

BUS DOWN ON LINE 1!

BUS... HEY, WE FORGOT TO START THE CHIEF AT 7 A.M.! IT TAKES 3 HOURS TO WARM HIM UP!

ZZZ

FINI

Home Hunting with the Niners

"Be it ever so humble, there's no place like home for wearing what you like." — George Aden

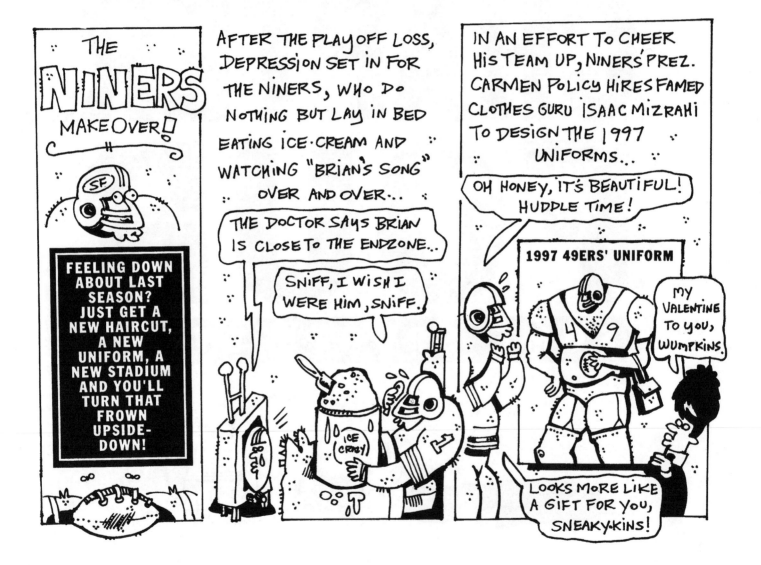

LEFT WITHOUT AN ADEQUATE HOME, THE NINERS ARE FORCED TO MOVE BACK IN WITH THEIR PARENTS BUT TROUBLE ERUPTS AT THANKSGIVING WHEN MOM ASKS SON TO PASS THE TURKEY...

HE OVERSHOOTS MOM BY 20 YARDS AND LOSES POSSESSION.

THROWN OUT OF THE HOUSE, THE NINERS ARE LEFT TEMPORARILY HOMELESS, BUT "STREET SHEET" SALES SKYROCKET...

"STREET SHEET" OR EAT CLEAT.

I'LL TAKE TWELVE.

PRESIDENT CARMEN POLICY DECIDES IT IS BETTER TO RENT THAN BUY A HOME. NATURALLY, HE CALLS "RENTAL SOLUTIONS,®" AN APARTMENT LOCATING SERVICE...

FIRST THINGS FIRST, DO YOU HAVE ANY CATS?

NO, BUT WE DO NEED A 72,000 SEATING CAPACITY AND PARKING.

NO PROBLEM AS LONG AS YOU DON'T HAVE CATS.

"The toughest thing about success is that you've got to keep on being a success." — Irving Berlin

SPECIAL REPORT!

THE 49ERS HAVE JUST ANNOUNCED THEY HAVE ALREADY FIRED NEW HEAD COACH STEVE MARIUCCI AFTER HE FAILED TO PRODUCE ANY WINS IN HIS FIRST THREE DAYS AS COACH.

MARIUCCI'S PROTEST THAT "NO GAMES HAD BEEN PLAYED" WAS DISMISSED AS "THE EXCUSE OF A LOSER."

NEWS

THE FANS ARE LIVID. THE NINERS QUICKLY CALL ANOTHER PRESS CONFERENCE AND ATTEMPT TO SHIFT THE MEDIA FOCUS FROM THE FIRINGS TO CLUB PRESIDENT CARMEN POLICY'S FREAKISHLY HUGE FEATHERED HAIRCUT...

CARMEN, WHY'DYA FIRE HIM?

FIRE WHO? RELAX AND ENJOY THE MAJESTY OF MY FEATHERED HAIR. IT IS FOR ALL OF US TO ENJOY..

YOU IGNORED MY...

DO NOT RESIST ITS PLEASURES. MY HAIR IS GOD'S GIFT TO US. SUBMIT TO MY HAIR!

..GETTING.. WEAK..MUST.. ..RESIST...

THE PUBLIC RELATIONS DISASTER BEGAN LAST WEEK WHEN THE NINERS FORCED OUT POPULAR HEAD COACH GEORGE SEIFERT, SCIENTIFICALLY PROVEN TO BE "THE NICEST GUY ON EARTH..."

S.F. EXAMINER

SEIFERT SAVES TINY KITTENS FROM BLAZE. NINERS STILL FIRE HIM.

REVIVES KITTY

SEIFERT CURES CANCER. STILL FIRED.

P. 12

S.F. CHRONICLE

SEIFERT DANCES WITH LONELY, RETARDED CHILDREN. STILL FIRED..

SPECIAL REPORT!

IT HAS BEEN CONFIRMED THAT THE NINERS HAVE APPROACHED THE MAIN LIBRARY'S CHIEF LIBRARIAN KENNETH DOWLIN TO TAKE OVER AS HEAD COACH. FANS SPIT UP BLOOD.

BAD SCOUTING IS BLAMED. AN ENRAGED CARMEN POLICY ANNOUNCES HIS HAIR IS NO LONGER SPEAKING TO THE PRESS.

NEWS

DESPITE PROTESTS, LIBRARIAN DOWLIN IS HIRED. HE QUICKLY FORCES THE OFFENSE TO USE THE "DEWEY DECIMAL SYSTEM" AND PROCEEDS TO BLOW THE ENTIRE BUDGET ON CLERKS. HE ALSO THOUGHTLESSLY THROWS AWAY VALUABLE PLAYERS HE CAN'T FIND SPACE FOR, AND MISFILES THOSE WHO ARE LEFT...

THE GAME'S STARTING ANY MINUTE! JEEEZ, WHO ☆ ✪ # PUT JERRY RICE UNDER "J"?

J K

IN TURN, EX-NINERS' COACH SEIFERT TAKES THE TOP JOB AT THE S.F. MAIN LIBRARY, BUT IS SHOCKED TO FIND THE "MODERN DAY LIBRARIAN" TO BE JUST AS OBSESSED WITH MILLION-DOLLAR CONTRACTS AND PRODUCT ENDORSEMENTS. THEIR AGENTS ARE SNAKES.

DON'T LOW-BALL US. SEVENTY PERCENT OF THIS LIBRARY'S BUSINESS IS PEOPLE COMING TO SEE MY CLIENT SHELVE BOOKS...

TELL HIM ABOUT NIKE.

FINI

"Never invest your money in anything that eats or needs repainting." — Billy Rose

SPECIAL REPORT!

IN AN APOLOGY, NINER'S PRESIDENT CARMEN POLICY SAYS HE NEVER MEANT TO THREATEN TO MOVE HIS TEAM OUT OF THE BAY AREA IF A NEW STADIUM WASN'T BUILT.

HE ADDS THAT IF THIS PERCEPTION PERSISTS, HE WILL MOVE HIS TEAM OUT OF THE BAY AREA.

NEWS

REALIZING HE'D DONE IT AGAIN, POLICY APOLOGIZES FOR THE APOLOGY, AND THEN THREATENS TO MOVE HIS TEAM OUT OF THE BAY AREA IF HIS APOLOGY FOR THE APOLOGY ISN'T ACCEPTED. FANS REVOLT.

FRIGHTENED, POLICY RETREATS INTO HIS FREAKISHLY HUGE HAIR...

In a live report, we watch as experts try to coax Policy back out of his hair with tasty turkey medallions..."

I'M NOT COMIN' OUT.

AT WEDNESDAY'S SUPERVISORS MEETING, COMPULSIVE MALL-BUILDER AND NINERS OWNER EDDIE DEBARTOLO TELLINGLY MISTOOK THE SEDENTARY ANTI-STADIUM CRUSADER JOEL VENTRESCA FOR A LANDFILL AND BUILT A SHOPPING MALL ON HIM...

THIS MALL ON MY HEAD IS JUST ANOTHER EXAMPLE OF A DEVELOPER OUT OF CONTROL!

macys

COME ON! IF I CAN REVIVE JOEL VENTRESCA, HUNTERS POINT WILL BE EASY!

THE STADIUM PROPOSAL IS RATHER DUBIOUS. THE NINERS ARE CONVINCED THEY CAN SELL OVER ONE THOUSAND "SPECIAL V.I.P. SPONSOR SEATS" LOCATED IN THE PRESTIGIOUS BANGS SECTION OF CARMEN POLICY'S HAIR...

VIP SECTION

PRO-BALLPARK SUPERVISOR REV. AMOS BROWN IS ON RECORD AS "ELEPHANT ELATED, PEACOCK PROUD AND HYENA HAPPY" OVER THE PARK, BUT BEHIND THE SCENES FRIENDS PAINT A VERY DIFFERENT PICTURE...

HE'S SCARED FOR HIS LIFE. IN TRUTH, HE'S "PLATYPUS PERPLEXED, ANTEATER AGITATED AND EVEN LHASA APSO APPALLED." I'M WORRIED ABOUT HIM.

ON A SHOCKING NOTE, THE WEDNESDAY MEETING WAS ATTENDED BY FAMED CITIZEN ANGELA ALIOTO, THE ONLY HUMAN WITH BIGGER HAIR THAN CARMEN POLICY. AN OPPORTUNISTIC DEBARTOLO QUICKLY BUILDS MALLS ON THEM...

MACYS   SEARS

THINK OF THE PARKING!

FINI

"Sports do not build character, they reveal it." — Haywood Hale Brown

THE CONTROVERSY SURROUNDING ROBERT DENIRO'S FILM THE **FAN** R

A TRI-STAR FILM ABOUT AN INSANE FAN'S OBSESSION WITH A GIANTS PLAYER. GIANTS VICE PRESIDENT PAT GALLAGHER SAYS THE FILM MISREPRESENTS THE TEAM...

FIRST OF ALL, THE TITLE. WE HAVE NO FANS. WAS THERE ANY RESEARCH?

GALLAGHER SAYS GIANTS FANS ARE SO SCARCE THAT, IN ACTUALITY, GIANTS PLAYERS ARE MORE LIKELY TO STALK THE FANS...

HELLO, POLICE? YEAH, BARRY BONDS IS HIDING BEHIND MY BUREAU AGAIN.

PLEASE COME TO THE GAME.

ANOTHER PROBLEM THE GIANTS POINT TO IS THE AMOUNT OF SWEARING IN THE FILM. GALLAGHER PRESENTS HIDDEN-CAMERA PROOF THAT THE GIANTS NEVER UTTER HARSH LANGUAGE.

A STRIKE?! WHAT ARE YOU, A POOPY FACE?

WATCH IT, MISTER!

UMPIRE'S A SILLY BILLY!

DON'T CROSS THE LINE!

DOUBLE POOPY FACE!

YOU'RE OUT OF THE GAME!

THE GIANTS WANT TRI-STAR TO REMOVE THE FOLLOWING OFFENDING SEQUENCES:

PLEASE REMOVE:

- ALL REFERENCES TO "BALLS."

- MONTAGE SCENE OF ATHLETES ADJUSTING THEIR CUPS TO THE CARS' SONG "MOVING IN STEREO."

- A SEXUALLY-CHARGED SCENE IN WHICH GIANTS PITCHER W. VANLANDINGHAM SUGGESTIVELY CROSSES AND UNCROSSES HIS LEGS TO DISTRACT THE OTHER TEAM.

GALLAGHER ALSO ARGUES THAT MOST GIANTS FANS LOOK NOTHING LIKE THE HANDSOME, TRIM DENIRO. HE SHOWS THIS DIAGRAM...

DENIRO 2"   REAL FAN 1 MILE

N

SEVENTH INNING STRETCH-MARKS.

GALLAGHER POINTS TO THE MOVIE'S REDESIGN OF THE GIANTS UNIFORM AS A SIGN OF HOLLYWOOD EXCESS...

WESLEY SNIPES' BULLETPROOF VACUFORM ECTOMUSCLE-PADDED GIANTS BASEBALL BODY ARMOR ®

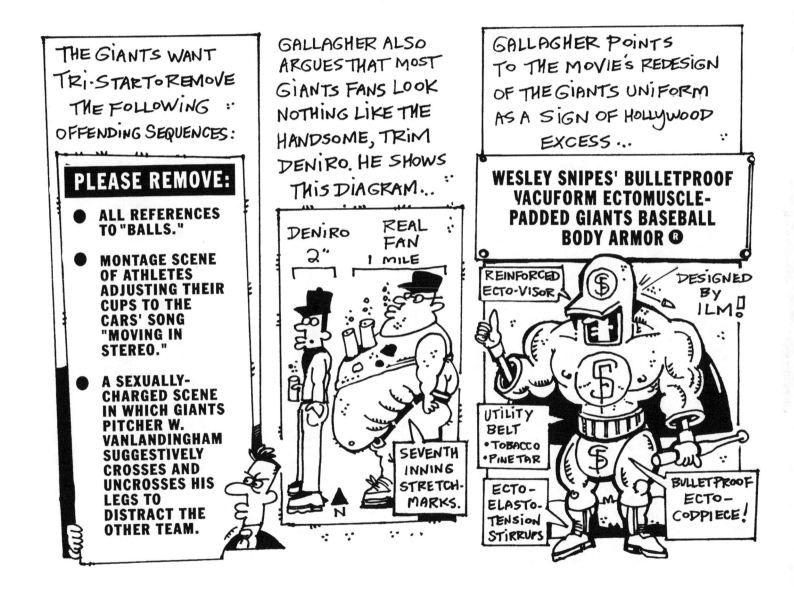

REINFORCED ECTO-VISOR

DESIGNED BY ILM!

UTILITY BELT
• TOBACCO
• PINE TAR

ECTO-ELASTO-TENSION STIRRUPS

BULLETPROOF ECTO-CODPIECE!

MAJOR LEAGUE BASEBALL® IS CONCERNED THAT SOME OF THE FILM'S VIOLENCE IS OVERDONE. THEY POINT TO ONE SCENE IN WHICH 42 PLAYERS DIE DURING A ROUTINE DOUBLE PLAY..

SCENE 43

RIDICULOUS! EVERYONE KNOWS ONLY 18 PLAYERS CAN DIE IN ANY GIVEN PLAY, 19 IN THE A.L. WITH THE D.H.

ALSO CONSIDERED UNREALISTIC WERE VIOLENT SCENES OF WESLEY SNIPES ROUNDING THE BASES IN A HEAVILY-ARMORED "SNIPESMOBILE"®, DESIGNED BY H.R. GIGER..

PROBABLY MOST SHOCKING WAS THE HOMOEROTIC SUBTEXT OF THE FILM, ESPECIALLY IN THE GROUNDSKEEPER SCENES. SEVERAL WERE SO HOT THEY HAD TO BE REMOVED TO ENSURE AN "R" RATING...

INFAMOUS EROTIC GROUNDSKEEPING LOST SCENE!
→
RENT THE NC-17 VERSION OF "THE FAN" TO SEE THIS SCENE'S SHOCKING LOST ENDING!

GALLAGHER REVEALS THAT NOWADAYS GIANTS GROUNDSKEEPERS TEND TO HAVE MORE GROUPIES THAN THE PLAYERS, 'CAUSE THEY MAKE MORE MONEY FROM BADLY-MANAGED OVERTIME..

AS HEAD GROUNDSKEEPER, I GOTTA WARN YOU, WOMEN ARE GONNA BE COMIN' ON TO YOU... PARTIES. BOOZE. I LOST A WHOLE YEAR ONCE, BUT THIS GRASS IS MY HOME.

SNFF

HEAD GROUNDSKEEPER BILL BUCKLEY'S POSTER SALES HAVE SURPASSED EVEN THOSE OF BARRY BONDS. ACROSS THE CITY, CHILDREN ARE SEEN DOING LAWN WORK IN HOPES OF STARDOM..

GROUNDSKEEPER BILL BUCKLEY
BASEBALL FEVER: RAKE IT!

BUOYED BY THE SUCCESS OF MAKING THE GIANTS SEEM EXCITING, TRI-STAR® BUYS THE FILM RIGHTS TO "BELMONT TOWN MEETINGS," TO BE DIRECTED BY ACTION DIRECTOR JOHN WOO...

MY NEIGHBOR'S TREE IS STRETCHING INTO MY YARD!

WE'LL HAVE TO REVIEW YOUR INFORMA..UNNH!

BULLETPROOF ECTO-ELDERLY TOWN MEETING BODY ARMOR

FINI

71

"If at first you don't succeed, try, try again. Then quit. No use being a damn fool about it." — W.C. Fields

THE TIME WAS RIGHT. THE NEW GIANTS BALLPARK PLAN WAS UNVEILED AT THE ST. FRANCIS HOTEL BY CONSULTANT JACK DAVIS...

SO WHAD'YA THINK, JOURNALIST SCUM?

WHAT ABOUT THE CHINA BASIN BUILDING HEIGHT RESTRICTIONS?

THIS IS ACTUAL SIZE, YOU IDIOT.

AND SO THE FIRST LIE, I MEAN PITCH, WAS THROWN IN

CHINA BASIN-BALL ®!

A GAME WITH MORE OUTS THAN THE S.F. GAY MEN'S CHORUS!

BASEBALL FEVER: CONTRACT IT!

OPPOSITION WAS ALMOST IMMEDIATE. POLITICIAN JOEL VENTRESCA, CHAIR OF "EEYORES AGAINST PRETTY MUCH EVERYTHING," SPEAKS OUT...

IT'LL NEVER WORK. PINE TAR COSTS ARE SKYROCKETING! AND WHAT ABOUT THE TOXIC WASTE?

OH POOH.

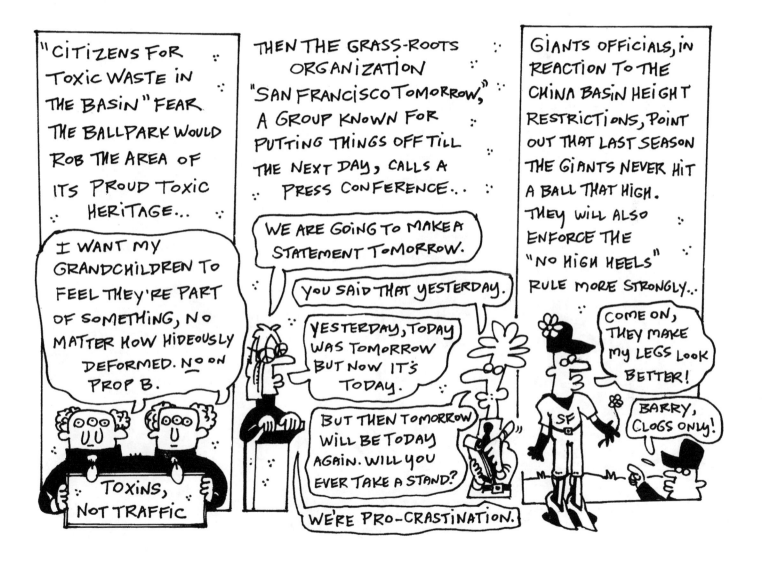

73

A NEW MUNI LINE WOULD BE ADDED THAT ACTUALLY STOPS AT THE NEW PARK'S BASES. THIS IS THE BEST CHANCE GIANTS HITTERS HAVE HAD OF GETTING HOME IN YEARS...

LINE 59

"HOK" INC.®, THE FIRM DESIGNING THE PARK, HAS CREATED AN ASYMMETRICAL FIELD FAVORING THE GIANTS' RIGHT-HANDED LINE UP...

GIANTS COULD AT LEAST BUNT A HOMERUN

490 FT

390 FT

4 FT

N

1 BUNT

ALSO, MONEY WOULD BE SAVED BY COMBINING THIRD BASE AND LEFT FIELD POSITIONS.

VERY LITTLE FOUL TERRITORY SEPARATES THE FANS FROM THE FIELD, ALLOWING BARRY BONDS AND HIS WIFE TO KICK EACH OTHER DURING GAMES WHEN NEEDED.

OOOF

OOOF

FINI

CHAPTER FIVE

SOME SEXUAL POLITICS STUFF

"God is with those who persevere." — Koran, Ch. VIII

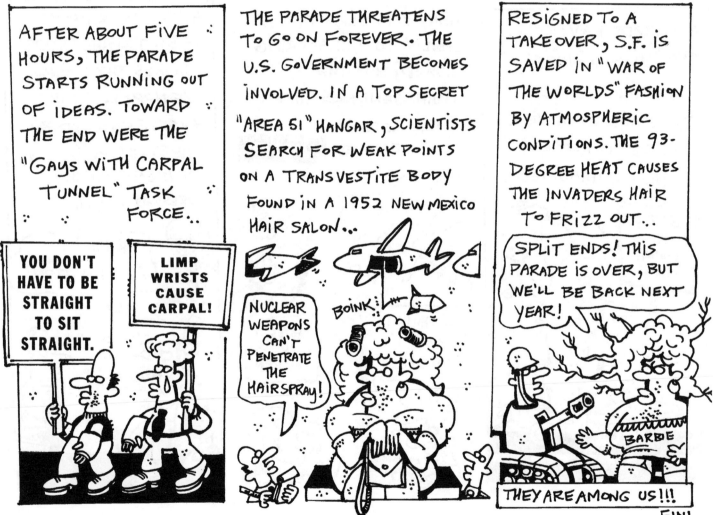

AFTER ABOUT FIVE HOURS, THE PARADE STARTS RUNNING OUT OF IDEAS. TOWARD THE END WERE THE "GAYS WITH CARPAL TUNNEL" TASK FORCE...

YOU DON'T HAVE TO BE STRAIGHT TO SIT STRAIGHT.

LIMP WRISTS CAUSE CARPAL!

THE PARADE THREATENS TO GO ON FOREVER. THE U.S. GOVERNMENT BECOMES INVOLVED. IN A TOP SECRET "AREA 51" HANGAR, SCIENTISTS SEARCH FOR WEAK POINTS ON A TRANSVESTITE BODY FOUND IN A 1952 NEW MEXICO HAIR SALON...

NUCLEAR WEAPONS CAN'T PENETRATE THE HAIRSPRAY!

BOINK!

RESIGNED TO A TAKEOVER, S.F. IS SAVED IN "WAR OF THE WORLDS" FASHION BY ATMOSPHERIC CONDITIONS. THE 93-DEGREE HEAT CAUSES THE INVADERS HAIR TO FRIZZ OUT...

SPLIT ENDS! THIS PARADE IS OVER, BUT WE'LL BE BACK NEXT YEAR!

BARBE

THEY ARE AMONG US!!!

FINI

"Give me chastity and continence – but not yet." — Saint Augustine

LEGALIZING **PROSTITUTION** IN S.F.?

LOCAL POLITICO MARGO ST. JAMES WANTS SEX OFF THE DESKS AND BACK ON THE STREETS WHERE IT BELONGS...

WANNA DATE?

HERE'S HOW THE CITY COULD RUN IT!

SAN FRANCISCO SHOULD SELL MONTHLY PASSES FOR PROSTITUTES, JUST LIKE MUNI!

IT'S MARCH, BABY.

GOOD TILL THE 3RD!

FEB 97

IF YOU PAY DAILY, YOU GET A PASS WHICH ALLOWS YOU TO SWITCH PROSTITUTES TWICE WITHIN TWO HOURS...

EXPIRED AT 4 P.M., BABY. THAT'LL BE ANOTHER FIFTY.

☆#&☆.

PROSTITUTES COULD BE ISSUED LETTERED STICKERS FOR THEIR SPECIFIC STREETS...

DAMN PIMPS NEVER MOVE THEM!

PROSTITUTES WITH A **G** STICKER MUST BE MOVED BY NOON ON MONDAY FOR STREET CLEANING

Homophobia vs. Heterophobia – Having It Both Ways

"Passion and prejudice govern the world; only under the name of reason." — John Wesley.

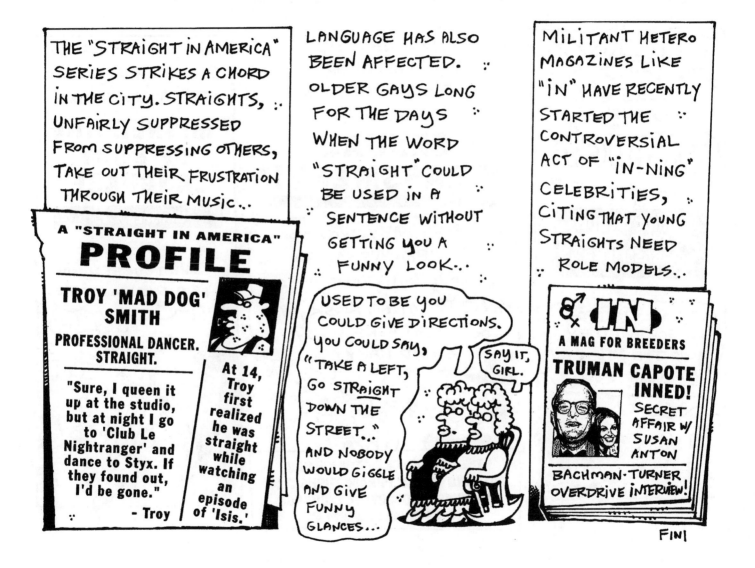

THE "STRAIGHT IN AMERICA" SERIES STRIKES A CHORD IN THE CITY. STRAIGHTS, UNFAIRLY SUPPRESSED FROM SUPPRESSING OTHERS, TAKE OUT THEIR FRUSTRATION THROUGH THEIR MUSIC...

A "STRAIGHT IN AMERICA"
PROFILE

TROY 'MAD DOG' SMITH

PROFESSIONAL DANCER. STRAIGHT.

"Sure, I queen it up at the studio, but at night I go to 'Club Le Nightranger' and dance to Styx. If they found out, I'd be gone."
— Troy

At 14, Troy first realized he was straight while watching an episode of 'Isis.'

LANGUAGE HAS ALSO BEEN AFFECTED. OLDER GAYS LONG FOR THE DAYS WHEN THE WORD "STRAIGHT" COULD BE USED IN A SENTENCE WITHOUT GETTING YOU A FUNNY LOOK...

USED TO BE YOU COULD GIVE DIRECTIONS. YOU COULD SAY, "TAKE A LEFT, GO STRAIGHT DOWN THE STREET..." AND NOBODY WOULD GIGGLE AND GIVE FUNNY GLANCES...

SAY IT, GIRL.

MILITANT HETERO MAGAZINES LIKE "IN" HAVE RECENTLY STARTED THE CONTROVERSIAL ACT OF "IN-NING" CELEBRITIES, CITING THAT YOUNG STRAIGHTS NEED ROLE MODELS...

IN
A MAG FOR BREEDERS

TRUMAN CAPOTE INNED!
SECRET AFFAIR W/ SUSAN ANTON

BACHMAN-TURNER OVERDRIVE INTERVIEW!

FINI

83

"Power takes as ingratitude the writhing of its victims." — Rabindranath Tagore (1916)

HARASSMENT IS SPLIT INTO TWO TYPES:

1. THE COVERT **"QUID PRO QUO"** — LATIN FOR "THIS FOR THAT" OR

2. THE OVERT **"TOPO GIGIO"** LATIN FOR "CHEESY MOUSE PUPPET," AN EXPERIENCE FROM WHICH FEW WOMEN RECOVER...

SUBMIT TO TOPO!

"MISREADING OF BODY LANGUAGE"

EXAMPLE # 2.

WOW. THAT'S THE FIFTH TIME SHE'S TOUCHED MY ARM. I'VE GOT IT MADE!

CHOP CHOP CHOP

MOST WORKPLACES NOW HAVE A "SEXUAL HARASSMENT OFFICER" THAT EMPLOYEES CAN REPORT INCIDENTS TO..

...AND THEN I COULD TELL HE WAS OBJECTIFYING ME BECAUSE HE WASN'T LISTENING TO ANYTHING I WAS SAYING..

I THINK SHE DIGS ME.

"MISREADING OF BODY LANGUAGE"

EXAMPLE # 3.

To combat sexual harassment in the workplace, a Fresno business replaced all its accused managers with sexually timid panda bears. Women have reported no come-ons, but question the gentle creatures' market instincts...

Johnson, your guess that bamboo shades would be the next big thing has put us in Chapter 11.

She's running her hands through my hair! Yes!

To counteract men's use of sex as a weapon, male babies born after 1997 will have a ten-day waiting period before they receive their penises, so hospitals can do a background check...

Bingo! Says here this one's been incarcerated for nine months and just escaped through some hole...

POLICE DATABASE

BABY TIM

SIGMUND FREUD'S (1856-1939) INFAMOUS ESSAY "ROTATING TOTEMS AND TABOO" (1913) SUGGESTED WOMEN'S UNCONSCIOUS FEAR OF KIOSKS, ESPECIALLY THE ROTATING ONES NEAR MARKET STREET. FROM THIS CAME FREUD'S THEORY ON "KIOSK ENVY."

I BELIEVE THE "ROTATING KIOSK" IS A CONSTANT REMINDER TO WOMEN OF MAN'S SUPERIORITY IN... OUCH! HMMM, SHE'S TOUCHED MY CHEST. SHE MUST DIG ME...

THUCK

"MISREADING OF BODY LANGUAGE"

EXAMPLE # 4.

YES! I KNEW SHE WANTED TO GET ME HORIZONTAL!

WHEW.

JERK
RIP

THERE WAS A SMALL BUT IMPORTANT STEP FORWARD FOR WOMEN THIS YEAR.

"BOBBIT" WAS INCLUDED AS A VERB IN THE 1997 EDITIONS OF WEBSTER'S DICTIONARIES...

BOB•BIT (bäb-it) verb
1. TO REMOVE
2. TO SEPARATE
3. TO CHANGE OUTLOOK SUDDENL[Y]
4. TO WHITTLE WITH PURPOSE

FINI

87

"You can do anything in this world if you're prepared to take the consequences." — W. Somerset Maugham

THE INFAMOUS POLITICAL CONSULTANT

JACK ~~DANIELS~~ DAVIS' 50TH BIRTHDAY BASH!

EXAMINER · 25¢

PARTY PHOTOS!

OUCH.

CHRONICLE

EXCLUSIVE INTERVIEW WITH WHISKEY BOTTLE

PAGE 3

"IT WAS SUDDENLY VERY DARK..." - W. BOTTLE

THE PARTY'S CONTROVERSIAL "INDIAN SODOMY PERFORMANCE ART" HAS BEEN CRITICIZED FOR BEING "INAUTHENTIC," BUT "INDEPENDENT" COLUMNIST WARREN HINCKLE POINTED OUT HISTORICAL PRECURSORS...

SHOCKING UNCROPPED FOOTAGE OF FAMED 1970'S ANTI-LITTER ADS SHOW THE REAL REASON THAT INDIAN WAS WEEPING.

OUCH.

SHOCKING UNCROPPED LOGO OF BASEBALL'S CLEVELAND INDIANS SHOWS THE REAL REASON 'CHIEF WAHOO' IS SMILING.

Ⓡ 'CHIEF WAHOO' IS THE PROPERTY OF THE CLEVELAND INDIANS

WHAT ACTUALLY HAPPENED AT THE PARTY WAS MUCH WORSE THAN REPORTED. IN TRUTH, THE APACHE PERFORMANCE ARTIST WAS SODOMIZED BY CARMEN POLICY WITH A 10' SCALE MODEL OF THE PROPOSED BALLPARK/MALL...

METAPHOR FOR RICH WHITE MAN FORCING EVIL STADIUM ON POOR, TRUSTING VOTERS.

SUBSIDIZE, SODOMIZE, SAME THING.

THE WORST WAS YET TO COME. SUDDENLY A FEMALE MUNI DRIVER CAME UP TO HIM, CARVED THE SATANIC MUNI LOGO INTO HIS BACK, AND THEN RELIEVED HERSELF ON HIM, ALL THE WHILE LEAVING HER BUS UNATTENDED. THE PERFORMANCE ENDS WHEN HER BUS ROLLED INTO AND DESTROYED A TEPEE...

CRASH!!

THIS IS, LIKE, ANOTHER METAPHOR, DUDE.

CLAP CLAP CLAP

IT'S FASCINATING HOW MANY POLITICIANS CLAIM TO HAVE LEFT BEFORE THE NAUGHTY STUFF STARTED. HERE ARE THE WINNERS OF THE "LEAVE EARLY OLYMPICS"...

WHO LEFT EARLIEST AT JACK DAVIS' PARTY

Third place - Carmen Policy:

Claims to have left at 5 p.m., right after the Bible-reading had concluded. Reported shocked and dismayed at news of later events.

Second place - Barbara Kaufman:

Claims to have left the party on April 22nd, a day before she received the invitation. Shocked, but not dismayed.

Winner - Mayor Willie Brown:

Claims to have left the party on March 20, 1933, a full year before he was even born. Dismayed, but not reportedly shocked.

EXAMINER GRAPHICS

THE BIG WINNER IN ALL THIS IS "ARTIST" APACHE STEVE JOHNSON LEYSA, THIS YEAR'S "MANNY THE HIPPIE." BAY•TV, NOTING HIS CURRENT POPULARITY, HAS SIGNED HIM TO DO A LOCAL KID'S SHOW..

OKAY TIMMY, GUESS WHICH OF MY HANDS IS HOLDING THE WHISKEY BOTTLE.

THE LEFT ONE?

WRONG! NEITHER! HA!

FINI

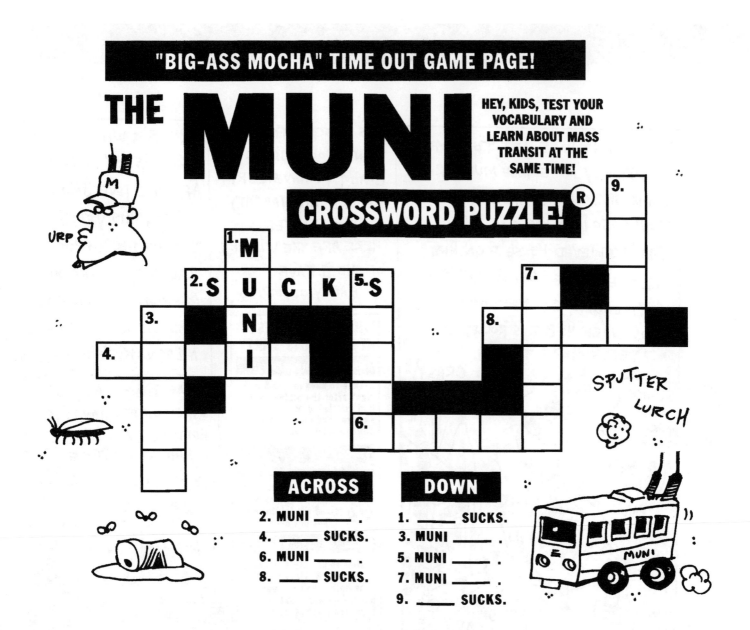

"BIG-ASS MOCHA" TIME OUT GAME PAGE!

THE MUNI CROSSWORD PUZZLE! ®

HEY, KIDS, TEST YOUR VOCABULARY AND LEARN ABOUT MASS TRANSIT AT THE SAME TIME!

URP

SPUTTER LURCH

MUNI

1. M
2. S U C K S
   U
3. N
4. I

5. S
6.
7.
8.
9.

ACROSS

2. MUNI _____ .
4. _____ SUCKS.
6. MUNI _____ .
8. _____ SUCKS.

DOWN

1. _____ SUCKS.
3. MUNI _____ .
5. MUNI _____ .
7. MUNI _____ .
9. _____ SUCKS.

CHAPTER SIX

SOME STUPID SPIRITUAL NEW AGE STUFF

"The Dreamer can know no truth, not even about his dream, except by awaking out of it." — George Santayana

I WENT TO A PSYCHIC FAIR in San Francisco! UNDERCOVER (I WORE A BLUE SHIRT INSTEAD OF MY USUAL WHITE) I WAS SENT TO EXPOSE THE SCAM!

WOW, THEY KNEW HOW MUCH WAS IN MY WALLET! I'M SOLD!

PSYCHIC FAIR $25.00

THE FIRST BOOTH I WENT TO WAS A FORTUNE TELLER. I ONLY HAD SOME CHANGE LEFT SO SHE'D ONLY LOOK ONE SECOND INTO MY FUTURE...

I SEE YOU REACTING TO WHAT I'M SAYING RIGHT NOW...

THANK...

..YOU.

NEXT I WENT TO A PALM READER. HE DEMANDED A REWRITE...

I DON'T GIVE A DAMN ABOUT ANY OF THESE CHARACTERS! AND YOUR GRAMMAR! YOU NEED A PALM PROOF-READER!

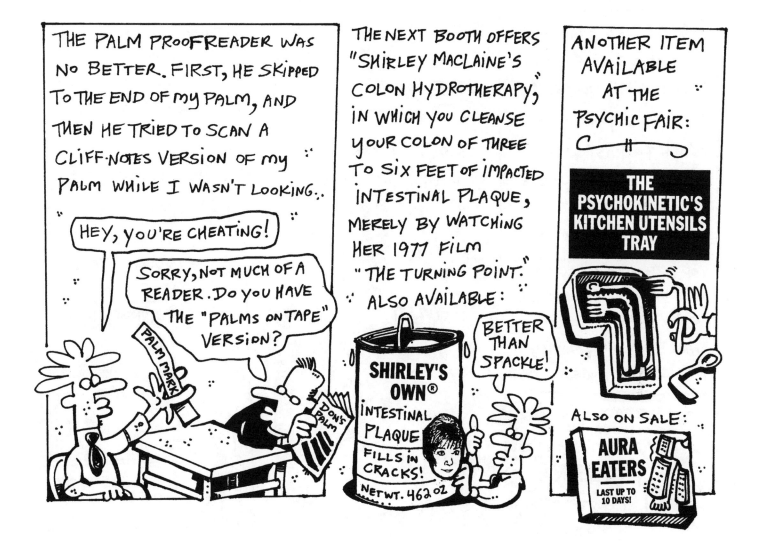

On UFOs, Cult Religions and Loony Eclipses

"Men will wrangle for religion, write for it, die for it; anything but live for it." — Charles Caleb

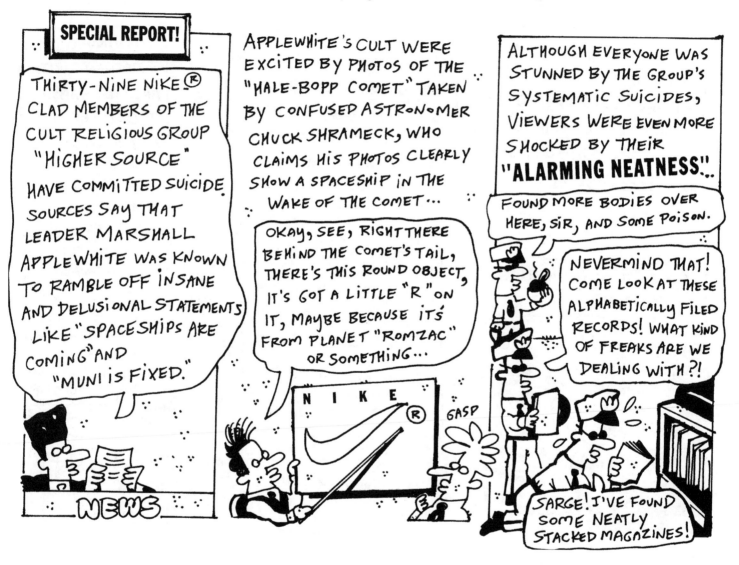

SPECIAL REPORT!

THIRTY-NINE NIKE® CLAD MEMBERS OF THE CULT RELIGIOUS GROUP "HIGHER SOURCE" HAVE COMMITTED SUICIDE. SOURCES SAY THAT LEADER MARSHALL APPLEWHITE WAS KNOWN TO RAMBLE OFF INSANE AND DELUSIONAL STATEMENTS LIKE "SPACESHIPS ARE COMING" AND "MUNI IS FIXED."

NEWS

APPLEWHITE'S CULT WERE EXCITED BY PHOTOS OF THE "HALE-BOPP COMET" TAKEN BY CONFUSED ASTRONOMER CHUCK SHRAMECK, WHO CLAIMS HIS PHOTOS CLEARLY SHOW A SPACESHIP IN THE WAKE OF THE COMET...

OKAY, SEE, RIGHT THERE BEHIND THE COMET'S TAIL, THERE'S THIS ROUND OBJECT, IT'S GOT A LITTLE "R" ON IT, MAYBE BECAUSE IT'S FROM PLANET "ROMZAC" OR SOMETHING...

NIKE ®

GASP

ALTHOUGH EVERYONE WAS STUNNED BY THE GROUP'S SYSTEMATIC SUICIDES, VIEWERS WERE EVEN MORE SHOCKED BY THEIR **"ALARMING NEATNESS"**...

FOUND MORE BODIES OVER HERE, SIR, AND SOME POISON.

NEVERMIND THAT! COME LOOK AT THESE ALPHABETICALLY FILED RECORDS! WHAT KIND OF FREAKS ARE WE DEALING WITH?!

SARGE! I'VE FOUND SOME NEATLY STACKED MAGAZINES!

FINI

"What after all, is a halo? It's only one more thing to keep clean." — Christopher Fry

THE FIRST STEP IN "REBIRTHING" IS TO THROW AWAY ALL YOUR "LEARNED FEARS" AND FOLLOW YOUR INNER-CHILD'S INSTINCTS..

FIRST SESSION: EATING THE LEAD PAINT OFF THE KITCHEN WALL. CONFRONT YOUR LEARNED FEARS!

CRUNCH CRUNCH

DAVIS' INNER-CHILD IS SO DEEP INSIDE THAT HE HAS TO USE **INNER CHILD RETRIEVAL**, A SYSTEM SIMILAR TO THAT WHICH SAVED BABY JESSICA...

RESCUE WORKER WITH COLLAPSABLE, DOUBLE-JOINTED BONES LOWERED ON ROPE INTO JACK DAVIS' INNARDS.

INNER CHILD LOCATION

N

UNFORTUNATELY, DAVIS DIGESTS THE RESCUE TEAM, FORCING EXPERTS TO EXTRACT HIS INNER-CHILD USING

THE JAWS OF LIFE...

SADLY, DAVIS ALSO DIGESTS HIS INNER-CHILD.

DAVIS IS LEFT WITH NO CHOICE BUT TO "REBIRTH," IN WHICH YOU RE-EXPERIENCE YOUR OWN BIRTH TO TRY AND FIND WHERE THINGS WENT WRONG. UNFORTUNATELY, DAVIS' INTENTIONS WERE QUESTIONABLE...

I THINK MY PROBLEMS STARTED WHEN THE DOCTOR SPANKED ME. CAN WE DO THAT PART AGAIN?

AND AGAIN!

THE REBIRTH UNSUCCESSFUL, THE HEALERS DECIDE TO TEACH DAVIS ABOUT LEVELS OF SPIRITUAL AWARENESS USING:

"THE JOHN TESH FOREHEAD CLIMB OF SPIRITUAL ENLIGHTENMENT." ®

"TESH MASTER"

YOUR OWN SHOW — 5
CELEBRITY — 4
ENLIGHTENMENT — 3
ONENESS — 2
CONFRONT FEARS — 1

DAVIS CLIMBS TO THE TOP OF JOHN TESH'S HEAD AND MEETS GOD. THEY COMPARE MIRACLES...

I CREATED LIFE ITSELF.

I GOT FRANK JORDAN ELECTED TO MAYOR IN 1992.

YOU WIN. HERE'S THE KEY TO HEAVEN.

FINI

CHAPTER SEVEN

SOME FAMOUS S.F. CELEBRITY STUFF

IRONIC DETACHMENT.

David Letterman Live in San Francisco Behind the Scenes

"A celebrity is one who is known to many persons he is glad he doesn't know." — H.L. Mencken

IN CASE YOU GET CONFUSED, THERE'S A HANDY TELEPROMPTER TO TELL YOU WHAT YOU SHOULD BE FEELING AT ANY GIVEN MOMENT...

APPLAUSE!

APPEAR DEEPLY TOUCHED BY ACTOR'S PLIGHT.

LAUGH AT THE COMEDIAN'S OBSCURE REFERENCE TO THE "ODESSA STEPS" SEQUENCE IN THE FILM "POTEMKIN" THAT ONLY YOU "GET."

DISASTER WAS BARELY AVERTED WHEN SUDDENLY THE TELEPROMPTER STARTED MALFUNCTIONING. THEY HAD TO SHUT IT DOWN BEFORE ANYONE GOT HURT...

SMELL LIKE A FISH

CHOP YOUR BEST FRIEND'S HEAD OFF

KILL! KILL! KILL!

AAAAA

FINALLY LETTERMAN COMES ON STAGE. HIS SMALL, SKINNY BODY IS NOT STRONG ENOUGH TO SUPPORT HIS LARGE HEAD, WHICH IS SUSPENDED FROM WIRES...

BIG SHOW... IRONIC DETACHMENT... HI YA...

LATENIGHT PUPPETEERS

"The tree of liberty must be refreshed from time to time with the blood of patriots and tyrants. It is its natural manure." — Thomas Jefferson

"Acting is merely the art of keeping a large group of people from coughing." — Ralph Richardson

SNEAKING INTO THE ALCATRAZ "THE ROCK!" PARTY!

HARDLY ANYBODY FROM S.F. GOT INVITED, JUST BIG HOLLYWOOD JERKS. BUT THAT DIDN'T STOP US AT "S.F. COMIX!"

I SMELL A STORY!

ONLY CELEBRITIES WERE INVITED, SO THE EXAMINER CREATES A STUNNINGLY REAL GEORGE KENNEDY DISGUISE. THEY LOWER ME IN...

HAIR-FLAP DOOR

COSTUME ENTRANCE

LOWER, LOWER..

TAKING ADVANTAGE OF GEORGE KENNEDY'S REMARKABLE RESEMBLANCE TO THE LOVELY MANATEE, I FOLLOW THE FERRY TO ALCATRAZ...

MANATEES, NATURE'S MERMAIDS.

FINALLY, I GET S.F. NATIVE NICOLAS CAGE'S ATTENTION IN A PORTA-POTTY..

NICK BABY, I GOTTA SCRIPT YA GOTTA SEE..

SCRIPT

ZIIIIP

A PORTA-POTTY PITCH..

MY SCRIPT IS CALLED **"LEAVING LOS LOBOS"**

A STORY ABOUT A MUSICIAN WHO LEAVES A CRITICALLY-ACCLAIMED BAND TO EAT HIMSELF TO DEATH WITH OREOS. NICK COULD PLAY HIM!

DON'T ASK ME TO STOP, BABY, I'M ALREADY ON THE "DOUBLESTUFF"

OREO DOUBLE

HE COULD MEET A DOWN ON HER LUCK FORMER PORNO "FILM STRIP" STAR, AND IN THE LAST SCENE HE COULD DIE AFTER THEY HAVE SEX, AND HIS LAST WORD COULD BE:

"GARP."

... THEN OTHER S.F. CELEBRITY ROBIN WILLIAMS COULD DO THE SEQUEL!

FINI

Don Johnson & Other Myths

"Better not to be a hero than work oneself up into heroism by shouting lies." — George Santayana

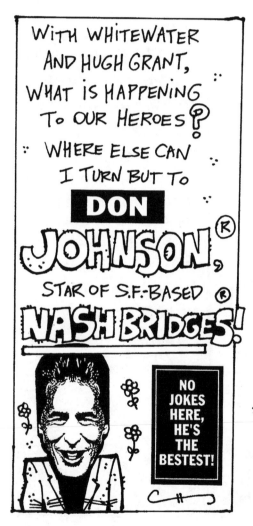

WITH WHITEWATER AND HUGH GRANT, WHAT IS HAPPENING TO OUR HEROES?

WHERE ELSE CAN I TURN BUT TO **DON JOHNSON**®, STAR OF S.F.-BASED ® **NASH BRIDGES!**

NO JOKES HERE, HE'S THE BESTEST!

I FOUND OUT THAT JOHNSON WAS FILMING HIS SHOW AT MARKET AND FIFTH. I RUSHED TO CATCH MY FIRST-EVER GLIMPSE OF OUR LAST GREAT HERO. I WAS SHOCKED TO FIND HE WAS ONLY 3 FEET 2 INCHES TALL, CONCEALED BY MISLEADING DIALOGUE...

NASH, IF THE KILLER SEES ME, HE'LL SHOOT ME DEAD!

QUICK, HIDE BEHIND ME!

DON JOHNSON IS THE FIRST ACTOR I'VE EVER SEEN WHO USES A STUNTMAN FOR DIALOGUE BECAUSE OF SOME RISKY SCENES USING "GERUNDS."

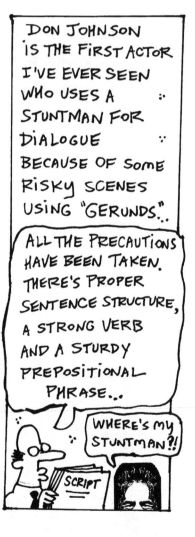

ALL THE PRECAUTIONS HAVE BEEN TAKEN. THERE'S PROPER SENTENCE STRUCTURE, A STRONG VERB AND A STURDY PREPOSITIONAL PHRASE...

WHERE'S MY STUNTMAN?!

SCRIPT

IT IS DECIDED THAT GEORGE LUCAS' "ILM" IS NEEDED TO CREATE THE ILLUSION THAT DON JOHNSON HAS ACTING ABILITY. A NEW SOFTWARE, "INCOMPARISON 3.1," IS USED, WHICH PLACES THE IMAGE OF ACTOR BOB DENVER NEXT TO ANY ACTOR, INSTANTLY MAKING THEM LOOK TALENTED.

SKIPPER!

TO BE OR NOT TO BE.

BEHOLD OUR MAGIC.

I HAD NOT BEEN THIS DISAPPOINTED SINCE I DISCOVERED THAT FAMED CONDUCTOR MICHAEL TILSON THOMAS WAS NOT THE TALL, MACHO DUDE HE APPEARED TO BE ON THOSE S.F. SYMPHONY BILLBOARDS...

MT2
MICHAEL TILSON THOMAS

I'LL BE BACH

MICHAEL TILSON THOMAS IS REPORTED TO BE, IN TRUTH, A LITTLE SMALLER THAN A BREADBOX, BUT A LITTLE LARGER THAN A TOASTER.

SCIENTISTS FEEL THAT THE DECLINE OF HEROES IN SOCIETY IS DIRECTLY LINKED TO THE PROLIFERATION OF ESTROGEN-BASED PESTICIDES. CHEMICALS SUCH AS "PCBs" AND "DDTs" CAUSE INFERTILITY IN MALES. TWO RESULTS: HERMAPHRODITIC FISH IN MICHIGAN AND RU-PAUL IN L.A....

FASCINATING! THIS FISH HAS EQUAL INTEREST IN FOOTBALL AND SHOPPING.

49ERS

GUCCI

NESSIE!

113

SCIENTISTS HAVE BEEN ABLE TO TRACK ESTROGEN'S GLOBAL IMPACT BY MONITORING ACTOR JEAN-CLAUDE VAN DAMME'S MOVIE TITLES THROUGHOUT THE YEARS...

VAN DAMME MOVIE TITLES SINCE ESTROGEN SPREAD

1984: "EXTREMELY HARD TARGET"

1985: "NOT QUITE AS HARD TARGET"

1986: "SOFT AND BOUNCY TARGET"

1989: "PASSIVE AGGRESSIVE"

1991: "MAXIMUM SHOPPING"

1994: "MAXIMUM COMPLAINING ABOUT HOW COLD IT IS"

1997: JEAN-CLAUDE VAN DAMME IS "CATTY!" R

IN SYMPATHY TO THE ESTROGEN-INFECTED INFERTILE MEN IN S.F., CHINESE RESTAURANTS QUICKLY PRINT UP NEW SIGNS SAYING "NO MSG, NO PCB AND NO DDT." PROBLEMS STILL ARISE...

IS ANYONE SAFE FROM PCB?

I'M SORRY ABOUT THE "SOFT NOODLE" REFERENCE, SIR.

IN RESPONSE TO THE ESTROGEN INFESTATION, DON JOHNSON'S SHOW "NASH BRIDGES" IS RETOOLED INTO "THE BRIDGES OF MARIN COUNTY," IN WHICH JOHNSON FALLS FOR PHOTOGRAPHER ROBERT KINCAID, PLAYED BY BOB DENVER.

FRANCESCA, IF YOUR HUSBAND SEES ME, HE'LL SHOOT ME DEAD!

QUICK, HIDE BEHIND ME!

FINI

CHAPTER EIGHT

SOME LOCAL POLITICS STUFF

"Wealth maketh many friends." — The Bible

"Intolerance itself is a form of egotism, and to condemn egotism intolerantly is to share it." — George Santayana

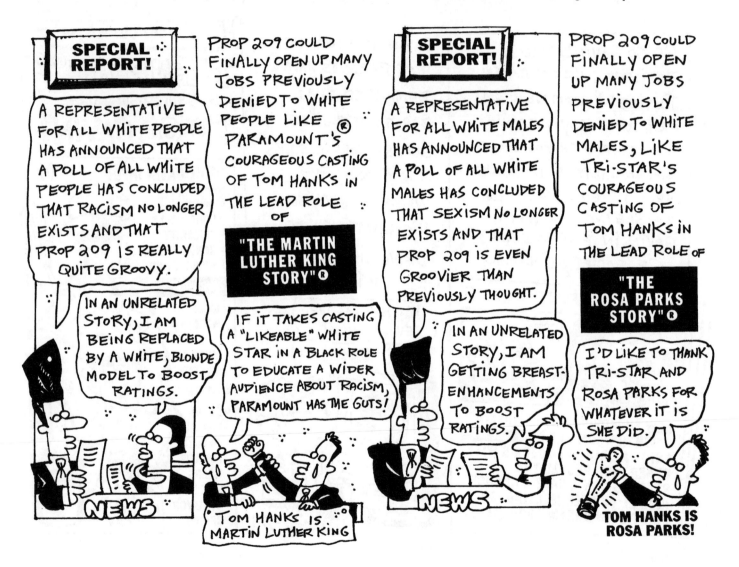

ANOTHER SPECIAL REPORT!

A REPRESENTATIVE FOR ALL WHITE, STRAIGHT MALES HAS ANNOUNCED THAT A POLL OF ALL WHITE, STRAIGHT MALES HAS CONCLUDED THAT HOMOPHOBIA NO LONGER EXISTS AND THAT PROP 209 SHOULD INCLUDE GAYS, TOO.

IN AN UNRELATED STORY, I AM BEING REPLACED BY THE "LIKEABLE" STRAIGHT TOM HANKS.

NEWS

YET ANOTHER SPECIAL REPORT!

A REPRESENTATIVE FOR ALL WHITE BLEEDING HEART LIBERALS HAS ANNOUNCED THAT A POLL OF ALL WHITE BLEEDING HEART LIBERALS HAS CONCLUDED THAT AFRICAN-AMERICANS ARE OUR EQUALS EXCEPT AFRICAN-AMERICANS WHO DISAGREE WITH WHITE BLEEDING HEART LIBERALS.

IN AN UNRELATED STORY, PROP 209 SPOKESMAN WARD CONNERLY HAS BEEN CAST IN THE LEAD ROLE OF "THE TOM HANKS STORY."

SATIRE WRAP-UP TIME!

ONCE AGAIN, "S.F. COMIX" HAS COURAGEOUSLY TAKEN THE UNPOPULAR "PREJUDICE IS BAD" STANCE! BUT PROP 209 STILL CONFUSES:

■ IF YOU VOTE FOR 209, YOU'RE A RACIST BECAUSE YOU DON'T WANT TO HELP MINORITIES.

■ IF YOU VOTE AGAINST 209, YOU'RE A RACIST BECAUSE YOU ASSUME MINORITIES NEED YOUR HELP.

■ IF YOU DON'T VOTE AT ALL, YOU'RE A LAZY, CYNICAL AMERICAN WHO THINKS VOTING IS A WASTE OF TIME AND IT WON'T CHANGE ANYTHING EITHER WAY.

THANK GOD FOR GERMAINE WONG! SHE SENT OUT TWO BALLOTS TO EVERYONE! VOTE BOTH! FINI

119

The Pathfinder Lands on Columnist Warren Hinckle

"I have nothing to say and I am saying it and that is poetry." — John Cage

SPECIAL REPORT

MISSION CONTROLLERS ARE ECSTATIC OVER THE SUCCESSFUL LANDING OF THE "HINCKLE PATHFINDER" SOMEWHERE IN THE NORTHERN REGION OF THE LONG DRIED-UP COLUMNIST. SCIENTISTS HOPE TO FIND EVIDENCE OF PAST CREATIVE LIFE THAT HAS LONG BEEN RUMORED.

NASA hopes that the low budget "Hincklefinder" will find clues to the origins of this stormy S.F. Independent columnist. Scientists claim this is only the first in a series of expeditions to the city's "farthest-out" journalists. And now a big-ass graphic:

THE HINCKLEFINDER LANDING

1. Entry

Earth

2. Parachute deploys. Heat shield protects the craft against over 8,000 miles of hot air.

3. The craft falls to the Hinckle surface, air bags protecting it against the volatile columnist's dangerous exterior.

4. Hincklefinder deploys the tiny "Muckraker" mobile.

LIFE ON HINCKLE?

NEWS

THE FIRST PICTURES WERE REMARKABLE. SCIENTISTS NOTED THAT THE HINCKLE MOUNTAINS SWING NOTABLY TO THE LEFT, PROBABLY DUE TO STRONG CURRENTS OF RIGHTEOUSNESS DURING HIS TIME AT "RAMPARTS" MAGAZINE IN 1969...

First photos back from the Hinckle surface. Landed within sixty yards of famed eye patch!

THE ROVER, "MUCKRAKER," VENTURED OUT ON THE "HINCKIS VALLIS", SITE OF AN ANCIENT FLOOD OF **"HINCKLE SPRINKLE"**, WHICH SCIENTISTS BELIEVE WAS CAUSED BY AN ALL-NIGHT DRINKING BINGE AT CITY MAGAZINE IN 1975. THE ROVER ANALYZES THE SPRINKLE'S COMPOSITION...

"HINCKLE SPRINKLE" IS MADE UP OF 50% MENCKEN, 35% TWAIN AND 15% KACZYNSKI, THE SAME MAKEUP OF THIS CHUNK FOUND ON AN ANTARCTIC BAR STOOL. THIS CONFIRMS HINCKLE BLEW THESE CHUNKS AS FAR BACK AS 1962.

NASA

NASA HAD A BIG SCARE WHEN THE HIGH LIQUOR CONTENT OF THE TESTINGS IMPAIRED THE ROVER, CAUSING A BLACKOUT THAT LASTED OVER TWELVE HOURS. WHEN THE SIGNAL WAS RESTORED, THE VEHICLE WAS FOUND LENS DOWN IN THE DIRT IN AN UNKNOWN SECTOR, COVERED WITH LIPSTICK AND REFUSING TO TRANSMIT THE NIGHT'S PHOTOS...

NATIONAL ENQUIRER
ROVING TOO FAR?
SEE THE HOT PHOTOS PATHFINDER WOULDN'T SEND BACK TO NASA!

NASA WAS MOST IMPRESSED WITH THE STUNNING PHOTOS OF THE MOON CYCLES. THESE SHOTS PROVED THEORIES THAT HINCKLE KISSES MAYOR BROWN'S MOON EVERY TUESDAY...

Scientists stunned by photos of weekly orbit of the Willie Brown Moon.

NEXT EXPEDITION: LOCAL ANCHORMAN PETE WILSON!

The "Big Homosexuality" $368 Billion Settlement

"It does me no injury for my neighbor to say there are twenty gods, or no God." — Thomas Jefferson

SPECIAL REPORT

GAY NEGOTIATORS HAVE ANNOUNCED A HISTORIC SETTLEMENT THAT WILL CHANGE FOREVER THE WAY HOMOSEXUALS ARE MARKETED IN THE UNITED STATES.

"BIG HOMOSEXUALITY" WILL HAVE TO PAY $368 BILLION TO DEVASTATED PARENTS, $160 BILLION EARMARKED FOR A NATIONWIDE ANTI-GAY PROGRAM FOR IMPRESSIONABLE YOUTHS.

NEWS

THE AGREEMENT WAS THE CULMINATION OF OVER TWENTY YEARS OF FIGHTING. IT ALL STARTED IN 1967 WHEN THE BRAVE "CHRISTIAN COALITION" RELEASED TEST RESULTS EXPOSING THE DEVASTATING EFFECTS OF **"SECONDHAND HOMOSEXUALITY"**

SUBJECT A. A GAY   SUBJECT B. TIMMY JR.   SUBJECT C. TIMMY SR.

WANNA PLAY CATCH, SON?

LET'S RENT A JUDY GARLAND FLICK.

OH GOD NO.

⌊— 4 FEET —⌋

THERE WAS ENOUGH CONCERN THAT THE SURGEON GENERAL FORCED THE NATION'S MOST POTENT HOMOSEXUALS TO CARRY A WARNING ON THEIR PACKAGES. UNFORTUNATELY, IT GAVE GAYNESS AN ATTRACTIVE "OUTLAW" MISTIQUE.

SURGEON GENERAL'S WARNING: HOMOSEXUALS MAY BE HAZARDOUS TO YOUR MORALITY

NOTHING WAS MORE HEARTBREAKING THIS YEAR THAN WATCHING VICE PRESIDENT AL GORE, AT THE DEMOCRATIC CONVENTION IN CHICAGO, TEARFULLY DESCRIBE WATCHING HIS SISTER SLOWLY TURN GAY RIGHT BEFORE HIS EYES...

AND THEN, CHOKE...SOB, I WATCHED...SNIFF..AS SHE...GOT..SOB.. REALLY GOOD AT SOFTBALL.. OH GOD..SOB..

AS PER THE SETTLEMENT, ALL HOMOSEXUALITY IS ABOLISHED BY 2009. UNFORTUNATELY, FASHION DESIGN IS ANOTHER VICTIM...

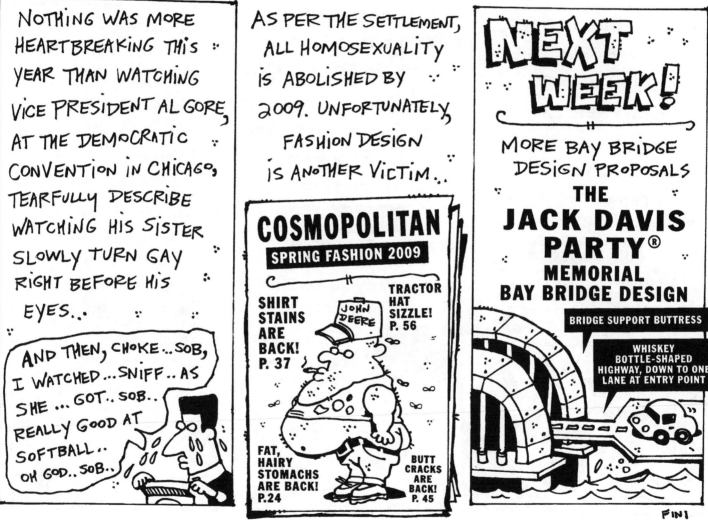

COSMOPOLITAN
SPRING FASHION 2009

SHIRT STAINS ARE BACK! P. 37

TRACTOR HAT SIZZLE! P. 56

JOHN DEERE

FAT, HAIRY STOMACHS ARE BACK! P.24

BUTT CRACKS ARE BACK! P. 45

NEXT WEEK!

MORE BAY BRIDGE DESIGN PROPOSALS

THE JACK DAVIS PARTY® MEMORIAL BAY BRIDGE DESIGN

BRIDGE SUPPORT BUTTRESS

WHISKEY BOTTLE-SHAPED HIGHWAY, DOWN TO ONE LANE AT ENTRY POINT

FINI

CHAPTER NINE

NATIONAL POLITICS STUFF

"An election is coming. Universal peace is declared, and the foxes have a sincere interest in prolonging the lives of the poultry." — George Eliot

THE S.F. COMIX ®

GOP '96 CONVENTION READER'S GUIDE ®

SAN DIEGO

A HANDY AND INFORMATIVE GUIDE WHICH WILL WIN US LOTS OF AWARDS BUT MEAN LITTLE OR NOTHING TO YOU, OUR READERS! READ ON! OR DON'T! WE DON'T NEED YOU!

WE APOLOGIZE FOR THE COCKY TONE OF THAT LAST PANEL. THE CIRCULATION DEPARTMENT JUST ALERTED US TO THE FACT THAT WE DO, IN FACT, NEED YOU. SO BEFORE YOU CANCEL YOUR SUBSCRIPTION, CHECK OUT THIS HUGE INFOGRAPHIC THAT WE COPIED OUT OF A BOOK.

THE SAN DIEGO CONVENTION CENTER

The San Diego Convention Center is a tri-level complex. The main hall will house the Republican National Convention.

Skyboxes and lounges

Podium

Delegates

Food stand   Media   Open bar

The addition of toys, ramps, ladders, and levels guards against boredom and makes watching your rat more enjoyable.

N

# of delegates: 5,000   Media: 15,000   Rats: 20,000

EXAMINER GRAPHICS

DAY ① OF THE CONVENTION: PROBABLY THE MOST ANTICIPATED RITUAL OF THE GOP CONVENTIONS: "THE BOB DOLE LIFTING OF THE BROW"

DOLE'S FURROWED BROW CAN COLLECT DIRT THAT RISKS INFECTION! CLEAN IT OUT AT LEAST EVERY FOUR YEARS!

Q-TIP READY.

KID'S PANEL! LEARN STUFF!

A GOP® CONNECT THE DOTS!

DRAW THE BIG TENT!

CONNECT THE DOTS AND FIND OUT WHO GETS UNDER THE GOP'S "BIG TENT OF INCLUSION." FOLLOWING THE PARTY LINE HAS NEVER BEEN THIS MUCH FUN!

6.
5.
7.
4.
3.
2.
1.

THE 3RD NIGHT'S RONALD REAGAN TRIBUTE WAS A HUGE TEARJERKER. NANCY REAGAN CAME OUT AND SHARED AN EXAMPLE OF RON'S LEGENDARY OPTIMISM...

RONNIE ALWAYS SAW MY HEAD AS HALF FULL AS OPPOSED TO HALF EMPTY.

CLAP CLAP CLAP CLAP CLAP

KID'S PANEL! LEARN STUFF!

KIDS, FIND BOB DOLE'S FURROWED BROW IN THE FLOCK OF SEAGULLS BELOW!

CIRCLE AND SEND TO THE EXAMINER!

FINI

127

More Fun Facts About The GOP Convention

"Politics, as a practice, whatever its professions, has always been the systematic organization of hatreds." — Henry Adams

THE S.F. COMIX ®

GOP CONVENTION READER'S GUIDE ®

PART DEUX

COMPARISON CHART

KEMP: CHIP ON HIS SHOULDER

DOLE: CHIP OFF HIS SHOULDER (WAR INJURY)

GOP SPORTS ANALOGIES CONVERSION CHART

Dole and Kemp's constant "quarterback" and "blocker" football analogies have left non-football fans in the dark. Here's a handy "analogy conversion chart" for those who follow other sports:

Football Analogy

- Dole is "Quarterback"
- Kemp is "Blocker"

Baseball Analogy

- Dole is "Pitcher"
- Kemp is "Catcher"

Basketball Analogy

- Dole is "Center"
- Kemp is "Guard"

Curling Analogy

- Dole is "that guy pushing that thing"
- Kemp is "that other guy sweeping in front of that thing"

Foosball Analogy

- Dole is "the drunk guy"
- Kemp is "the other drunk guy"

☆ GOP ☆ SOUVENIR PRODUCTS!

HERE ARE JUST A FEW OF THE HOTTEST GOP SELLERS!

❶ THE BOB DOLE FURROWED BROW CLOCK ®

BOTH ON SALE!

❷ THE JACK KEMP KITTY SCRATCH POST ®

REPUBLICANS HAVE PROMISED TO SHOWCASE "REAL" AMERICANS THIS YEAR. "WILD KINGDOM'S" JIM HANNA HOSTED THESE SEGMENTS...

BOB DOLE'S NEVER BEEN SO CLOSE TO ONE BEFORE. CAN I PET IT?

SURE, BOB. THIS IS A CALLED A VOTER. ALMOST EXTINCT.

GRRR

WK

GOP INFOGRAPHIC! HOW TO TELL WHEN JACK KEMP IS FINISHED SPEAKING:

EVERYONE KNOWS WHEN KEMP GETS TALKIN' HE CAN GO ON ALL NIGHT. HERE'S A HANDY CHART TO CLUE YOU IN ON WHEN HIS SPEECH HAS REACHED ITS CLIMAX...

A POPPING A BIG TENT:
Kemp filled with adrenaline.

BLAH BLAH BLAH

B SPEECH CLIMAX:
Kemp instantly falls asleep, refuses to cuddle.

ZZ

TO COMBAT THE LACK OF DRAMA IN THE TIGHTLY-SCRIPTED SHOW, THE GOP HIRED QUENTIN TARANTINO TO WRITE A FEW OF THURSDAY'S SEGMENTS TO SPICE THINGS UP...

☆#◊#, THE ADRENALINE SHOT TO DOLE'S HEART DID NOTHING!

BOB DOLE SAYS ☆#◊ SCHWAG.

FINI

129

The GOP Convention's Inclusion Delusion

"The great masses of the people...will more easily fall victims to a great lie than a small one." — Adolf Hitler

"All politics are based on the indifference of the majority." — James Reston

CLINTON'S SLIDE TOWARD THE MIDDLE HAS FORCED DOLE TO CAMPAIGN AGAINST HIMSELF..

VOTE FOR ME BEFORE CLINTON DOES ALL THE THINGS I'D DO IF ELECTED! DO YOU WANT THAT?!

KID'S PANEL!

CAN YOU SPOT **SENATOR EDWARD KENNEDY** HIDDEN AMONG THE **CHEESY 'STAR TREK' ROCK FORMATIONS?**

JIM, THIS ROCK FORMATION HAS A HIGH VODKA READING.

CLINTON'S LOVE OF CELEBRITIES IS WELL KNOWN. THERE'S A RUMOR HE'S NAMING **RICHARD GERE®** AS SECRETARY OF DEFENSE..

COME ON EVERYBODY, WE GOTTA SEND GOOD VIBES TO BOSNIA! COME ON!!

FUN FUN FUN!

HEY KIDS, CAN YOU TELL THE DIFFERENCE BETWEEN **SENATOR JOE BIDEN®** AND **LINUS?®**

FINI

133

The Democrats and "I Feel Your Pain, Inc."

"Virtue will not go so far if vanity did not keep it company." — La Rochefoucald

SEEING THAT TEARS EQUAL VOTES, CLINTON DOES HIS ACCEPTANCE SPEECH FROM A THERAPIST'S COUCH INSTEAD OF A PODIUM.

SO WHAT DO YOU WANT TO TELL THE VOTERS?

I WANNA TELL 'EM I LOVE 'EM.

AND WHY DON'T YOU?

THEY EXPECT STUFF. LOVE SHOULD BE UNCONDITIONAL.

NEW AGE SLOGANS ARE QUICKLY PRINTED UP FOR THE FEEL-GOOD DEMOCRATS.

CLINTON/GORE
A $500 TAX CUT FOR EVERY INNER CHILD

CLINTON/GORE
ELECT US TO ANOTHER "TERM OF ENDEARMENT"

CLINTON/GORE
THE CHICAGO SEVEN
HABITS OF HIGHLY EFFECTIVE PEOPLE!!

ON STAGE, CLINTON UNCOVERS A HORRIFIC SUPPRESSED MEMORY OF BEING A "LIBERAL."

HE JOINS A THERAPY GROUP TO BATTLE IT...

I'M BILL CLINTON AND I'M A REPUBLICAN. THERE, I SAID IT.

ADMITTING IT IS HALF THE PROBLEM.

"The trouble with our age is that it is all signpost and no destination." — Louis Kronenberger

YET ANOTHER INFOGRAPHIC!!

OTHER UNEVENTFUL DATES THROUGHOUT OUR HISTORY

Here's a list of dates in history when nothing of any interest happened:

January 27, 1902

The only living witness, Jim Smith, says it was a particularly long and uneventful day.

June 12, 1928

Probably the most uneventful day in history. Say "June 12, 1928," and people will tell you where they were on "The Day Nothing Happened."

April 19, 1996

San Jose Mercury News announces the closing of The San Francisco Examiner. Nothing happens.

August 1996

15,000 jounalists go to San Diego and Chicago to cover the conventions. Nothing happens.

October 7, 1997

Cartoonist Don Asmussen's "The San Francisco Comic Strip: Big-Ass Mocha" book comes out. Nobody buys it.

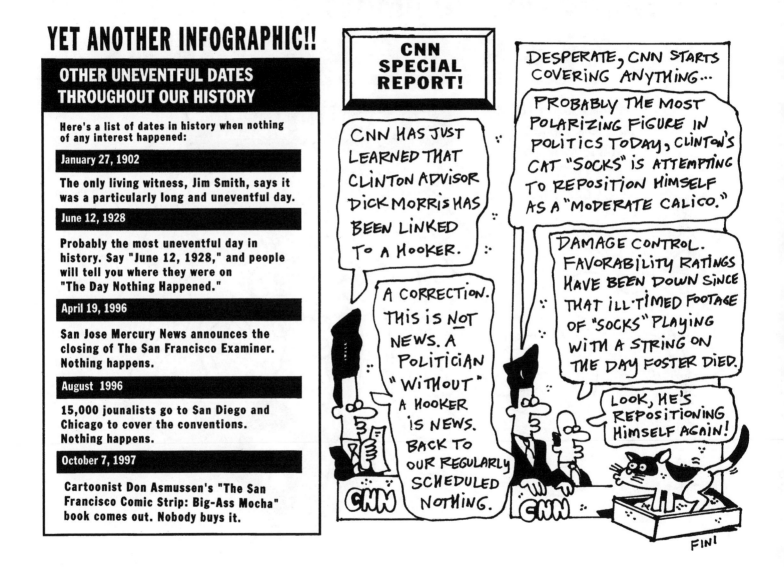

CNN SPECIAL REPORT!

CNN HAS JUST LEARNED THAT CLINTON ADVISOR DICK MORRIS HAS BEEN LINKED TO A HOOKER.

A CORRECTION. THIS IS NOT NEWS. A POLITICIAN "WITHOUT" A HOOKER IS NEWS. BACK TO OUR REGULARLY SCHEDULED NOTHING.

DESPERATE, CNN STARTS COVERING ANYTHING...

PROBABLY THE MOST POLARIZING FIGURE IN POLITICS TODAY, CLINTON'S CAT "SOCKS" IS ATTEMPTING TO REPOSITION HIMSELF AS A "MODERATE CALICO."

DAMAGE CONTROL. FAVORABILITY RATINGS HAVE BEEN DOWN SINCE THAT ILL-TIMED FOOTAGE OF "SOCKS" PLAYING WITH A STRING ON THE DAY FOSTER DIED.

LOOK, HE'S REPOSITIONING HIMSELF AGAIN!

FINI

138

CHAPTER TEN

SOME BIG BUSINESS STUFF

"There are no moral phenomena at all, but only a moral interpretation of phenomena." — Nietzsche – Beyond Good & Evil

ROBERT J. SAMUELSON, AUTHOR OF "THE GOOD LIFE & ITS DISCONTENTS," A PRO-BUSINESS DIATRIBE, JUMPS TO SKINNER'S DEFENSE...

THE STAN SKINNER I KNOW HAS NEVER STEPPED ON A KITTEN. EATEN ONE, SURE. THEY'RE TASTY AS HELL, BUT HE'S NEVER STEPPED ON ONE! STOP PAINTING HIM AS A VILLAIN!

STAN, PASS THE KITTENS.

CRUNCH CRUNCH

PG&E'S SELF-IMAGE HAS IMPROVED SO MUCH SINCE ITS REDUCTION THAT IT IS CONSIDERING WEARING A TWO-PIECE SWIMMING SUIT FOR THE FIRST TIME IN YEARS...

OOOOH BABY, YOU'RE RIGHT-SIZED!

GIGGLE.

OH STOP IT!

IN A TRAGIC TURN REMINISCENT OF KAREN CARPENTER, PG&E KEPT LOSING WEIGHT, BECAME ADDICTED TO CAFFEINE PILLS AND MISSED CRUCIAL RECORDING SESSIONS. PG&E DENIED THE RUMORS WITH A CRYPTIC PRESS RELEASE...

PG&E PRESS RELEASE

DEAR EVERYONE,
PG&E IS JUST FINE. LOST A LITTLE WEIGHT DUE TO THE FLU, THAT'S ALL. FEELING MUCH BETTER NOW. THANKS. WE'RE BETTER THAN EVER, WE PROMISE. OOPS, WE JUST DIED.

TO GET THE REAL STORY, RENT "SUPERSTAR: THE TRAGIC DEATH OF PG&E," STARRING ANN JILLIAN AS "PG&E" AND BOB DENVER AS "RICHARD CARPENTER"..

I CAN'T SING, I'M TOO FAT. I NEED A ROUND OF LAYOFFS.

HONEY, DO SOME HIRING BEFORE IT'S TOO LATE!

PERHAPS THE MOST FRIGHTENING SCENES IN THE MOVIE WERE OF PG&E'S TRIPS TO THE BATHROOM AFTER HAVING MADE SEVERAL HIRES. SHE WOULD INDUCE LAYOFFS BY LOOKING AT PROFIT MARGINS..

OH, THE MESS I'VE MADE..

STOCKS

FORMER "SCOTT PAPER®" CEO "CHAINSAW AL" DUNLAP SPOKE AT PG&E'S FUNERAL, AND QUOTED THE BIBLE..

...AND GOD CREATED THE EARTH IN SIX DAYS, THEN LAID EVERYONE OFF ON THE SEVENTH, AND THEN PUT HIS SON IN CHARGE, WHO HAD NO EXPERIENCE IN THE BUSINESS, AMEN.

THE HEALING HAD BEGUN..

LAID-OFF PG&E WORKERS HAVE USED THE ARTS TO HEAL, FORMING A THEATRE TROUPE PERFORMING SUCH CLASSICS AS "ROSENCRANTZ & GUILDENSTERN'S POSITIONS HAVE BEEN COMBINED" AND "THE CARPAL TUNNEL VERSION OF HAMLET..."

IT IS HAMLET, THOU ART SLAIN, NO MEDICINE IN THE WORLD CAN DO THEE GOOD, IN THEE LIES THE CARPITH TUNNEL...

POSTURE HATH SEALED THY FATE.

MEANWHILE, CEOS START TO MARKET THEMSELVES AS ROLE MODELS. "CEO TRADING CARDS" TAKE OFF LIKE A BULLET...

I'LL TRADE YOU AT&T'S CEO ALLEN FOR SCOTT'S DUNLAP.

IF IT WASN'T FOR A TORN LIGAMENT, ALLEN WOULD HAVE LAID OFF 20,000 INSTEAD OF JUST 10,000 LAST YEAR!

AN APOLOGY

DUE TO S.F. COMIX CUTBACKS, THE STAFFER WHO WAS SUPPOSED TO WRITE THIS PANEL WAS LAID OFF. IN ITS PLACE, WE HAVE SUBSTITUTED AN INEXPENSIVE PIECE OF CLIPART. ENJOY!

FINI

143

"The basic law of capitalism is you or I, not you and I." — Karl Liebnicht

MY TRIP TO THE HOME DEPOT IN DALY CITY, U.S.A.!

EVEN THE WORST CYNIC CANNOT HELP BUT BE TOUCHED BY THE FOUR HUNDRED POSTERS OF THE AMERICAN FLAG HOME DEPOT HANGS IN THEIR STORES!

HOME DEPOT
THE AMERICAN DREAM: NOW AVAILABLE IN BULK.

THE FIRST THING YOU NOTICE AT HOME DEPOT IS THE BIG-ASS AMERICAN SHOPPING CARTS! 20 FEET BY 20 FEET! I HEAR IN OTHER LESS DEMOCRATIC COUNTRIES LIKE INDIA THAT THE SHOPPING CARTS ARE MUCH SMALLER.

I BOUGHT TWENTY OF HOME DEPOT'S "MASTER PLUNGERS"® 'CAUSE LEAVING ITEMS IN THEIR STORES IS LIKE LEAVING FOOD ON YOUR PLATE. AT THE REGISTER, THEIR HI-TECH SCANNERS ARE AMAZING!

OUR SCANNER SHOWS THAT YOU ATTENDED A SOCIALIST RALLY IN 1987.

I WAS AFTER A CHICK!

DO THE PLEDGE OF ALLEGIANCE, PINKO.

MASTER PLUNGER

CHECK OUT

SHOPPING WORKS UP AN APPETITE! FORTUNATELY EVERY HOME DEPOT® COMES WITH A SIZZLER® RESTAURANT (THE HOME DEPOT OF FOOD) RIGHT NEXT TO IT! YOU HARDLY HAVE TO GO OUTSIDE (WHERE THERE'S CRIME 'N' STUFF). GET A LOAD OF SIZZLER'S BIG-ASS AMERICAN PLATES!

ENJOY OUR SIZZLER FOOD DUCTS!

VEGGIE

MEAT

THE BEAUTY OF U.S. CONSUMERISM BLOSSOMS WHEN YOU LEAST EXPECT IT. A FELLOW SIZZLER PATRON STARTED CHOKING ON SOME SWEDISH MEATBALLS, BUT FORTUNATELY I HAD JUST BOUGHT "MASTER PLUNGER®"

GOD BLESS AMERICA!

PUCKA PUCKA PUCKA

HOME DEPOTS ARE EVERYWHERE! S.F., ALWAYS IN THE SHADOW OF DALY CITY, IS GETTING ONE, TOO! SOON THERE'LL BE SO MANY STORES THEY'LL CONNECT 'EM ALL AND WE'LL TRULY BE A UNITED STATES!

THE HOME DEPOT

CELEBRATE YOUR FREEDOM TO CHOOSE TO HAVE ONLY ONE CHOICE!

FINI

WHERE IN THE WORLD IS
CARMEN POLICY? ®

FOR A WHILE THERE, FORTY NINERS PRESIDENT CARMEN
POLICY WAS THREATENING TO MOVE HIS TEAM TO ALL SORTS
OF PLACES IN THE WORLD IF WE DIDN'T GIVE HIM A STADIUM.
HERE'S A NEW EDUCATIONAL GEOGRAPHY GAME BASED ON
HIS THREATS!

WHERE IN THE WORLD IS CARMEN POLICY THREATENING TO MOVE THE NINERS NOW, KIDS?

WRITE YOUR ANSWER HERE:

_____

CHAPTER ELEVEN

SOME MEDIA STUFF

A Softer, Gentler S.F. Comic Strip

"A difference of taste in jokes is a great strain on the affections." — George Eliot
"Impropriety is the soul of wit." — W. Somerset Maugham

BOY, DID I GET A TON OF HATE MAIL LAST WEEK..

TO S.F. COMIX,
YOU ARE A BITTER AND MEAN-SPIRITED JERK, I HOPE YOU DIE! YOU SUCK!
A READER

TO S.F. COMIX,
YOUR STRIP HAS A RESPONSIBILITY TO SPREAD POSITIVE MESSAGES, YOU PIECE OF CRAP. ROT IN HELL!
A READER

TO S.F. COMIX,
YOU ARE A MISANTHROPE! HOW ABOUT SOME POSITIVE MESSAGES, YOU SCUM BAG!
A READER

ALL YOU DO IS CRITICIZE, YOU UNTALENTED LOSER.
A READER

THE TASTE POLICE HAD FINALLY NABBED ME. I WAS PUBLIC ENEMY #1. I QUICKLY HIRED THE IMAGE CONSULTANTS WHO DEVISED THE TIM McVEIGH AND TED KACZYNSKI "SYMPATHETIC HAIRCUT MAKEOVERS.."

OUR RESEARCH SHOWS THAT A '70s FEATHERED HAIRCUT MAKES EVEN HITLER ENDEARING.

JEEZ, I WANNA HUG 'EM.

STUDY #1246B-C
HITLER MAKEOVER
HATED   CUDDLY

I'M STILL UNCONVINCED, BUT THEN THEY SHOW ME HOW AN ENORMOUS FEATHER-CUT MADE THE PHILIPPINES' MOUNT PINATUBO APPEAR LESS THREATENING TO THE VILLAGERS BELOW..

STUDY #1246C-C
MOUNT PINATUBO MAKEOVER

WHAT A NICE VOLCANO!

I'M SOLD!

DURING MY MAKEOVER MY BROTHER FROM OHIO CONSENTS TO TALK ABOUT ME TO THE PRESS...

HAVEN'T SEEN HIM IN FIFTEEN YEARS. HE'S A LONER. I SENT MONEY TO HIM TWO TIMES. I HATE TO THINK MY MONEY PAID FOR THE PENS USED FOR HIS BITTER, MEAN-SPIRITED COMIC STRIP ATTACKS.

MY NEW HAIRCUT WORKS WONDERS. THE EXAMINER PROMOTES MY MAKEOVER WITH TIME AND NEWSWEEK MAGAZINE INTERVIEWS. TALK OF MY TORTURED CHILDHOOD EXPLAINS MY HURTFUL CARTOONS. OVERNIGHT, I BECOME AN OBJECT OF SYMPATHY...

TIME
THE ASMUSSEN INTERVIEW
SERIAL JOKER ASMUSSEN SHOWS SOFT SIDE, GREAT NEW HAIRCUT

I WAS SPANKED.

CAT FANCY
DON LOVES KITTENS!

NEWS
ASMUSSEN EXCLUSIVE
ACTUALLY GREAT GUY, HAIRCUT FRAMES FACE MUCH BETTER

I LOVE ENYA.

I RENOUNCE MY SATIRIC PAST ON A HISTORIC "LARRY KING LIVE SHOW...

LARRY, WE NEED MORE POSITIVE MESSAGES! SATIRE ONLY TEARS DOWN! DON'T BE SEDUCED BY ITS DARKNESS! JUST SAY NO TO SATIRE!

BY THE WAY, YOUR HAIR LOOKS GREAT, DONNY.

150

UNTIL SCIENTISTS FINALLY FIND THAT ELUSIVE "ESKIMO GENE", NO JUDGMENTS CAN BE MADE, ALTHOUGH ONE HAS TO WONDER WHY THERE ARE SO MANY ESKIMO HAIRDRESSERS IN S.F....

.. SO I SAID TO HIM, "IS THAT THE NORTH POLE OR ARE YOU HAPPY TO SEE ME?"

GET ANY NANOOKIE?

AN APOLOGY
FOR THE LAST THREE JOKES.

I APOLOGIZE FOR MY TRANSPARENT ATTEMPTS AT DISGUISING INSENSITIVE GAY JOKES AS INSENSITIVE ESKIMO JOKES. AS PUNISHMENT, I WILL SUBJECT MYSELF TO "A CLOCKWORK ORANGE" - TYPE TORTURE, WATCHING ELDERLY PEOPLE PIN MY CARTOON TO REFRIGERATORS AND SMILING WARMLY.

"S.F. COMIX" IS A BEAM OF SUNSHINE THROUGH MY WINDOW.

OH DEAR GOD...

SF COMIX

GAR FIELD

*ASMUSSEN HAS MANY ELDERLY FRIENDS...

AS A FINAL TEST TO SEE IF HE'S FREE OF SATIRICAL DESIRES, ASMUSSEN IS PLACED IN FRONT OF A NUDE FORMER MAYOR NAMED FRANK JORDAN..

NO JOKES? HE'S CURED!

HIS PERSONALITY ABOLISHED, ASMUSSEN IS READY FOR SYNDICATION!

FINI

151

"A precedent embalms a principle." — Benjamin Disraeli

SPECIAL REPORT!

ATTORNEY GENERAL DAN "DOLPH" LUNGREN AND THOUSANDS OF ARMED AGENTS RAIDED THE OFFICES OF MAJOR CARTOON SYNDICATES TODAY, FINDING OVER 200,000 POUNDS OF "MORALLY BANKRUPT" COMIC STRIPS...

AMONG THEM WERE THE DEADLY, ADDICTIVE "NANCY" STRIPS THAT HAVE TAKEN SO MANY TEENAGE LIVES.

NEWS

NUMEROUS PRO-DRUG "DOONESBURY" STRIPS WERE CONFISCATED, BUT DAN LUNGREN SINGLED OUT A VIOLENCE-PROMOTING "PEANUTS" STRIP TO SHOW HOW "AMORAL" COMICS HAVE BECOME...

E X H i B i T A.

"YOU'RE A COP KILLER, CHARLIE BROWN!"

100 COPS TO GO, CHUCKY B.

GOOD GRIEF, SNOOPY DOG DOG!

NOT SO FUNNY NOW, HUH?

PLAYING THE "POLITICS OF FEAR," THE REPUBLICANS RUN "WILLIE HORTON-STYLE" ADS SHOWING THE COLD, PREDATORY STARE OF CHARLES SCHULTZ...

KEEP THESE MONSTERS AWAY FROM OUR CHILDREN!

SCHULTZ: NUTS OR WHAT?

152

THE GOVERNMENT SETS UP "THE WAR ON COMICS." UNFORTUNATELY, INSTEAD OF BUSTING THE BIG FISH, COPS JAIL MILLIONS OF "SMALL-TIME STREET SYNDICATORS".

WHADD'YA IN THE JOINT FOR?

SOLD "BABY BLUES" TO AN UNDERCOVER COP.

CARTOON PARANOIA GRIPS THE POPULACE AS THE NATION SWINGS TO THE RIGHT. SEEING HIS FAVORABILITY RATINGS PLUMMET, "DOONESBURY" CREATOR GARRY TRUDEAU CALLS A MEETING OF THE STRIP'S 742 ARTISTS AND WRITERS.

I AM HIRING POLITICAL CONSULTANT DICK MORRIS TO HELP REPOSITION "DOONESBURY" TOWARD THE CENTER OF CARTOON IDEOLOGY.

GASSSP!

"DOONESBURY" STAFFERS ARE SHOCKED. MORRIS HAD JUST WORKED ON THE ULTRA-CONSERVATIVE "MARMADUKE" TEAM. BUT THE MOVE WORKS...

"DOONESBURY'S SLIDE TO CENTER HAS FORCED "GARFIELD" MORE TO THE RIGHT WITH THE EXTREMISTS!

WHO WILL LUNGREN BLAME NOW?

SPECIAL REPORT!

SINGER ROBERTA FLACK NARROWLY ESCAPED INJURY TODAY WHEN A DERANGED FAN ATTEMPTED TO KILL HER SOFTLY WITH HIS SONG...

ATTORNEY GENERAL LUNGREN AND 1000 AGENTS HAVE RAIDED COLUMBIA RECORDS TO CONFISCATE ALL "MID-TEMPO" BALLADS.

FINI

153

"A man must first despise himself, and then others will despise him." — Mencius – Works

EVERYBODY **HATES** THE **PRESS!**

FROM WILLIE BROWN TO HILTON KRAMER, THE VERDICT'S IN!

BREAKING THE NEWS WE SUCK. J. FALLOWS

THE MEDIA CIRCUS WE SUCK, EXCEPT ME. HOWARD KURTZ

MEDIA ARE FROM MARS, READERS ARE FROM VENUS.

THIS PHENOMENON IS NOT NEW. IN THE '70s, IDEOLOGUE FAVE NOAM CHOMSKY HOSTED A HIT GAMESHOW CALLED:

"BEAT THE PRESS,"

IN WHICH COCKY, UNSUSPECTING JOURNALISTS WERE LURED TO THEIR HILARIOUS DEMISES!

LECTURE TOUR

SNIFF SNIFF

PRESS

MANY READERS COMPLAIN ABOUT JOURNALISM'S FOCUS ON THE NEGATIVE. A QUICK PEEK AT 1997 PULITZER CATEGORIES CONFIRMS THIS...

PULITZER CATEGORIES

25. INSPIRATIONAL STORY IN WHICH BLOOD SQUIRTS OUT OF SOMETHING.

26. UPLIFTING STORY IN WHICH BRAINS POUR OUT OF SOMETHING.

27. RIVETING STORY IN WHICH THE WORD "CARNAGE" IS USED MORE THAN ONCE.

"The report of my death was an exaggeration." — Mark Twain

FACT: AS A SHOW OF GOOD FAITH TO THE CITY, THE CHRONICLE WOULD ALLOW THE HOMELESS TO LIVE IN THE NOW USELESS EXAMINER BOXES...

HEY BABY, MY BEST NEWS IS BELOW THE FOLD..

ONE VAGRANT PER QUARTER

FICTION: THE EXAMINER EDITORS ARE SO SICK OF A SAN JOSE REPORTER'S CONSTANT MERGER STORIES THAT THEY START RUNNING RUMORS ABOUT HER...

S.F. EXAMINER   25¢

SAN JOSE REPORTER TO MERGE WITH NEW BOYFRIEND BY FRIDAY, IF YOU KNOW WHAT WE MEAN, NUDGE, NUDGE, WINK.....

S.F. EXAMINER   25¢

MERGER IMMINENT, BOYFRIEND'S BUDDIES BRAG. BREAD ALBUM PURCHASED...   P. 4

THE MERCURY NEWS HAS RUN SO MANY RUMORS THEY'RE RUNNING OUT OF HEADLINES TO USE..

MERGER HEADLINES

2/91: "EXAMINER TO CLOSE"

3/92: "EXAMINER TO REALLY CLOSE"

4/93: "EXAMINER ON LAST LEGS"

6/94: "EXAMINER ON SECOND PAIR OF LAST LEGS"

4/95: "EXAMINER ON LAST KNEES"

5/96: "EXAMINER SPITTING UP BLOOD"

9/96: "EXAMINER ON LAST SPIT"

9/96: "REALLY, ANY DAY NOW, JUST WATCH"

FACT: THE POSSIBILITY OF A ONE-NEWSPAPER TOWN CONCERNS MANY PEOPLE, ESPECIALLY THE OWNERS OF BIRD SHOPS...

I LINE MY CAGES WITH THE CHRONICLE IN THE MORNING AND THEN THE EXAMINER IN THE AFTERNOON. IN A ONE-PAPER TOWN, MY SHOP WOULD STINK TO HIGH HEAVEN.

A LOT CAN HAPPEN BETWEEN 9 AND 5.

FACT: MERGER NEGOTIATIONS ARE GOING ON. RUMORS ARE FLOATING THAT ONLY ONE SNAG IS KEEPING THE MERGER FROM HAPPENING...

THE MERGED PAPER MUST CARRY "ZIPPY."

NO. "BABY BLUES."

"ZIPPY."

"BABY BLUES."

TO QUICKEN THE NEGOTIATIONS, MAYOR WILLIE BROWN BRINGS IN YOUTH GANG MEMBERS...

"BABY BLUES" IT IS.

FINI

161

"Thanks to the interstate highway system, it is now possible to travel across the country from coast to coast without seeing anything." — Charles Kuralt

BUDGETED AT $1.97, MORSE, PHOTOGRAPHER KIM KOMENICH AND I RIDE DOWN THE INTERSTATE-5. THE ONLY RADIO STATION WE CAN GET PLAYS "MUSKRAT LOVE" OVER AND OVER. I TRY TO BREAK THE ICE..

I DON'T KNOW ABOUT YOU, BUT I'D DO MUSKRAT SAM OVER MUSKRAT SUZIE ANY DAY.

GET IN THE BACK!

IN BAKERSFIELD, WE MEET A SPANISH-SPEAKING TRACTOR OPERATOR. SEEING AN OPPORTUNITY FOR A "REAL MOMENT," MORSE ATTEMPTS TO SPEAK SPANISH, BUT MISTAKENLY ASKS:

UH, PUEDO ROTATA SU KIOSKA?*

* MAY I ROTATE YOUR KIOSK?

USTED ES UN MUCHACHO NANCYO!*

* YOU ARE A NANCY-BOY!

MI KIOSKA ESTA' CONTENTO.*

* MY KIOSK IS VERY HAPPY

WE RUN TO NEARBY COLUSA, A TOWN WITH 132.7 PERCENT UNEMPLOYMENT (BLAMED ON THE SCHOOL'S POOR MATH PROGRAM). I TRY TO BEFRIEND A RICE FARMER...

YOU KNOW IF YOU GUYS ALLOWED SAME-SEX MARRIAGES, RICE SALES WOULD DOUBLE.

SAY WHAT?

I DON'T KNOW 'BOUT YOU, BUT I'D DO THE CAPTAIN OVER TENNILLE ANY DAY.

"We feel and know that we are eternal." — Benedict De Spinoza

THE UNAUTHORIZED BIOGRAPHY OF HERB CAEN®

WHAT THE CHRONICLE WON'T TELL YOU

COLUMNIST HERB CAEN WAS BORN IN 1916. DOCTORS WERE STUNNED THAT HE WAS ALREADY NOSTALGIC AT BIRTH...

BACK THEN, A WOMB WAS A WOMB. YOU FELT SAFE AND WARM. IT WAS THAT KIND OF WOMB.

SLAP HIM ALREADY!

CAEN HAS ALWAYS SHOWED A GIFT FOR WORDPLAY. SOME CAUGHT ON, SOME DIDN'T...

CAENISMS THAT CAUGHT ON:

- BEATNIK
- BERSERKLEY

CAENISMS THAT DIDN'T CATCH ON:

- KIOSKNIK
- SAN FRANKIOSKO
- CANDLESTICKNIK POINTNIK AT 3COMNIK PARKNIK

165

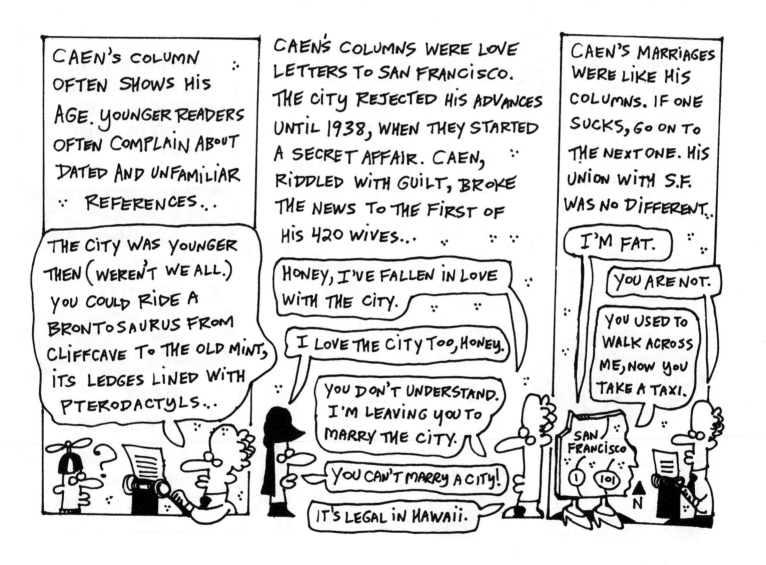

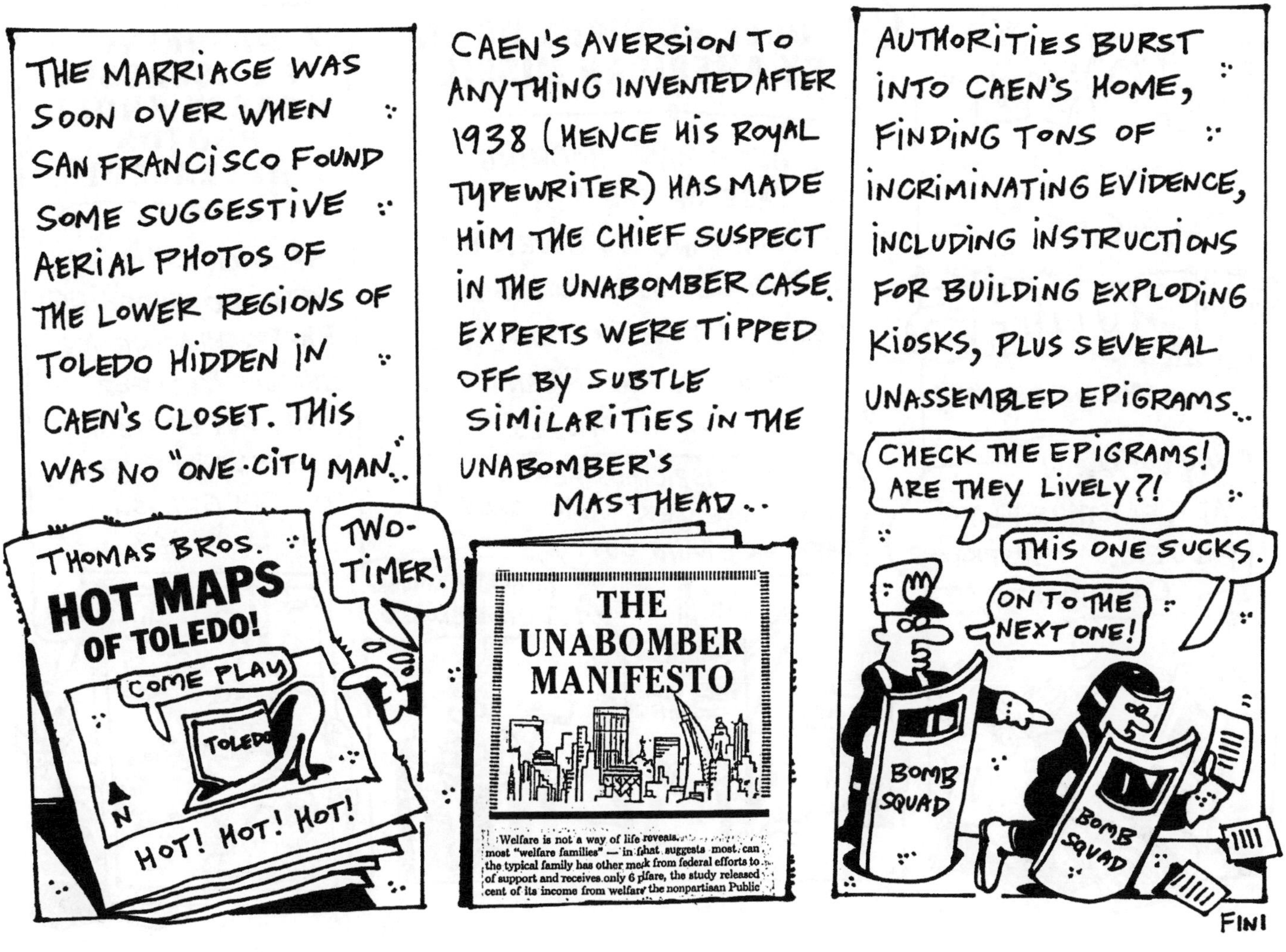

THE MARRIAGE WAS SOON OVER WHEN SAN FRANCISCO FOUND SOME SUGGESTIVE AERIAL PHOTOS OF THE LOWER REGIONS OF TOLEDO HIDDEN IN CAEN'S CLOSET. THIS WAS NO "ONE-CITY MAN"..

THOMAS BROS.
HOT MAPS OF TOLEDO!
COME PLAY
TOLEDO
N
HOT! HOT! HOT!
TWO-TIMER!

CAEN'S AVERSION TO ANYTHING INVENTED AFTER 1938 (HENCE HIS ROYAL TYPEWRITER) HAS MADE HIM THE CHIEF SUSPECT IN THE UNABOMBER CASE. EXPERTS WERE TIPPED OFF BY SUBTLE SIMILARITIES IN THE UNABOMBER'S MASTHEAD..

THE UNABOMBER MANIFESTO

"Welfare is not a way of life reveals, most "welfare families" — in that suggests most can the typical family has other meak from federal efforts to of support and receives only 6 plare, the study released cent of its income from welfare the nonpartisan Public"

AUTHORITIES BURST INTO CAEN'S HOME, FINDING TONS OF INCRIMINATING EVIDENCE, INCLUDING INSTRUCTIONS FOR BUILDING EXPLODING KIOSKS, PLUS SEVERAL UNASSEMBLED EPIGRAMS..

CHECK THE EPIGRAMS! ARE THEY LIVELY?!

THIS ONE SUCKS.
ON TO THE NEXT ONE!

BOMB SQUAD
BOMB SQUAD

FINI

"There are no whole truths; all truths are only half-truths. It is trying to treat them as a whole truths that plays with the devil." — Alfred North Whitehead

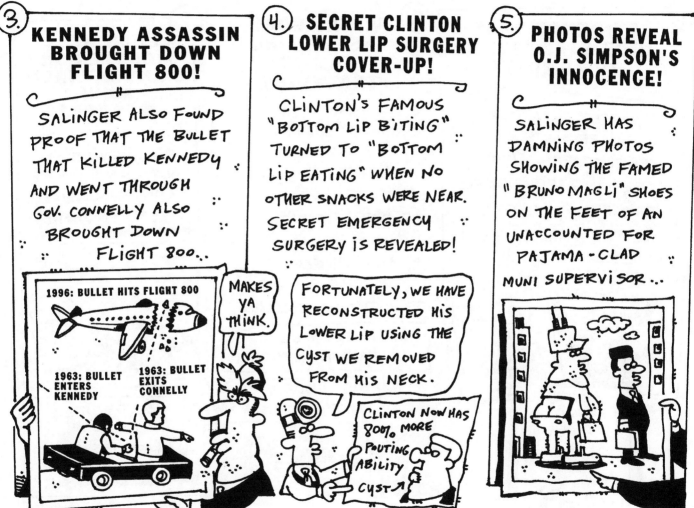

3. KENNEDY ASSASSIN BROUGHT DOWN FLIGHT 800!

SALINGER ALSO FOUND PROOF THAT THE BULLET THAT KILLED KENNEDY AND WENT THROUGH GOV. CONNELLY ALSO BROUGHT DOWN FLIGHT 800...

1996: BULLET HITS FLIGHT 800

1963: BULLET ENTERS KENNEDY

1963: BULLET EXITS CONNELLY

MAKES YA THINK.

4. SECRET CLINTON LOWER LIP SURGERY COVER-UP!

CLINTON'S FAMOUS "BOTTOM LIP BITING" TURNED TO "BOTTOM LIP EATING" WHEN NO OTHER SNACKS WERE NEAR. SECRET EMERGENCY SURGERY IS REVEALED!

FORTUNATELY, WE HAVE RECONSTRUCTED HIS LOWER LIP USING THE CYST WE REMOVED FROM HIS NECK.

CLINTON NOW HAS 80% MORE POUTING ABILITY

CYST →

5. PHOTOS REVEAL O.J. SIMPSON'S INNOCENCE!

SALINGER HAS DAMNING PHOTOS SHOWING THE FAMED "BRUNO MAGLI" SHOES ON THE FEET OF AN UNACCOUNTED FOR PAJAMA-CLAD MUNI SUPERVISOR...

6. EVIDENCE THAT ROCK STAR "STING" IS HUMBLE!

SALINGER HAS SUPPOSEDLY FOUND ABSOLUTE PHOTOGRAPHIC PROOF OF STING BEING HUMBLE, THOUGH EXPERTS FEEL THE PHOTOS ARE DOCTORED.

I'VE SUCKED SINCE THE POLICE BROKE UP...

THE INDIANS HATE ME.

STING? CALL ME STINK.

7. V.P. AL GORE INSTIGATING FAMILY TRAGEDIES!

SALINGER HAS PROOF THAT AT RECENT FAMILY PICNICS, AL GORE HAS BEEN ACTIVELY TRYING TO DRUM UP PERSONAL FAMILY TRAGEDIES TO USE IN FUTURE TEAR-JERKING SPEECHES.

HEY TIMMY, GO GET THAT BALL IN THE HIGHWAY.

HEY UNCLE, EVER TRY THIS ODWALLA STUFF?

8. LOCH NESS MONSTER OR UNDISCIPLINED MUNI WORKER?

THE JURY'S STILL OUT ON THIS CONTROVERSIAL PHOTO ON THE NET:

YOU DECIDE! CHECK ONE!

☐ LOCH NESS MONSTER
☐ UNACCOUNTED FOR MUNI SUPERVISOR

SEND TO THE EXAMINER!

170

EXTRA: CHAPTER TWELVE!!

S.F. COMIX "BIG-ASS MOCHA" SUPPLEMENTARY SECTION!

CRITERION® EDITION

SPECIAL FEATURES

VIDEO

- EXCLUSIVE RESTORATION OF ORIGINAL S.F. COMIX "BIG-ASS MOCHA" DOWNBEAT ENDING!
- OTHER OUTTAKES (INCLUDING LEGENDARY LOST TOILET SCENE!)
- ORIGINAL PRELIMINARY S.F. COMIX "BIG-ASS MOCHA" PRODUCTION DESIGNS BY H.R. GIGER!
- ORIGINAL ADVERTISING PROMOTIONAL POSTER DESIGNS!
- ORIGINAL "UNICORN DREAM SEQUENCE" WHICH HINTED THAT ASMUSSEN MAY BE A REPLICANT!

AUDIO

- ANALOGUE TRACK 1 FEATURING S.F. COMIX CREATOR DON ASMUSSEN RUNNING COMMENTARY
- ANALOGUE TRACK 2 FEATURING IRRITATING HIGH-PITCHED NOISE
- ANALOGUE TRACK 3 FEATURING ANGELA ALIOTO COMMENTARY (SEE ANALOGUE TRACK 2)

BIG-ASS MOCHA

CRITERION SECTION 1: WIDE PANEL FORMATTING

THE SAN FRANCISCO COMIC STRIP © HAS ALWAYS BEEN MEANT TO BE SEEN IN ITS ORIGINAL PANEL RATIO OF 1.85, OR "WIDE PANEL" FORMAT. DON ASMUSSEN ® HAS ALWAYS FELT THE NORMAL COMICS PAGE "1.35 RATIO" LEAVES OUT TOO MUCH VISUAL INFORMATION. SEE THE EXAMPLE BELOW OF THE LETTERBOXED VERSION VERSUS THE NORMAL S.F. COMIX PAN & SCAN PANELS. YOU MAKE THE CHOICE.

A. ORIGINAL PAN & SCAN S.F. COMIX PANEL

B. LETTERBOXED S.F. COMIX WIDE PANEL VERSION

UNEXPLAINED EWOK WARRIOR CHANGES ENTIRE DYNAMIC OF SCENE

MAKE MINE MILK.

MAKE MINE MILK.

CRITERION SECTION 2: PANEL OUTTAKES

ALONG THE WAY, ASMUSSEN HAS HAD TO CUT MANY S.F. COMIX PANELS THAT, ALTHOUGH STRONG, TENDED TO SLOW DOWN THE PACING OF THE COMIC. BELOW ARE PROBABLY THE MOST FAMOUS OUTTAKES, OFTEN SEEN CIRCULATING AT S.F. COMIC STRIP® CONVENTIONS.

A. THE "STAIRS" OUTTAKE

FROM STRIP #134, THIS TRANSITIONAL PANEL OF THE MAIN CHARACTER CLIMBING THE STAIRS TO THE NEXT SCENE/JOKE WAS ORIGINALLY CUT TO TIGHTEN THE COMIC'S PACING. WE NOW PRESENT IT HERE, FOR THE FIRST TIME, IN ALL ITS RESTORED GLORY.

B. THE "TOILET" OUTTAKE

FROM STRIP #325, THIS PANEL, THE MOST WIDELY SOUGHT BY "S.F. COMIX" COLLECTORS, SHOWS THE MAIN CHARACTER USING THE TOILET BETWEEN TWO OTHER PANELS CONTAINING GREAT JOKES. CUT WHEN CONSIDERED EXTRANEOUS, THOUGH IT DID SHOW UP IN SOME FOREIGN PRINTS.

MOST AVID "S.F. COMIX" FANS ARE CONSTANTLY DEBATING ABOUT THE INFAMOUS "LOST UNICORN DREAM SEQUENCE," WHICH SUPPOSEDLY "HINTED" TO THE FACT THAT THE MAIN CHARACTER WAS ACTUALLY A REPLICANT (SYNTHETIC ROBOT). HERE IS THE ORIGINAL SEQUENCE OF PANELS, WHICH ASMUSSEN ORIGINALLY CUT BECAUSE OF BAD LINE WORK. YOU DECIDE THE DREAM'S "MEANING."

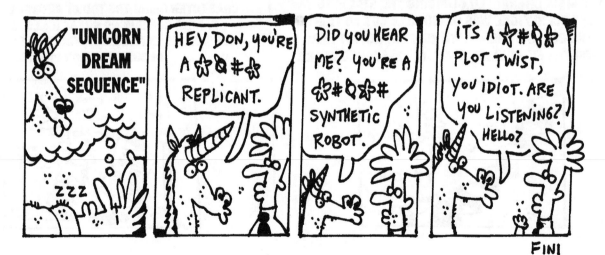

CRITERION SECTION 3: "BIG-ASS MOCHA" ORIGINAL DOWNBEAT ENDING

TEST AUDIENCES FOR THIS BOOK FOUND ITS ORIGINAL ENDING TO BE A DOWNER. AFRAID THIS WOULD AFFECT THE SALES OF THE BOOK, WE SUBSTITUTED AN ENDING WHICH INCORPORATED MANY ADORABLE KITTENS WITH TINY HATS AFFIXED TO THEIR HEADS. BELOW IS THE ORIGINAL ENDING, WHICH ASMUSSEN PREFERS. YOU DECIDE.

∴ WHEN THE S.F. COMIC STRIP ® WAS IN THE PLANNING STAGES, SEVERAL WORLD FAMOUS ARTISTS WERE COMMISSIONED TO DESIGN THE "LOOK" OF THE PROPOSED STRIP. ONE SUCH ARTIST WAS THE SCIENCE FICTION AND FANTASY ILLUSTRATOR H.R. GIGER. BELOW ARE GIGER'S PROPOSED S.F. COMIX DESIGNS, LATER REJECTED FOR BUDGETARY REASONS..

A.
H.R. GIGER DESIGN FOR MAIN CHARACTER/ "BIOMECHANI-DON"

B.
H.R. GIGER DESIGN FOR MAYOR BROWN/ "BIOMECHANI-WILLIE"

C.
H.R. GIGER DESIGN FOR SHOWERING EX-MAYOR FRANK JORDAN

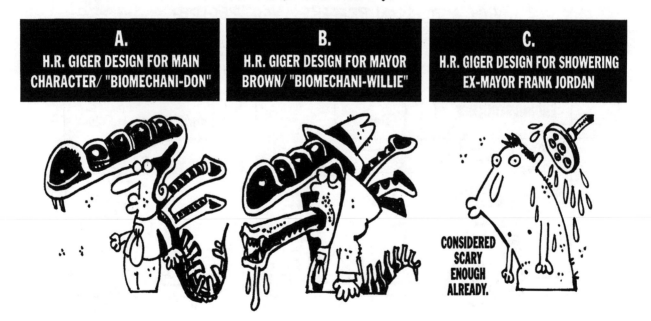

CONSIDERED SCARY ENOUGH ALREADY.

CRITERION SECTION 5: PROMOTIONAL DESIGNS

HERE ARE SOME OF THE ORIGINAL PROMOTIONAL DESIGNS DEVELOPED FOR THIS BOOK. SEVERAL DESIGNS WERE TESTED BEFORE THE ONES BELOW WERE CHOSEN.

"BIG-ASS MOCHA" PROMOTIONAL POSTER A. (TEASER)

S.F. COMIX "BIG-ASS MOCHA" BOOK! → BUY IT NEXT WEEK!

"BIG-ASS MOCHA" PROMOTIONAL POSTER B. (1st WEEK)

S.F. COMIX "BIG-ASS MOCHA" BOOK! → BUY IT NOW!

"BIG-ASS MOCHA" PROMOTIONAL POSTER C. (4th WEEK)

S.F. COMIX "BIG-ASS MOCHA" BOOK! WHY DIDN'T YOU BUY IT?

177

"Remarks are not literature." — Gertrude Stein

An Extra Strip That Never Got Used About Doggies

"I never saw a wild thing sorry for itself." — D.H. Lawrence

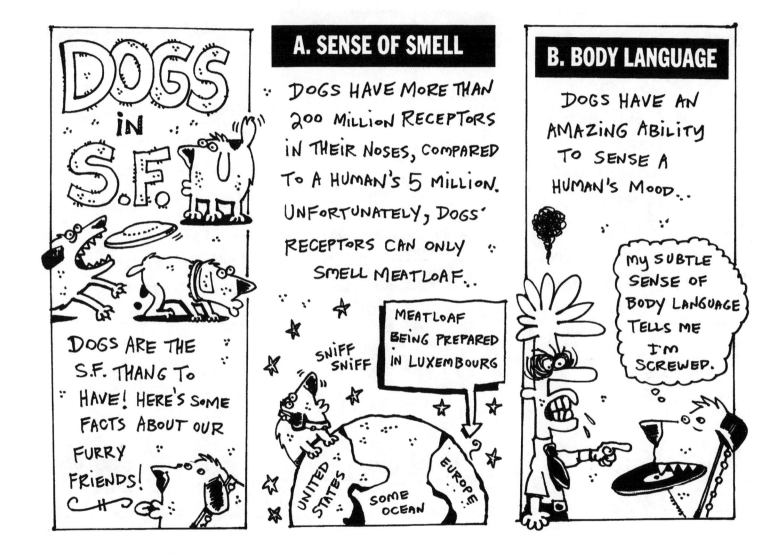

181

C. SELF-AWARENESS

DO DOGS THINK ABOUT "SELF" AND OTHER ABSTRACTIONS?

INDIVIDUALITY, PERSONALITY IS DEVELOPED FROM WITHIN. LIFE IS A DEED CONCERNED WITH THE DUALITY OF AGENT AND OBJECT. OOOOOOOH A BONE!

D. SAFETY

IN SAN FRANCISCO, NEVER EVER TIE YOUR DOG TO A ROTATING KIOSK...

SAN FRANCISCO

E. MARKETABILITY

ONE OF THE MOST SUCCESSFUL EVENTS AT CANDLESTICK PARK THIS YEAR WAS "LHASA APSO DAY." THE FIRST 1,000 FANS RECEIVED A FREE LHASA APSO AT THE GATE...

FINI

QUESTIONS FOR DISCUSSION:

 1. WHAT GOOD COULD A BOOK THIS CRAPPY BRING TO THIS WORLD? DISCUSS.

 2. HOW COULD THE BOOK BE OVER IF THERE HASN'T BEEN ANYTHING FUNNY YET? DISCUSS.

3. WHAT ARE THE CHANCES OF THERE BEING A SECOND BOOK IN MY TWO-BOOK DEAL WITH RUSSIAN HILL PRESS? DON'T BOTHER DISCUSSING.

4. WAS THERE REALLY A "SEVERED PENIS TASTES LIKE CHICKEN" JOKE ON PAGE 77 OR WAS THAT A TYPO? DISCUSS.

5. WAS A "MUNI RIDE IS LIKE A UFO ABDUCTION" JOKE REPEATED ON PAGES 24 AND 56? IS ASMUSSEN THAT LAZY? DOES IT MATTER? DID ANYONE READ THAT FAR ANYWAY?

WATCH FOR THE NEXT "SAN FRANCISCO COMIC STRIP" BOOK CALLED "STUFF NOT GOOD ENOUGH FOR THE FIRST BOOK," COMING EVENTUALLY...

IN AN EFFORT TO KEEP UP WITH THE CURRENT TREND OF FALSE ENDINGS AND SURPRISE SHOCKS, WE AT "S.F. COMIX" ARE PROUD TO PRESENT TO YOU OUR OWN "SURPRISE BOOK ENDING." IN THE TRADITION OF THE FILM "CARRIE," WE HOPE TO GIVE YOU A SHOCK THAT YOU'LL STILL BE TALKING TO FRIENDS ABOUT FOR YEARS TO COME. ENJOY!

AND NOW, THE "BIG-ASS MOCHA" SURPRISE SHOCK ENDING!

THANKS FOR READING MY BOOK, NOW LEAVE ME ALONE.

ONE OF THOSE BLANK PAGES AT
THE END OF BOOKS.